Democracy's Lot

RHETORIC, CULTURE, AND SOCIAL CRITIQUE

SERIES EDITOR
John Louis Lucaites

EDITORIAL BOARD
Jeffrey A. Bennett
Barbara Biesecker
Carole Blair
Joshua Gunn
Robert Hariman
Debra Hawhee
Claire Sisco King
Steven Mailloux
Raymie E. McKerrow
Toby Miller
Phaedra C. Pezzullo
Austin Sarat
Janet Staiger
Barbie Zelizer

Democracy's Lot
Rhetoric, Publics, and the Places of Invention

CANDICE RAI

The University of Alabama Press
Tuscaloosa

The University of Alabama Press
Tuscaloosa, Alabama 35487–0380
uapress.ua.edu

Copyright © 2016 by the University of Alabama Press
All rights reserved.

Inquiries about reproducing material from this work should be addressed to the University of Alabama Press.

Typeface: Scala

Manufactured in the United States of America
Cover design and illustration: Michele Myatt Quinn
∞

The paper on which this book is printed meets the minimum requirements of American National Standard for Information Sciences—Permanence of Paper for Printed Library Materials, ANSI Z39.48-1984.

Cataloging-in-Publication data is available from the Library of Congress.
ISBN: 978-0-8173-1900-7
E-ISBN: 978-0-8173-8946-8

To Joel, Sanchaman, and Junot Felix.

In loving memory of my father, Mani Lall Rai,
and my dear friend Leane Dostaler.

Contents

List of Illustrations ix

Acknowledgments xi

Introduction: Democratic Persuasions 1

1. Places of Invention 31

2. Democratic Persuasions in Contested Publics 66

3. Public Art and the Rhetorics of Diversity 110

4. Positive Loitering and the Ambivalence of Democracy 143

5. Democratic Affects and Public Formations 172

Conclusion: From the Thicket 198

Epilogue: Exiting the Parlor 211

Notes 217

Works Cited 227

Index 239

Illustrations

FIGURES

1. An Empty Lot   1
2. Rehabbed Vintage Brownstones in Uptown   3
3. Broadway Street in the Heart of Uptown   4
4. Broadway Street near Wilson Yard   4
5. Empty Uptown Theater in the Background in 2007   46
6. Wilson Yard in 2004   68
7. Map of Uptown Neighborhood Area   69
8. Target at Wilson Yard, 2010   70
9. Affordable Housing and Retail at Wilson Yard, Target on the far right, 2010   70
10. Roots of Argyle Mural, "Transition Area"   111
11. Uplift Mural (the face of Che Guevara is painted over with the word "community")   112
12. Uplift Mural   119
13. Roots of Argyle Mural   129
14. Argyle Street in Uptown   129
15. Roots of Argyle Mural, Native American figure as "spiritual guide"   132
16. Sidewalk Across from U-Haul   145
17. Screen shot of initial "gang riot" Uptown Update post   181

TABLES

1. Foreign-Born Persons in Uptown, 1970–2009   48
2. Uptown's Racial and Ethnic Composition by Percentage of Total Population Compared to Chicago's, 1990–2010   55
3. Uptown Poverty Rates, 1970–2000   55
4. Index Crime Statistics for Districts 20 and 23   150
5. Lowest Crime Statistics Rankings   150
6. Comparison of Reported Crimes in Uptown and Surrounding Lakefront Neighborhoods   151

Acknowledgments

Above all, I would like to thank the men and women of Uptown for sharing their stories with me and for their truly remarkable practices of citizenship.

Being in the field—this field—has taught me to be a more generous listener of perspectives I would have too easily dismissed prior. I may have lost sharpness to the political edge that I started with, but I have gained a depth of empathy that has forced me to engage with a broader range of political questions and engagements with the world. In the end, I remain most aligned with politics that question how to intervene in human-made designs that result in and naturalize any number of pernicious things: poverty, shame, disenfranchisement, and the like; I have also, however, become thoroughly disenchanted by the manner in which we have often approached these questions: by dehumanizing and vilifying people who hold political positions we may oppose.

One day, an informant asked me to "summarize my research findings." I replied, "I guess, if anything, I am trying to resist. . . . clarity about what the right thing to do is, trying to muck it up. Somehow the clarity of what democracy is is part of the problem for me. I think my hope is to backup and slow people down and model a complex way to look at language and arguments working in the world, to muck up the easy way we think we know democracy or justice or our own positions."

My inclination to muck things up comes also from working with my mentor and colleague at the University of Illinois-Chicago, Ralph Cintrón. Ralph's support over the years was central to my development as a scholar and to the formulation of this book. Beyond his expertise as a storyteller, rhetorician, and ethnographer, Ralph is a master of asking good questions—the mucking up sort that need to be asked, that derail and unhinge, that are uncomfortable, that catalyze inquiry. Whatever this book offers emerges, in part, from the inquiries sparked long ago by questions he posed to me.

At UIC, I also must thank Todd DeStigter, Robert Fairbanks, Kevin Barnhurst, and Janet Smith for their wisdom; Jamie Daniel, who taught an inspirational class on the public sphere that continues to influence me; and Ann Merle Feldman, who had a profound impact on the shape of my career. And I am grateful to colleagues and friends who are flung far and wide: Ellyzabeth Alder, Alicia Castellanos, Caroline Gottschalk Druschke, Sarah Ford, Pamela Fox, John French, Annie Knepler, Lindsay Marshall, Rebecca de Wind Mattingly, erin mcclellan Nayda Pittendrigh, and Sue Weinstein. Thank you also to Marlia Banning and John Ackerman for intervening at a critical juncture early on.

At the University of Washington, I am fortunate to have many supportive and inspiring colleagues, including Miriam Bartha, Nancy Bou Ayash, Kimberlee Gillis-Bridges, Gary Handwerk, Gillian Harkins, Carrie Mathews, Colette Moore, Suhanthie Motha, Priti Sandhu, Sandy Silberstein, Gail Stygall, Anu Taranath, John Webster, and Kathy Woodward. A special thanks to Juan Guerra, who provided guidance, to Elizabeth Simmons-O'Neill for her modeling of ethical ways to engage the academy, and to Anis Bawarshi, who offered moral and intellectual support from the very beginning through to the end.

I would like to acknowledge UW's Royalty Research Fund and the Simpson Center's Society of Scholars program for supporting this project. I discovered the bravery and tools to write Chapter five in a seminar on multimodality at the 2010 RSA Institute: a thank you to Anne Wysocki and Dennis Lynch for organizing us and to the fantastic participants for their brilliance. I also want to thank Daniel Waterman and the team at the University of Alabama Press for their extraordinary guidance, and I am grateful to the anonymous reviewers at UAB Press for their sage advice. Chapter three draws from my essay "Power, Publics, and the Rhetorical Uses of Democracy," in *The Public Work of Rhetoric: Citizen-Scholars and Civic Engagement*, edited by John M. Ackerman and David J. Coogan, and published by the University of South Carolina Press (2010). Chapter four draws on my essay "Positive Loitering and Public Goods: The Ambivalence of Civic Participation and Community Policing in the Neoliberal City," published in *Ethnography* (2011). Both pieces are used with permission.

I would like to thank my friends and family for their good cheer, support, and companionship. I would especially like to thank Margaret Gonzalez for her general hilarity, for her spunk, and for sticking it out with me;

Megan Marie Bolinder for her strength, brilliance, and friendship; and Leal Ridgway for being there from the very beginning. And, then, there is Leane Dostaler—wherever her life energies may have traveled, she urges us all toward living fully and with grace.

And, finally, I want to thank my brothers, Andrew, Robert, and Nathan, for their love and support, my father, Mani, for being a model teacher, and my mother, Linda, for making it all possible. Most preciously, I want to thank Joel Felix who offered support and companionship through it all and for his many contributions to this project, and to express my profound gratitude for the blessings of Sanchaman and Junot. All of my love.

Democracy's Lot

Introduction

Democratic Persuasions

Admittedly, democracy's meanings and uses are many, and some are at odds with others. But a concept that brings to life cultural concerns, commitments, and enduring tensions that people need to navigate is not meaningless. Democracy is an ideal with traction, a tool useful in multiple situations.
>> Karen Tracy, *Challenges of Ordinary Democracy*

If words serve to blur things, it is because the conflict over words is inseparable from the battle over things . . . To understand what democracy means is to hear the struggle that is at stake in the word: not simply the tones of anger and scorn with which it can be imbued but, more profoundly the slippages and reversals of meaning that it authorizes, or that one authorizes oneself to make with regard to it.
>> Jacques Rancière, *Hatred of Democracy*

1. An Empty Lot. Photo by Author.

Nothing stands out as noteworthy in this photo of an empty lot. If not for the elevated commuter train speeding by in the background, this place would be indistinguishable from any other such lot. Here, we have a perfectly mundane urban space—trashy, weedy, circumscribed by a plain chain link fence: one of thousands of "non-places" largely invisible in daily life. And yet, as you will learn, *this place* catalyzed a remarkable set of public events. This place has much to teach us about democracy. And, because I am a rhetorician, I will also make the case that this place has much to tell us about the power of rhetoric and its significance in everyday life. While democracy has had critics since its inception in Classical Greece, and while countless human atrocities have been performed in its name, a powerful sense of its presumed virtue continues to persuade people to sacrifice their lives to pursue this hallowed thing we call democracy. Yet, the capacity of democratic rhetoric to marshal power, stitch together diametrically opposed ideologies, and mobilize people toward incommensurable public goods suggest that one cannot know democracy in the abstract. This idea that democracy and the public work of rhetoric can only be captured by inhabiting particular places—where one might observe democracy's concrete uses, evocations, and practices—lured me into the field to study the workings of democracy as it is practiced by ordinary citizens in a radically diverse and politically charged gentrifying neighborhood.

This empty lot in question, known as Wilson Yard, is located in Uptown, a Chicago lakeside neighborhood that is as notorious for its diversity as for its striking level of political strife. With over forty languages fluently spoken, stark economic, cultural, and ethnic diversity, and passionate and sustained civic action across the political spectrum—this is a neighborhood that cannot explain away democratic shortcomings by pointing to a lack of diversity or apathy. Uptown's population ranges from the very affluent to the very poor—an economic disparity easily read in the built environment, where mansions sit near Section 8 public housing, rows of new condos are next door to homeless shelters, and upscale pet stores are adjacent to transient cage hotels. Throughout are businesses representing Uptown's immigrant cultures—Middle-Eastern, Guatemalan, Mexican, Vietnamese, Ethiopian, to name a few. In the everyday comings and goings of this urban landscape, one encounters hipsters searching for a nightcap, homeless men pushing carts, affluent gay couples off to work, tourists seeking ethnic fare, recent immigrants returning home, new parents strolling infants, sketchy men making it their business to sexually harass women, students spilling into classrooms, drug addicts in search, and so on. Indeed, Uptown is a poster child for Zukin's argument that "gentrification makes inequality more visible by

2. Rehabbed Vintage Brownstones in Uptown. Photo by Author.

fostering a new juxtaposition of landscape and vernacular, creating 'islands of renewal in seas of decay'" (188).

Beneath the surface of such "diversities" visible to eye—in the form of architecture, aesthetics, and bodily and spatial markers of race and class—Uptown has a long history of competing publics engaged in passionate, politically volatile battles over public space, urban development, and neighborhood identity. Diversity does not exist peaceably here, and harmonious consensus is nowhere to be found. Intense civic participation has been endemic since the midtwentieth century, punctuated by cycles of investment and disinvestment that have sustained citizen movements to spurn market-driven commercial development, on the one hand, and counter movements to halt and redirect the processes of gentrification on behalf of disenfranchised citizens, on the other. Suffice it to say here that Uptown's competing publics provide an exemplary opportunity for observing how the contradictory uses of democratic rhetoric materialize in everyday life, and for testing the limitations and possibilities of the liberal democratic project.

The history of Wilson Yard as a site of democratic contest began after a fire destroyed a public transit repair shop in 1996, leaving behind the empty lot featured above. When the city opted to sell the lot, the local alderman ini-

3. Broadway Street in the Heart of Uptown. Photo by Author.

4. Broadway Street near Wilson Yard. Photo by Author.

tiated a controversial community-led development plan to determine what to build there that might capture Uptown's radical diversity. This planning process spanned over a decade (1998–2010), and through the years ignited hostile publics that engaged in countless meetings, protests, town halls, blueprint roll outs, and media stunts; the writing of thousands of blog entries, online comments, news articles, petitions, and protest letters; the formation of community organizations centered explicitly on promoting or thwarting one plan or another for the lot; and the launch of lawsuits related to developing the lot, among other civic activities. Public discourse has largely over-simplified the battle as a class war. For example, Lydersen characterizes Wilson Yard as a wrangle between "people who want to see primarily low-income housing" and people "who want mostly commercial development" (8). Roeder noted that Wilson Yard pits "property owners. . . . against people with lower incomes" ("Wilson" 47). Yielding neither consensus nor capitulation among Uptown's conflicting interests, the now-developed lot is a spatial monument to the contest itself. Reflecting something for everyone while completely satisfying no one, the lot is now home to a Target, mixed commercial retail, and 178 subsidized affordable apartments for "low," "very low," and "extremely low-income" households.

The competing publics of Wilson Yard transformed the lot into a metaphor for democracy—and, like all good metaphors, it took on a powerful force all its own because people with very different sensibilities invested it with their own contradictory dreams, evoking it to fight for justice as they understood it, and twisting the metaphor this way and that to accommodate various uses. As more arguments, stories, experiences, human energies, and public memories became implicated in and tethered to its evocation, this lot increasingly absorbed and vibrated with *rhetorical force*. It might sound strange to say that rhetoric has a force, given the most common definitions of rhetoric as mere words, flowery language, vacuous discourse, or utilitarian strategies of persuasion. Such denigrating or reductive definitions of rhetoric do not capture what I mean when I say that part of what this book is about is studying rhetorical force and how people use rhetoric in their everyday lives to get things done. Let me say a word more on rhetorical force by returning to the lot. The mundane materiality of dirt, fence, train, and weed that you saw in the opening photo soon served as a lighting rod for all kinds of contradictory arguments about the good life, about who constitutes a good neighbor, and about how best to collectively work toward a brighter, more inclusive future.

The empty lot was transformed into symbolic stuff that people endowed with all manner of meanings that were, in turn, hinged to myriad felt encounters and public observations that citizens experienced while moving through Uptown's built environment; to people's personal emotions, fears, and hopes; and to broader concerns over everything from the welfare state to the proper uses of tax monies. The lot (or rather talk and activity around it) was soon overflowing with contested ideas about democracy, citizenship, and social justice. A symbol has rhetorical force; then, when it becomes so freighted with meaning, simply evoking it summons all of the networked webs of associations, dispositions, identities, affects, practices, and contested beliefs attached to it within our collective, public memories.

But, something also has rhetorical force because it maintains a relationship to (and, perhaps, exists as) materiality in at least two ways—first, to have force, rhetoric (along with the tagalong meanings that adhere to it) must be remade through our everyday practices, institutions, and spaces (in this sense, too, to have rhetorical force, an argument must have material vehicles such as bodies, genres, institutions, newspapers, and so on to carry it, circulate it, maintain it, reproduce it, keep it in mind). But, to extend this thinking: rhetoric is not only made visible and transported by material carriers, but also emerges from and is brought to life by the particular environs already present in the world. Rhetoric is emplaced, embodied, and embedded in the places and practices—indeed, in the very forms of being of everyday life. If this is simply a way of saying that rhetoric is situated and that rhetors must consider context, then this perception must be pushed to its radical extreme as profound immersion in and understanding of the immanent enmeshments of all that constitutes the world—the histories, discourses, environments, spaces, ideologies, subjectivities, bodily impulses, visual habits, dreams, biological imperatives, public memories, collective emotions, human designs, nonhuman things, technologies, tools, stuff, textures of power and politics, ways of knowing and doing, forms of engagement, mechanisms of suffering, doxa, material scaffolding, and so on. While no one can possibly access all of these enmeshments, the point is that rhetoric necessarily emerges from and attunes to them and is thus also a tool of attunement, orientation, and intervention within the social thicket.

Second, to have force, rhetoric must be consequential and have a strong affective capacity—which is to say that it must have a potential for producing social effects, like changing minds, maintaining status quo, producing emotional responses, or mobilizing civic action. It must live in bodies, vibrate between bodies. It must compel and move us. Therefore, this book is also about how such shared meanings and rhetorical forces inhabit and emerge from our spaces and bodies, acting as guides, nudges, seductive whispers that persuade us to move, feel, and think this way, but not that way. Perhaps I am simply describing how ideology works, but I do so to get at how we might think of rhetoric—not simply as razzle-dazzle style or verbal bullshittery—but also as intimately tied to our suasive public narratives and shared material conditions, as a force that not only orders our lives but also animates our bodies. Gets under our skin. Puts things into motion through and beyond human will. Emerging from and wedded to the co-constitutive interactions of language, people, things, matter, and all other presences and forces in the world, so I am also trying to get at a theory of persuasion that (includes but also) extends beyond a concern for symbols, symbolic content, argument, language, rational logic, and human intention. Diane Davis helps us take this a step further, arguing for a more fundamental "originary (or pre-originary) rhetoricity—an affect*ability* or persuad*ability*—that is the condition for symbolic action" (2) and that suggests already-existing "structure(s) of exposure" embedded in the world's entanglements and relations that "precede and exceed symbolic intervention" (3).

My unfolding and expansive description of rhetoric as a powerful constellation of forces in and of the world points to the sheer complexity involved in attempting to learn the arts of persuasion and wield rhetoric's power. This human attempt to locate, reproduce, alter, and deploy the powers of rhetoric to resolve the problems of collective living would have been familiar to ancient rhetoricians; indeed, the capacity to find or craft symbols that resonate with rhetorical force within everyday life is what Aristotle referred to as rhetorical invention. Understood as the capacity to discover the available means of persuasion in any situation, invention requires one to "invent" from within what Jenny Edbauer Rice calls "rhetorical ecologies" ("Unframing" 19) that are already invested with material constraints, political textures, ideological vectors, affective valences, normative social relationships, and salient rhetorical structures. This book, in the broadest sense, is about reconceiving rhetorical invention within what Thomas Rickert calls the "infinitesimal encounters, direct, indirect, and emergent, ongoing in the world" (163) and, more specifically, within the democratic imaginary—which is to say that I have studied the rhetorical forces specific to democracy, how democratic rhetoric becomes invested with meaning, how democracy is practiced and manifest in and through materiality, the arsenal of contradictory arguments hinged to the democratic project, and the power of democratic rhetoric to support productive and pernicious human endeavors.

Therefore, infusing ethnographic detail into the study of democracy, publics, and rhetorical invention within democracy is the first objective of this book. As a rhetorician, I include in this book observations of how the rhetorics of democracy are situated and evoked within Uptown's contested publics and, specifically, within various related field examples that center on controversial affordable housing developments, cycles of real estate speculation, community policing campaigns, public art initiatives, public policies, street protests, grassroots efforts, and online organizing. My second objective is to offer a contemporary theory of rhetorical invention that attunes to the profound complexity involved in the deceivingly simple act of discovering the motors, conditions, and resources for persuasion within everyday life. Beyond locating publicly salient rational arguments or powerful rhetorical topoi that circulate in a social space, the resources for invention we might consider include the genres that facilitate participation, activity, and contest; the mechanisms that reproduce macro structural forces in the local; extralinguistic bodily knowledges, affects, and emotions; the political agency and shaping power of things, environments, and spaces; historical, spatial, political, ideological, material, and environmental recalcitrancies, constraints, and levers; the subjectivities that align with or resist dominant powers—and so on. The rhetorical forces that circulate and the resources that manifest within social spaces constitute, then, what I call the *places of invention*—a simple concept intended to capture the radical complexity of rhetorical situations by evoking multiple and interrelated meanings of "place" (as the raw materialities of concrete places; the social narratives and histories we invest in those places; the genres, practices, and institutions that emerge and help people act within places; and the rhetorical commonplaces, or topoi, that travel within places).

My third objective is to theorize rhetorical ethnography as an ideal method for studying the places of invention (and rhetoric-in-action, generally), which requires a focus on rhetoric's consequences; the material conditions that produce and constrain rhetorical force; how rhetorics map onto cultural narratives, ideologies, and affective forces within social spaces; and how rhetorics evolve, manifest, and circulate. Such objects require one to study persuasive qualities that lie in excess of and in tension with textual analysis, and lend themselves to embodied methodologies that facilitate long-term presence. This book engages in rhetorical ethnography to document how the ideals of democracy materialize in the everyday, and how democratic rhetoric is operationalized to various ends in situ. I see ethnography as an ideal method for studying not only what rhetoric means but also what it does and how, as Carole Blair puts it.

This book, therefore, offers an ethnographic account of how clashing citizens use democratic rhetoric in their struggle to define the future of their neighborhood. Opposed to polite debates about matters of the public good,

Uptown's competing publics use democratic discourse in passionate and hostile enactments of democracy. Such contest, as countless political theorists have attested, resides at the very heart of the democratic project itself, and, accordingly, I do not aim to locate more polite, just, or better forms of democracy. While democracy offers powerful rhetorical resources that inspire and facilitate citizen participation, the range of incompatible political projects that can be legitimately pursued in its name suggests that we can only understand democracy in the contexts of its practice, and that no amount of earnest labor or theorizing will undo the paradoxes of democracy. Therefore, another idea threaded throughout the book is a wondering over how to build a politics forged in the ambivalence of democratic practice, rather than in its presumed virtue. Ultimately, this book seeks to deepen our understanding of the work that democratic rhetoric does and the promises and pitfalls of everyday democratic practice.

On Publics and Everyday Democracy

While it is impossible to pinpoint the reasons why such robust, competing publics formed and persist in Uptown, a good starting place for understanding this emergence is the neighborhood's radical diversity (ideological, political, racial, ethnic, cultural, sexual, religious, economic, aesthetic), coupled with the material foundation for maintaining such diversity (varied housing stock, powerful support from governmental and other agencies, and activist networks that represent various positions). To these reasons for public formation, we must add Uptown's sustained venues and mechanisms for debate and civic action—including active block clubs, grassroots groups, local organizations, social service agencies, and active blogs, community boards, and websites. Finally, and maybe most salient, Uptown has faced a sustained, tangible, immediate, and felt exigency of threat to everyday lives across, and because of these diversities, material conditions, ways of knowing and doing. As Larry Bennett writes, "Political conflict is so commonplace in Uptown that it is sometimes supposed that personal animosities, organizational competition, and intergroup mistrust are inherent features of the community" (165). Such dynamics are the motors and lifeblood of democratic practice, some would argue.

In the Federalist No. 10, James Madison argued that warring factions are a permanent feature of democratic society, and one of its most serious threats. Rejecting the use of force to prevent factions, on the grounds that this would sacrifice liberty, and ruling out lasting consensus, he advocated the maintenance of diverse talents, opinions, and practices that could temper a tyrannous majority through checks and balances. The problem posed in the Federalist Papers—that is, how to contend with the threat of proliferating competing public interests without resorting to violence—is a permanent contention in democratic theory and practice. While this fractured quality of the public may be definitive, the desire for consensus and collective action is equally characteristic. Whether it is accomplished by Hobbes's Leviathan, via Rousseau's social contract, from behind Rawls's veil of ignorance, or through debate within Habermas's public sphere, one of the enduring commonplaces of democracy is the question of where foundations for collective decision-making across radical diversity and political incommensurability may arise. Rational talk (conversation, debate, verbal wrangle) has been figured as the primary mechanism through which a public will might be crafted.

As there are countless books devoted to theorizing democracy, I focus here only on those features of democratic publics most prevalent to this study: (1) I offer a *conceptualization of the public* as dynamic, emergent, contested, multiple, crafted through ongoing activity, and profoundly situated in, manifest from, and tethered to particular contexts, times, and materiality conditions; (2) I focus on both the *centrality of everyday "talk," communicative labor, and discursive artifacts* in rhetorical models of the democratic public and on *how materialities, affective valences, and nonhuman agencies both shape and enact democratic persuasions*: (3) I consider the *formation and qualities of democratic subjects* that are capable of engaging in democratic practice, and, more generally, what *forms of democratic subjectivities emerge within the concrete, ideologically infused spaces* of the field site; and (4) Implicating the previous points, I study the *relationship between rhetoric and materiality* within everyday democratic practice and public formation.

First, then, I understand publics as multiple, dynamic, and radically situational emergences defined by activity, intensity, and contest. Liberal democratic publics are defined by inherent conflict in that they are both infused with diverse, incommensurable conceptions of the public good and held together by shared ways of knowing, doing, and speaking that are idiosyncratic to places and time. While it has been widely criticized,[1] Jürgen Habermas's early conception of the public sphere remains a central heuristic for discussing the possibilities and limitations of democracy. Offering a model for liberal democracy, he conceives the public sphere as an autonomous, open, and egalitarian space existing between the state and civil society where private individuals generate—through rational debate—democratically derived public opinion that might influence state power.[2] The public sphere, in short, crystallizes the "people's public use of their reason" (*The Structural* 27). Common critiques highlight his model's preoccupation with consensus at the expense of pluralism; its restriction of debate to matters of public concern, which favors those rhetorically savvy enough to translate private interests into public matters; its idealized speech situation and norms, which cannot capture how debate really occurs; its failure to account for ways that systemic inequalities (and power) result in informal exclusions rooted in race, class, gender, and so forth; and its insistence on disinterestedness and rationality at the expense of passion, embodiment, "non-rational" appeals, and vernacular/marginal epistemologies (see Calhoun, Daniel, Eliasoph, Fraser, Fleming, Hauser, Montag, and Tracy, to name a few).

Within rhetorical studies, the turn toward studying the "everyday," "rhetoric in culture," and the "vernacular" has inspired conceptions of the public that supposedly ameliorate some of these criticisms by better reflecting the raw grittiness of how democratic publics really work and that acknowledge the profound situatedness of rhetoric and the norms of discursive exchange. The interest in studying the "everyday" presents itself as an attunement to the rhetorical practices of the local, nonofficial, marginalized, counter-cultural, disenfranchised, spatial, ecological, and material. The "everyday" public is radically immanent, not transcendent or idealized, which points to a model that is grounded, emergent, and responsive to the contextual dynamics in which rhetoric circulates. Gerard Hauser's important work on public spheres offers a "rhetorical model," conceived as "*emergences* manifested through vernacular rhetoric" (*Vernacular* 15) that represent "actual communicative practices in actually existing democracies" (46). Karen Tracy offers "ordinary democracy" as an "empirically anchored concept" that is "observable," "not a normative ideal," and "connects to how people actually talk" (*Ordinary* 3–7).

Such preoccupation with the immanent character of publics leads to a focus on the crafting of publics through ongoing, everyday rhetorical acts. Brouwer and Asen, for example, forward "public modalities" as their metaphor of choice for the public, which emphasizes "multiplicity, movement and activity" and "foregrounds the *productive arts of crafting publicity*" (3). These scholars stress the centrality of technê in public formation, which refers to an art, a "process of productive knowledge," and "cunning reason and good timing" that "recognizes the roles of individuals and groups in crafting their lives, even as people act amid constraints" (19–20). Publics scholars working within ecological and network perspectives share this emphasis on the active crafting of publics. To study the public from these orientations—as I am inclined to do—is to consider the co-constituency of ideologies, rhetorics, materialities, activities, and cultural/social/economic/affective forces that influence and circulate within an environment.

For example, Latour understands the public as an "assemblage" of practices and as salience that can be traced through activity. Grabill sees the "public" as a "type of connection that is visible because of movement" and as "associations that are actively created and re-created" (195). Edbauer imagines publics as "rhetorical ecologies" in which rhetoric is perceived as a "verb" such that we may say that "we *do rhetoric*" (13) or that we *do publics*. In sum, I share with these theorists a desire to examine how democracy really occurs within concrete contexts through the ongoing activity of human and nonhuman agencies that shape and are shaped by the material conditions, rhetorical forces, and ideological pulls of specific places and times. In this book, therefore, I argue that democracy is best studied on the plane of immanence, rooted in the places where democratic rhetoric is evoked, and where one can account for the radically situated and kairotic nature of rhetorical action.

Second, at the core of the public sphere and its derivatives is the hope that people might discover shared norms to guide everyday politics through debate (as opposed to the use of force, the sway of social status, or raw power). Ordinary talk is the lifeblood of democratic publics, and within rhetorical studies, figured as one of the most prevalent objects of study and sites of invention and intervention. Rice, for example, refers to publics as "active manifestations of talk" that occur in "ordinary spaces of encounter" (*Distant* 19). Tracy similarly focuses her study of "ordinary democracy" on everyday talk, arguing, "Through talk people make, resist, and change policies; cement or endanger relationships; and soothe or intensify conflicts" (5). Hauser locates the "local norms of *reasonableness*" in everyday vernacular talk because "arguments have no force apart from satisfying those standards that particular publics are prepared to summon" (*Vernacular* 52).

More recently, scholars have expanded our understanding of the public agents capable of "talking" beyond humans. Braun and Whatmore argue that "things are not merely instruments," but "talk" and at "once enable and constrain meaning" (xxi), thus, "we must be willing to speak of the performances of things and not just the actions of humans" and accept that "material culture carries emotions and ideas" (xx). Jane Bennett conceives "things" as public actors that can "make things happen" (39). Rather than inert matter, they constitute "vibrant materiality"—indeed, the concrete matter that influences the more abstract matters of public concern in a democracy. In this book, I build on these publics approaches by looking at and beyond human-centric talk to include a focus on how nonhuman public agencies, affective forces, and visual rhetorics constitute the everyday democracies I observe.

Third, given the demands of participating in public life, rhetorical scholars have also asked what kinds of subjects can engage in democracy. Indeed, theorizing how to cultivate public subjectivities capable of doing democracy (more justly, inclusively, and persuasively) is another way rhetoricians have articulated their own capacities for political agency. Not surprisingly, such public subjectivities are figured as super rhetoricians, akin to Cicero's ideal orator—rhetorically dexterous, empathetic, disciplined, and systematic, yet flexible enough to adapt, jab-jab, and pounce when the moment requires responsive action. This democratic subject must be disposed to act within profoundly complex, situational, vexed, and politically ambivalent circumstances, and must do so ethically—where ethical means being open to Others and forever amenable to debate and change. Crowley's preferred democratic subject, for example, "privileges movement, flexibility, contingency, and difference" (56), and seeks not to "shut down argumentative possibilities but to generate all the positions that are available. . . . in a given moment and situation" (*Towards* 56). Fleming calls for citizens with the "habits and disposition of politics, of dealing nonviolently with conflict, of managing social differences without either separation or assimilation" (xiv). Hauser valorizes democratic subjects with "*rhetorical competency*, or a capacity to participate in rhetorical experiences" (33–34). Rice critiques democratic subjects that are "thoroughly grounded in *feeling*," seeking a "publicness" rooted in action and commitment to sustainable collective futures (*Distant* 6).

While such qualities of an ideal democratic subjectivity are ones I also admire, my fieldwork suggests that cultivating super rhetoricians would not resolve the kinds of paradoxical tensions at the core of the democratic project. In Uptown, there are many citizens who exhibit these characteristics and who are engaged in situated, thoughtful, rhetorically minded civic action, all driven by a desire for social justice and deploying strikingly similar rhetorical tools, yet at loggerheads in radically incommensurable political projects. So, while I do not advocate an ideal subjectivity, my work does investigate the emergence and circulation of democratic subjectivities that manifest in everyday life with myriad ideological dispositions and tethered to various material conditions that shape and are shaped by people who inhabit such subjectivities. Accordingly, this project is not just about democratic rhetorics but also about democratic subjectivities (as well as about how rhetoric and subjectivity are entwined in situ). My aim is to render visible how, why, and when various democratic subjectivities emerge, to document the histories, ideological tendencies and rhetorical habits that such subjectivities exhibit, and to trace the consequences of different subjectivities.

Finally, in my publics approach, I am driven to examine the relationship between rhetoric and materiality. A rhetorical materialist approach examines, as Selzer argues, the "rhetorical dimension in the material" and "the material dimension in rhetoric" (9), taking "very seriously the material conditions that sustain the production, circulation, and consumption of rhetorical power" (9–10). McGee's influential work on materiality urges us to "think of rhetoric as an *object*, as material and omnipresent as air and water" (19), which "permits interactivity among people" as a "bridge. . . . [or] the social equivalent of a verb in a sentence" (21).[3] Blair critiques the treatment of materialities as mere vehicles of symbolic content (19), insisting that we "ask not just what a text means but. . . . what it does" (23). Biesecker and Lucaites attune to the "signifier and its constitutive effects," rather than simply to its capacity to "communicate meaning" (4–5).

The rhetorical materialist project, in short, is a useful analytic for exploring the co-constitutive relationship between (democratic) rhetoric and materiality; how rhetoric latches onto ideologies in the contexts of its use; the rhetoricity and agency of materiality itself—including the rhetorical qualities and political agency of things, aesthetics, bodies, and spaces; how material conditions catalyze, transport, constrain, and constitute rhetorical forces that, in turn, shape materialities; the circulations, enactments, modes of reproduction, affects, contexts, and consequences of rhetoric; not only the symbolic but also the material means of persuasion available in a social space; and the "techniques and technologies," as Greene puts it, through which people are transformed into rhetorical subjects that emerge "within a specific apparatus of production" (44).

In sum, in looking at how democracy is evoked and practiced in everyday life, I share Cruikshank's aim to "undermine the self-evidence of the notion that democracy is a good thing, pure and simple" (18). As she argues, "Democratic relations are still relations of power and as such are continually recreated, which requires that democratic theory never presuppose its subject but persistently inquire into the constitution of that subject" (18). I conceive the democratic public not merely as an entity, site, or process for coordinating collective action, but as a heuristic for generating salient questions and inquiries that help us examine, theorize, and intervene in publics. While we require metaphors for the public to help us pinpoint things to study, engage, refine, and act within, we also lament the tendency of these metaphors to flatten the complexities of publics in action. My turn to ethnography, as I speak to next, is conceived as a way not only to capture the dynamic immanence of a public through extended observation but also to make use of a genre capable of representing this dynamism and serve as a heuristic for thinking about democracy. When I say that I study democracy-in-action, democratic persuasions, democratic rhetoric, or everyday democracies, I signal my interest in how (democratic) rhetorical structures (topoi, commonplaces, icons, symbols, practices) are evoked in situ, and how such structures emerge from, circulate within, and adhere to broader ideological structures, affective valences, materialities, and public subjectivities.

Rhetoric, Fieldwork, and the Places of Invention

Dwight Conquergood observed that ethnography's "long-standing interest in meaning-making cultural practices and the suasory function of symbols" has led to a "thriving alliance between ethnography and rhetoric" (80). Anthropologist Michael Carrithers echoes this idea, arguing that "rhetoric sharpens the ethnographic eye" (577), making possible an analysis of everyday acts of persuasion wherein the "eventfulness of life. . . . is moved by the rhetorical will, the *energeia*, of those who. . . . aim to realize a plan or intention through, and upon others" (578). But what exactly does it mean for a rhetorician to do fieldwork? What constitutes data, research questions, or objects of study for a rhetorician fieldworker? What kinds of rhetorical phenomenon are best captured through fieldwork? How do rhetorical ethnographies differ from other kinds of ethnographies? What ethical commitments and liabilities do rhetorician fieldworkers share? While I don't have simple answers to these questions, I want to devote some space to exploring the field practices of rhetoricians (and others engaged in ethnographic studies that figure language, symbols, discourse, and persuasion as their primary objects).

For now, let me define rhetorical ethnographic methods as qualitative research engaged by those studying rhetorical phenomenon in a field site over a substantial period of time. Rhetorical field research facilitates an investigation not only into how symbols, language, and discourse order life, but also into the ways that individuals use rhetoric in fleeting everyday instances to get things done. Fieldwork helps us examine the ways that rhetoric manifests from and circulates consequentially within the dynamic places, practices, ideologies, relationships, and material conditions of everyday life. A growing interest in qualitative methods within rhetorical studies has researchers taking to the field to examine a range of rhetorical objects and problematics, including vernacular rhetoric (Hauser); rhetorics of everyday life (Cintrón); live rhetorics (Middleton, Senda-Cook, and Endres); everyday democracies and publics (Fleming, Rai, Rice, Tracy); the embodied, affective, material, and kairotic aspects of rhetoric in situ (Hess, LeMesurier, Pezzullo, Trainor); the everyday performances of rhetoric within dynamic public contexts, spaces, and places (Ackerman, Clair, Lindquist, mcclellan); the ways in which rhetoric facilitates and is situated within networks, social ecologies, and workplaces (Grabill, Read and Swarts, Rice, Spinuzzi);

and the possibilities for engaging rhetoric as a means of pragmatic action in the world (Hess, Druschke, Endres, Sprain, and Peterson, Herndl et al.).

While they have distinct political and intellectual commitments, these various projects tend to share conceptions of rhetoric that are amenable with field approaches—namely: (1) Rhetoric is kairotic, eventful, agonistic, emergent, dynamic, consequential, situational, and bound to materiality, thus, can only be fully understood in the contexts and moments of its everyday use where one can observe the dynamic interplay of the myriad elements of the rhetorical situation; (2) Being present in the field facilitates the observation of how and why rhetoric travels and evolves over time, how rhetoric and its resources invent culture, and how people inventively put existing rhetorical structures, genres, topoi, affective forces, salient symbols, objects, and so on to work; and (3) Given the complexity of rhetoric, discovering the available means of persuasion, as Aristotle defined rhetorical invention, calls for immersive methodologies and the inhabitation of the sites of rhetorical production where one might study the *places of invention*.

This term, *places of invention*, which I will explore in depth in Chapter one, provides a theory and method for studying rhetoric-in-action that foregrounds the relationship among rhetoric, power, agencies, materialities, ideologies, and contexts. To capture these amalgamations, this concept plays on the relationship between two conceptions of "place": first, it evokes the concept of rhetorical common*places*, or topoi, as salient discursive structures that emerge from and shape the social imagination; and, second, it draws on a more tangible idea of place that comprises the materialities, spaces, and locations that facilitate, inspire, and inhibit various forms of rhetorical action—as well as the tools, institutions, genres, and so on that manifest and enable (inter)action within particular places. This all presumes that the power of commonplaces can only be comprehended and deployed in concrete places where arguments emerge in everyday life and that, once discovered, might be put into play improvisationally in myriad situations; as such, one must, as Quintilian put it, discover the "secret places where arguments reside, and from which they must be drawn forth" (5.10.21). The idea that one must inhabit the places of rhetorical production to comprehend rhetoric goes far in explaining the impetus for rhetorical ethnography. In fact, ethnographies are replete with field practices devised to collect contextual data through inhabitation and with genre conventions designed to represent that context once gathered in ethnographic narratives that approximate inhabitation. Let me say a bit more about rhetorical ethnography as an exemplary method and as an ideal genre for studying and representing the *places of invention*, in turn.

Methodologically speaking, rhetorical field methods (and specifically rhetorical ethnography in my case) provide a good vantage point for observing rhetoric-in-action because they demand the sustained inhabitation (presence, immersion, engagement, and embodiment) of a researcher, who must go to the places where rhetorics are produced and circulate. The ethnographer's journey to the "field" as a body joining other bodies in concrete times and places affords the opportunity to examine any number of rhetorical objects only possible by "being there." As Conquergood assesses, ethnography is an "*embodied* practice" and an "intensely sensuous way of knowing" (180). Middleton, Senda-Cook, and Endres see the "potential for rhetorical field methods to analyze situations in which meanings depend on places, physical structures, spatial delineations, interactive bodies, and in-the-moment choices" (388). From the field, one might see how commonplaces (are made to) perform in places (that simultaneously perform on them) through the observation of ordinary acts of persuasion that reveal the workings together of rhetoric and materiality in dynamic yet nonetheless patterned forces that enable and constrain, punish and reward, obscure and reveal particular forms of being, ideologies, modes of thought, means of circulation, and ways to inhabit over time.

In terms of genre, Clifford refers to ethnographies as "fictions" and "economies. . . . of truth" that are inventions of "things not actually real" (6–7). Ethnographies are "caught up in the invention, not the representation, of cultures" (2), and they "cannot avoid expressive tropes, figures, and allegories that select and impose meaning as they translate it" (7). In this sense, rhetorical ethnography might be thought of as both a method that studies how rhetoric orders the world and a genre that fashions a miniature ordering of that ordering. Oft-repeated postmodern insights teach us that despite careful representations of field events, it is impossible for ethnographers to avoid "inventing" their objects through "expressive" language; however, the literary allowances of the ethnographic genre provide the inventive wiggle room required for complex representations of rhetoric-in-action through writing conventions that necessitate detailed contextual descriptions (thick description, informant quotations, narrative). Such conventions can *approximate* the places of invention through deeply situational representations of rhetorical force in a social field of action. In this sense, ethnographies perform a ("fictionalized") version of one's inhabitation of a field, enabling readers to witness the power of rhetoric within second-order approximations of its contexts of circulation and consequence.

Most generally, the rhetorical ethnographic genre provides a kind of depiction of rhetoric doing work in the world that captures the intensely situational and kairotic rhetorical forces generated when symbols interact with the particularities that exist in concrete places and times. By presenting rhetoric doing work in context, the ethnographic write-up represents not merely symbolic content but also a depiction of how power is (or social energies are) both manifest, leveraged, and reproduced in and by rhetoric *and* how these processes of reproduction are intimately linked to materiality (material practices, bodily habits, institutional practice, spatial arrangements).[4] If rhetoric both emanates from and shapes everyday life, and if rhetoric always exists in relationship to power, ideology, and materiality, and thus, if rhetoric and rhetorical situations are profoundly tethered, then it makes sense that studying rhetorical invention requires deep and sustained inhabitation of social spaces afforded by field researchers.

I see what follows as interrelated theoretical touchstones that might inform but not delimit how one might situate oneself within a rhetorical approach to field research. Rhetorical ethnographies and field methods, generally, provide methodological tools and theoretical orientations that enable researchers to:

Foreground the relationship between rhetoric and materiality. Studying how, why, and to what end rhetorics, materialities, and ideologies interact in everyday life is one possible aim of rhetorical ethnography. Within social spaces/places, these interactions occur as patterned forces that can be observed, even as they remain fickle. Documenting how rhetoric travels within and changes in relation to material conditions, moreover, is itself an object of study for rhetorical ethnographers. Rhetorical ethnographic methods also facilitate an analysis of how the built environment, objects, spaces, bodies, things, and various other nonhuman entities shape arguments, create rhetorical constraints and possibilities, and function as persuasive engines in and of themselves (beyond human agency).

Capture the vernacular, multiple, and conflicting perspectives and experiences in a fieldsite that may not be available to researchers relying on official discourses, public statements, archival documents, or other publicly available artifacts already in circulation. In short, by drawing on field methods, such as interviewing and participant observation, researchers are able to locate contested and diverse arguments and experiences within a social space, even within groups that may seem rather homogenous and unified in publicly available artifacts. Field methods help researchers study in situ reception of and audience responses to rhetoric-in-action. However, I do not see rhetorical field research as undercutting, wholly distinct from, or privileged over the goals of the traditional rhetorical critic. Rather, I see a field orientation as yielding additional and complementary tools that enable certain lines of sight not readily available through textual analysis of artifacts already in public archives.

Study rhetoric's flux, portability, timeliness, force, and consequences in rhetorical ecologies, networks, assemblages, and publics, and how macro and micro forces collide in rhetoric's emplacement and production. This lends itself toward ecological (and networked) rhetorical perspectives that stress the connectedness among "elements of rhetorical situations," as Rice argues ("Unframing" 9). Ecological orientations resist overly myopic views of rhetoric by questioning how micro and macro forces and processes link up; such theoretical inclinations also call for the observation of the active crafting, circulation, and consequences of rhetoric within the places of persuasion.

Capitalize on and respect the embodied presence of the researcher, as well as bodily and other extra-linguistic qualities of persuasion. Researchers go to the field to do more than gather up more static texts to perform analysis on, but are driven by questions and by the desire to capture rhetorical objects that require inhabitation. The researcher's (and informant's) intuition and embodied sense of the world provides important insights and yields knowledge not possible without going to the field. As such, fieldwork might focus on the affective, embodied, sensual, aesthetic, kairotic, performative, and consequential qualities of rhetoric; the materiality of rhetoric; the rhetoricity (and rhetorical agency) of bodies, objects, things, and spaces; and so on.

Study rhetoric and not cultures and people per se. As a human technê, readers might point out that human motivation is at the core of rhetorical practice. I agree. However, it means something different to say that you study rhetoric but not people or culture. To displace the cultural as the central object of ethnography need not ignore the significant relationship between culture and rhetoric, but it shifts one's focus. Rhetorical field research might, then, theorize and examine rhetoric itself, which is a something different than studying people or culture. To say that you study rhetorics and not people comes with its own ethical quandaries, of course, but it is also to say that your focus may exceed human motivations and culture, even while these remain central and meaningful. In short, rhetorical field methods can help reveal certain insights about rhetoric in excess of human culture.

Capture rhetorical forces and effects, not merely rhetorical intentions, truthfulness, or symbolic content. While the attention to what is "fact" and what is "fiction" in the field is important, the *rhetorical force* and *effects* of what is said and done is equally important, regardless of the "truthfulness" of an utterance. The truth of the matter, in other words, sometimes matters less than the force of the matter. In this sense, a rhetorical ethnographer might find herself paying more attention to what rhetoric does (or how it morphs, evolves, and circulates) than to what it means. Therefore, if one is interested in the power of language to do things, one might shift focus to understanding the nature and qualities of the forcefulness and consequences of language as the primary object, of which "truth" of an argument need not factor into its power—or, at any rate, is but one concern among others.

Craft field write-ups that function metaphorically, heuristically, as technê. Rhetorical ethnography, as a genre that attempts to capture rhetoric-in-action, might be thought of as a heuristic mapping of the available means of persuasion. This idea is inspired by Cintrón, who refers to ethnography as heuristical through and through. He conceives the ethnographic text as constituting a "worldview, an interpretative frame, a heuristic" (*Angel's* 6), as the "making of an order, a neat and clean" whose "borders are not geographic landmarks but, instead, paper and the imagination of the reader" (232). While the connection to actual fieldsites always exists, the ethnographic text operates generatively to help us see, study, and, if so inclined, intervene within the *places of invention*. Beyond the unpacking of symbols' meaning, reading cultural significations, or unmasking the operations of power (all worthy pursuits), write-ups of rhetoric-in-action can increase our capacities to recognize, trace, and respond to the available means of persuasion present within a fieldsite that are rendered visible by the ethnographic text. Theoretical insights, moreover, about how rhetoric works in the world might be rendered more tangible, see-able in narrative form. But if rhetorical ethnography is a heuristic (as opposed to or in addition to an objective reporting of social truths, a vehicle of "voice" for marginalized peoples, or some other such[5]), what exactly is this heuristic designed to do? And, if the fieldsite that the ethnographic genre renders visible is itself a tool of visibility, what exactly is the value of the vision afforded by such heuristics?

In sum, if rhetorical ethnography is distinguishable from other types of ethnographies, the distinction lies less in nitty-gritty field practices, and more in its theoretical dispositions toward studying rhetorical phenomenons and yielding rhetorical knowledge that can only be captured through the sustained presence of the researcher. By presenting powerful rhetorics doing work in context, the rhetorical ethnographic write-up represents not merely circulating rhetorical forms, content of arguments, or the contexts and conditions of rhetorical situations, but the interplay of forms, contents, and contexts that constitute rhetoric-in-action. This means that within the ethnographic genre, the field becomes a synecdoche of, if not a metaphor for, the available means of persuasion in the field, offering a generative springboard for thinking about and responding to the *places of invention* within the democratic imagination, in my case.

Field Orientations

I was initially drawn to the field by personal curiosities about an Illinois tax policy and by a compulsion to think about publics (how they form, what holds them together, why people act publicly, and so on). As it turned out, these two interests collided in Uptown. In the 1990s, I started reading about Tax Increment Financing (TIF)—a policy that was increasingly (and controversially) used in Chicago to generate money to spur development in depressed areas, often at the expense (or exclusion) of the city's most disenfranchised citizens (whom the policy is supposed to assist). In spare terms for now, TIFs work by diverting property tax increases within designated blighted "districts" to fuel development in the area for twenty-three years. The justification for funneling property tax increases to pay for public projects is that development (and thus property value increases) would not have occurred "but for" public subsidies.

To compensate for the revenue loss resulting from this twenty-three-year tax diversion, taxing bodies like public schools, park districts, and so forth (e.g., that rely on property taxes), layer in "hidden" tax increases that are passed on to property owners living in and nearby the TIF district. So, rather than operating as property tax diversions, TIFs function as property tax hikes without exactly seeming so—these practices no doubt help explain why Illinois, which has used the policy liberally, has the second highest property tax rate in the nation. While the TIFs flew under the radar for decades, by the time my fieldwork was wrapping up, public demands for "transparency" and "accountability" were gathering force. Not surprisingly, TIFs have commonly been used in areas where gentrification is already well underway—as opposed to in blighted, low-income areas in need. Loose definitions of "blight," among other things, has allowed the City of Chicago to capitalize on what Kenneth Burke would call "strategic ambiguity" in order to institute TIF districts "flexibly."

Former mayor Daley, for example, diverted nearly $100 million of TIF money to partially fund the stunning Millennium Park along the glittering lakefront in downtown Chicago. Beautiful and publicly valuable: yes. Blighted and aiding the disenfranchised directly: no. Under the reign of Mayor Rahm Emanuel (2011–present), TIFs have been publicly scrutinized as the city's "shadow budget." The *Chicago Sun-Times* called TIFs a "mad money pot of off-the-books spending" (Roeder, "Taming"), and county assessor Jim Houlihan called TIFs "funny money" (Joravsky, "Right Fight"). As a catalysis for what I'll just call creative funding in late-capitalism, Tax Increment Financing has been a powerful tool and seemingly the only game in town that helped Chicago live up to its motto as a "city that works" during financial crisis.

But back in the 1990s, the general public had little interest in or knowledge of the policy. Much of what I read about TIFs at that time focused on the class politics underscoring the policy and centered on housing. It was a moment of intense real estate speculation in Chicago, and gentrification politics were salient in public discourse, as many neighborhoods near Uptown—such as Wicker Park, Lincoln Park, Lake View, and Edgewater—were rapidly developing throughout the 1980s, 1990s, and beyond. Such wide-scale urban restructuring led to the displacement of thousands of Chicago residents and business owners who were priced out, igniting protests initiated by diverse neighborhood groups, community organizations, and artists. While TIFs were only one factor in these processes, they were commonly framed as engines of gentrification that displaced the poor, in part, because they often resulted in rent increases, promises of urban renewal, and infrastructural improvements that facilitated upscale housing development. Not surprisingly, the construction and preservation of affordable housing became a key issue tied to TIFs as a way to counteract the consequences of this frenzied moment of gentrification[6] and land speculation leading up to the housing bubble and burst.

In this roundabout way, my reading about a tax policy became my entry for thinking about housing and its links to democracy—a key issue threaded throughout this book. I ended up learning much more about TIFs when it became clear that the subsidized affordable housing at Wilson Yard would be partially funded by the policy. Because much more is said on this issue in subsequent chapters, suffice it to say here that Uptown's contentious politics led to novel uses and criticisms of the TIF. Suddenly, the TIF was being used to mitigate (not catalyze) gentrification on behalf of the poor, and rather than a tool that reinforced class inequity, its use at Wilson Yard was critiqued for its denigration of middle-class interests and as an unjust use of public policy to redistribute wealth via property taxes to fund public ("welfare") projects that harmed the property owners (who were "fitting the bill"). Interesting to me at the time, and now central to this project, was the way that democratic rhetoric (with its powerful topoi, attendant civic practices, and moral virtuousness) was the pervasive driver in the work of affordable housing activists and those activist working against housing at Wilson Yard. Democracy, in other words, proved a capacious topos capable of being put to use by people with strikingly different worldviews. Tracing how this works itself out on a micro-level is another prominent thread in the book.

This tracing of micro-democratic practices leads me to my interest in publics that I mentioned earlier. Uptown's longstanding contested and robust publics captured my imagination long before I fancied myself a rhetorician or an ethnographer. My introduction to Uptown's politics came in the late-1990s through my interaction with activists involved with the St. Francis Catholic Worker House, a collective that has offered "hospitality" to the poor in the neighborhood since 1974. The activists I knew were involved in any number of issues, mostly centered on antipoverty, affordable housing, environmental, and nonviolent measures, and taken up through a radical leftist perspective. I lived in Uptown on Wilson Avenue intermittently between 1995 and 2000. I was very young then, and to be frank, energized by the visceral experience of being involved with people "doing democracy." I say this with a certain amount of embarrassment, in part because identifying with activists does not an activist make (and I was no activist), but more to the point, because an emotional freight (as opposed to political compulsion) underscored my desire to be involved. While the politics of these activists were similar to my own concerns with the systemic injustices of capitalism—to be blunt—which have informed my own ways of engaging the world through teaching and scholarship, the choice to focus on affect in my description is no accident.

I would go so far as to say that this deeply felt sense of wanting to be part of something happening when that something is doing democracy (in solidarity with an effectual public of like-minded people engaged in a fight for justice) is one of the more significant motors of Uptown's sustained and robust publics. Of course, myriad historical, ideological, material, and circumstantial textures explain why ordinary people have sustained very public and laborious battles over the contested spaces of Uptown for so many decades, but these publics congealed, in part, because there is a strong undertow of palpable immediacy, passion, excitement, nostalgia, and invigoration associated with being involved in democracy that tends to pull people into politics here. As one informant put it: "I never really paid much attention to what was going on in my neighborhood or the city, politics wise. But there are people involved here in making things better. Getting out there and working together. And that feels good. To be part of that." As I'll argue throughout these pages, within the spaces of everyday democracies, the persuasive power of such feelings (of justice, collective will, publicness, belonging, moral righteousness) becomes evident within my fieldsite where such emotional forces become entangled with rhetorical structures, ideology, material practices, spatial arrangements, aesthetics, and arguments about urban development and the public good. And so, my interest in the TIF policy dovetailed with this curiosity about why publics with starkly divergent politics were passionately moved by analogous impulses to be involved in doing democracy in solidarity with others, and driven by similar transcendent moral motors rooted in a yearning for social justice, all the while making use of the language, practices, logics, and symbols of democracy. In short, while the political content and ideological undercurrent of arguments differed dramatically among Uptown's publics, the rhetorical workings looked alarmingly similar.

This talk of alarm brings me to a final bit of biography that is relevant to the making of this text. While there were many times that I encountered political perspectives in Uptown that, quite honestly, horrified me personally, I also grew increasingly wary of the tendency in urban ethnographies to portray the disenfranchised as "paragons of morality," as Loïc Wacquant phrases it, within texts that reproduce, whether consciously or not, the "moral schemata and expectations of its audience" (1469–1470). To be brief, I did not want to craft an ethnography peopled with familiar heroes and moustache-twirling bad guys at the expense of analysis located at the level of the system, of immanent dynamism of everyday life, and with respect to how the forces of capitalism (or power more generally) shape all of our collective experiences at all levels (and, more importantly, how language and its deep enmeshments with ideology and materiality propels such shaping forces, which are also affecting the contested uses and meanings of language in practice). If I first entered the field with a type of critically edged project in mind that engaged in something of a left-leaning hermeneutics of suspicion, I exited it with the desire to perform something more akin to mapping the available means of persuasion as they circulated within complex and ambivalent contexts with as much empathy as possible.

So, while there remains an underlying urge to understand the pernicious manifestations of capitalism in everyday life (and, more specifically, within democracies), there is an attendant compulsion to both better understand its positive productiveness and to extend an empathetic analysis of its negative consequences to those positions and people often characterized as enemies of social justice by the left (the affluent, the dominant, those in power, homeowners, business owners, gentrifiers, capitalists, Republicans, and so on). The longer I was in the field, the more facile such characterizations felt, given the dire material realities many people faced who were dismissed along these lines, yet were also negatively affected and seduced by the mechanisms of capitalism (e.g., homeowners drowning in mortgage debt, business owners barely scraping by, young parents disillusioned by daily encounters with drug deals, etc.). In the messy details of Uptown's everyday democracy, I found ambivalence, complicity, *and* reasonableness around every corner. Everybody was doing democracy, driven by a sense of moral righteousness, evoking similar terms, drawing on shared logics, and marching to the same chants while holding poster boards with the same slogans, etched with the same black sharpies.

Given this ambivalence of democracy I rather like Brouwer and Asen's charge that, in recognizing the "processes of public engagement" as "value-laden.... we should not artificially confine our interest only to sympathetic cases" (21); however, by not situating one's "critical project" within a "specific point along an ideological continuum" (namely, one that resonates with readers' dispositions), researchers "risk losing.... secure normative ground" (21). In my case, this implies that in crafting the "field" as you will encounter it, I sought to capture and render visible how democratic rhetoric and practice—in all of its politically incommensurable enactments—work in a specific place over time and to what consequences. As Crowley phrases it, I have attempted to study "good rhetoric," which "looks for all available arguments," as opposed to "bad rhetoric," which is "static and univocal," "favors the status quo and extrapolates predictions from it," and "shuts down alternatives and hides the proliferation of differences created by its very formulation" (56).

But, what does one risk in extending generosity to political positions one (and one's readers) may abhor and in questioning celebrated and cherished positions? One thing at risk, in particular, is losing one's own moral orientation within the social thicket or, worse, capitulating into political paralysis. Swirling in the undercurrents of this book, then, is a desire to imagine what collective action and public rhetoric (aimed to work against systemically produced harm and toward shared public goods) might look like that neither replicates unchecked venerations of democracy, nor surrenders to critiques that portend the complete undoing of "democracy" in the neoliberal era. At heart, then: a pondering (and invitation to ponder) over what may serve as an ethical and political framework that might help us evaluate and engage in democratic practice from within the radical ambivalence of the democratic project.

Finally, in nitty-gritty terms, this is a multisite, mixed-method, rhetorical ethnography that engages in interviews, (participant) observation, and rhetorical, archival, visual, new media, and Internet analysis. My two concentrated periods of fieldwork occurred while I was studying at the University of Illinois-Chicago between the years 2005 and 2008, and then again between 2010 and 2011 as faculty at the University of Washington. However, in one way or another, I was "in the field" between 2005 and 2014, as throughout this time I conducted follow-up interviews, read local blogs, and tracked Uptown's politics throughout this time. This research involved interviews with homeowners, renters, public officials, proponents and protestors of gentrification, community organizers, and business owners. I formally interviewed forty-two informants, several times in many cases, who were in some way staked in Uptown politics—totaling around seventy hours of recorded data.

I informally spoke to many others at and after meetings and on the fly during events, asking questions like, "Are you here to support this urban development project? Why? Why do you think this project is so controversial? What are your thoughts about such and such argument for affordable housing?" to add general texture to my understanding of why people were invested in various public actions. I made an effort to interview both perceived leaders and participants of groups/organizations across various political positions to get a sense of "the official party line," as well as the variety of contested opinions within supposedly unified groups. Interviews focused on people's experiences with and perceptions of their neighborhood, neighborhood politics, gentrification, contested public spaces, urban development, democracy, civic participation, and community organization.[7]

I attended and observed at least fifty public events, meetings, and activities: protests, marches, community policing meetings, public town halls, city hall discussions, urban planning charettes, blueprint roll outs, information sessions, and so on. Most of these events directly related to urban development projects, the regulation of contested public space, and affordable housing in Uptown. I did some ambient observation of everyday street goings-on in various Uptown places, like the Wilson el stop, blood alley, public parks, and Wilson Yard pre and post construction. I sifted through hundreds of primary, archival artifacts (something like fifty linear ft. worth) at the Chicago Historical Society between 2006 and 2008, and again in 2010 on Uptown and Chicago history and organizations, particularly around issues of urban renewal and Chicago public/affordable housing.

I analyzed countless public artifacts related to Uptown's past and contemporary history, most of which relate to tax policies, gentrification, local politics, neighborhood activism, and affordable housing—these artifacts included brochures, news articles, organizational meeting minutes and emails, petitions, maps, websites, blogs, online community boards, flyers, white papers, development blueprints, photos, radio show transcripts, subpoenas, and more. Remarkably, this amassment represents a mere glimpse of the dynamic social space that is Uptown, Chicago. And yet, even within this amassment, there remain many untold stories, field accounts, observations, and research insights. If ever there were proof of ethnography's heuristical and thoroughly rhetorical status, it should glare boldly from the coherence that I fashion here from this or that document, captured performance, recorded narrative, or observed everyday happening. Ethnography is always already an exercise in capturing partialities and an attempt to earnestly present them in a manner that reflects the life energies of the field while resonating beyond the particularities of the local, the everyday, and the concrete.

The central driver of my fieldwork, data analysis, and theory building has been to better understand (map, capture, intuit, study, represent, visualize, theorize) the conditions and qualities of public formation and to forward a concept of rhetorical invention predicated on a sense of persuasion as a three-dimensional force that moves us (through us, in spite of us, beyond us). Studying such a force implicates envisioning everyday life as a deep interplay of people, desires, bodies, senses, emotions, objects, biology, symbols, arguments, ideologies, spaces, institutions, materialities, public memories, contexts, timing, and rhetoric. In fact, there was a turning point in my fieldwork when I became substantially more interested in persuasive forces—namely, material ones—that may be tethered to but live beyond what people say or write (which is to say, beyond discursive, alphabetic, strictly symbolic, logos-based, rational, human-centric argument). While I never considered this a project about people per se (rather, I initially perceived it as an ethnography of a "social space" or of "publics in action," having been heavily influenced by Henri Lefebvre and Jürgen Habermas), increasingly, my attunement to the field shifted to a more ecological sensibility, such that my "looking" began orienting toward locating amalgamations, circulations, enmeshments, multidimensional and layered stickings together of bodies, rhetoric, things, materialities, ideologies, spaces, histories, contested worldviews, and everyday practices. I began wondering about, among other things, matters like how people's arguments jibe with and emerge from affective and emotional responses to their environs; how the spaces of debates factor into what people can say, do, and believe; and how, why, and to what consequence rhetoric, ideologies, and materialities entangle.

In short, my initial interest in how rhetoric becomes emplaced (in bodies, spaces, practices, things, etc.) and how places become rhetorical—intensified. Clearly, these sorts of things are not easy to perceive, let alone triangulate in objective terms. One intuits and attunes to such things, experiences them with one's body and mind, making rhetorical ethnography a reasonable tool of observation, as I've said. Clearly, accounting for the intricate and dynamic enmeshments of body and mind, rhetoric and materiality, subjects and objects, and the like can never be complete, but this book *as a whole*, spanning its many pages, is an attempt to look at such matters from different angles, perspectives, and degrees of abstraction such that *as a whole* it suggests a way of looking at rhetoric as profoundly and radically situated and emplaced, as emergent from, dispersed across, and also shaping of the many things, people, arguments, spaces, feelings, memories, and forces of this sort and that which constitute our world. The comings together of such things and forces suggest what it means (in a spiralingly deep sense) to exist here or there and, indeed, comprise the places of invention. Any lines of sight into these places is offered here more than anything as an orientation toward how rhetoric might be perceived, as a method for looking at rhetoric's emplacements, and as a hope that, in doing so, we might expand our tools for intervening in the thickets that find us.

Lay of the Land

In the broadest terms, then, this is a study of rhetorical invention and, more specifically, the places of invention within the democratic project. The invention and work of democratic persuasions can only be understood within the exigencies from which rhetorical forces emerge and circulate. Contestation draws the mechanisms of democratic persuasions more starkly into focus, and in contested spaces, qualitative researchers can learn not only about how people talk about democracy but also how the language people use to talk about and enact democracy reveals and obscures certain "truths," possibilities, and limitations about how democracy is or might be practiced. Rather than drawing conclusions about which versions of democracy are truer or more just, my inclination is empirical with arrows aimed at capturing democracy as it occurs through emergent, immanent, and dynamic public activity. In the chapters that follow, I use various methodological approaches to study rhetorical invention in everyday democracies.

In Chapter One, I turn to Uptown's history of public contention as grounding for a study of rhetorical invention within democracy. Drawing on historical, rhetorical, and ethnographic methodologies, this chapter contextualizes Uptown's current politics within a genealogy of the rhetorics that have circulated around disinvestment, urban development, and gentrification for nearly a 100 years. These rhetorics—which are heavily reliant on democratic topoi (rights talk, citizen responsibility, equality vs. freedom)—provide some of the rhetorical stuff from which individuals draw within contemporary politics. In this chapter, I argue that affordable housing has played a central role in Uptown, providing both literal places and rhetorical commonplaces where politics about the neighborhood's future get played out. Chapter Two traces the tensions and contradictions in democratic and publics theory within the context of Wilson Yard, the mixed-use affordable housing development project described in the opening. In this gentrifying neighborhood, the evocation of democratic rhetorics just as easily dovetails with neoliberal discourse to justify market-driven development as with social welfare discourses that advocate government intervention in the housing market to produce affordable housing to counteract such development. Tracing the nuances of democratic rhetoric and subjectivities as they are evoked, circulated, and inhabited in public discourse and in the everyday practices of democracy is my aim.

Chapter Three melds visual rhetorical and ethnographic approaches to study "diversity" as a powerful, capacious topos and visual icon in democracy. Given the many forms of Uptown's diversity, the topos is deployed both to foreground cultural, ethnic, and racial diversity (e.g., identity-based diversities) as signs of justice achieved (to the detriment of class politics) and to draw attention to the systemic injustices of capitalism. Like democratic rhetoric, more broadly speaking, the diversity topos contains and supports such competing positions, providing persuasive force to both by offering readymade blueprints for aligning to morally righteous social justice agendas. Specifically, I trace the rhetorics of diversity as they manifest in the creation of two public murals in Uptown, which reveal divergent and competing conceptions of democracy. Chapter Four draws on spatial, material, and affective rhetorical approaches to examine a community policing practice called "positive loitering"—a strategy devised by Uptown homeowners in collaboration with the police—to eradicate the "negative loitering" associated with informal day labor markets in contested public spaces. By examining "positive loitering" protests, I consider overt and subtle ways that both systemic inequities and productive public goods are (re)produced by citizens in the name of democracy. Chapter Five considers how public emotional valences contribute to democratic persuasions in the field by tracing the role that a popular Uptown blog played in mobilizing a movement against crime. Drawing on fieldwork and scholarship on affect, materiality, and network perspectives, I study how affective structures become tethered to the material, nonhuman, nonrational, bodily, emotional, visceral, ideological, and rhetorical, as well as how these enmeshments lead to public formation and action in both the online and offline world.

By book's end, any hope for clearly distinguishing—let alone valorizing—a leftist, rightist, radical, or conservative politic dissolves in the hurly-burly of everyday democratic practice, where tactics, appeals, and arguments bleed and exist as radically ambivalent and complicit. The Conclusion considers what a politic might be that emerges from this stalemate. Ultimately, if the transcendent virtue of democracy is unraveled in the everyday, it is also in the everyday that we find the most innovative practices for intervening in politics in small, but significant ways. In its most distilled form, this project aims to locate the places of invention within democracy, to capture the work of rhetoric in ordinary life, and to ask where, in what form, and to what consequences people have found or may yet discover discursive resources for intervening in public life. Every remaining chapter orients toward these concerns.

I
Places of Invention

> It is unconscionable that in the 21st century, upwards of 100 million people in the United States live in housing that is physically inadequate, in unsafe neighborhoods, overcrowded or way beyond what they realistically can afford. . . . . The call to adopt. . . . a Right to Housing not only has an ethical basis in principles of justice and ideals of a commonwealth. It is also based on a highly pragmatic perspective—the central role that housing plays in peoples' lives.
>
> Rachel G. Bratt, Michael E. Stone, and Chester Hartman, *A Right to Housing*

> Traditionally, the "rights" of a citizen were a negative concept: they were freedoms "from" (from religious persecution, arbitrary arrest, censorship, and the like). Now they acquired a positive meaning in the sense of "claims to" (to housing, health care, etc.), which. . . . the government had a duty to satisfy. . . . Setting aside the nebulous and rather meaningless slogan "freedom from fear," "freedom from want" meant really not a freedom but a right—the right to the necessities of life at public expense, i.e., the right to something that was not one's own.
>
> Richard Pipes, *Property and Freedom*

Within the context of American democracy, housing is understood as both a commodity and a universal welfare right, as private property and a public good, as a literal place where we dwell and the conceptually rich place we call home. The contention that arises from these dual-articulations makes housing a particularly good lens through which to examine the incommensurable pulls of democracy. Housing has persistently served as one of the central *places of invention* in the local politics and contested publics of Uptown. The sentiments expressed in the opening quotations go far in explaining why. In the first, housing is understood as a basic human "right to" a universal public good that democratic governments should protect and provide. As Eleanor, a representative of an Illinois affordable housing financing institution, explained to me: "From a fair housing perspective, housing should be available for everyone. [. . .] Do people have a right to safe, decent, and affordable housing? Yes!"

In the second, this social justice claim of "rights to" is redefined pejoratively as the right to something "not one's own" at "public expense," a perspective that underscores critiques of the welfare state and represents a desire to return to a traditional sense of "rights" as "freedoms (read: protections) from." Alfonso, a longtime Uptown resident and landlord, crystallizes a stark version of this claim when he classifies affordable housing advocates as wanting "something for nothing for everyone" by "helping the downtrodden who would likely not get off their rear-ends at the expense of anyone else." In the first sentiment, the state is a mechanism for redistributing public goods (driven by the motor of social equity); in the latter, state power, which should be limited as much as possible, is a mechanism for protecting private property and defending man from government exploitations and from fellow man (driven by the motor of individual freedom). These competing discourses not only reside at the core of countless contemporary U.S. political debates over matters such as government-mandated healthcare and welfare entitlements, but also circulate within my fieldsite, where they have been grafted onto any number of local issues for decades.

Within the context of a gentrifying neighborhood, housing is one of the most tangible sites for generating contested arguments about citizenship, rights, and democracy, because it plays a central role in either propelling or protecting against displacements from class-based urban change, and thus, literally determines who can afford to remain part of the "demos." Housing (whether it is new upscale homes that promise social mobility or the protection of affordable housing[1] to counteract gentrification) becomes the quintessential "place" (materially, figuratively, topically) where arguments are catalyzed about the public good. As Lyons and Hardy put it, a "house is more than just the building and its qualities" (10). Because of its "immobility," they argue, housing is unlike most commodities—it is a socially relational investment that creates interpersonal and economic bonds between neighbors whose perceived return on investment is dependent on one another's "quality" (aesthetics, culture, public behavior, class standing). The innate contentiousness of such bonds is seen in Uptown, where one's investment can threaten another's livelihood and one's lifestyle another's investment.

I focus on housing as a core topos for understanding rhetorical action in Uptown's everyday democracies for three key reasons. First and foremost, while I did not enter the field with an explicit focus on housing,[2] informants consistently identified housing as a lynchpin topic. During my time in the field, longtime affordable housing activists worried about the consequences of gentrification for low-income residents, and pushed for new low-cost housing in the name of equality and democracy. The formidable opposition that rose against these initiatives understood additional affordable housing as working against its goals to improve the business core, upgrade public aesthetics, and create safer streets. The fieldsite itself, in short, announced that housing was a magnet for broader political, ideological, moral, and economic concerns; a catalyst for civic action across the spectrum; and a key rhetorical battleground where differences were wrangled: which are all concepts that will be traced throughout this chapter and book.

Second, the historical prevalence of housing discourse in Uptown politics is long-lived—preceding my fieldwork by a hundred years. The questions of how, where, and in what manner to house the poor, where the responsibility lies to ensure balanced development, and how affordable housing is either threatened by or threatens "neighborhood improvement" have been common and reoccurring threads in Uptown's public discourse since the 1920s. The historical prominence of housing discourse and the pervasive linking of housing to democracy and its various attendant topoi (rights, equality, publics, citizenships, property ownership, taxpayers, freedom) constitute what Celeste Condit calls a *rhetorical formation*. Drawing on Foucault's discourse formation, Condit's term conceives public rhetoric as comprised of myriad dynamic and agonistic rhetorical structures that are crafted through a continual process of persuasion and seduction in the ongoing wrangle to exert control over public discourse (252–56). Her work also attunes us to how new forms of seduction are invented, and to how shifting material conditions change the persuasive lures that move people.

Third, and related, it is through the rhetorical formation that links housing and democracy that I will orient you to the rhetorical history of my fieldsite, which is the central aim of this chapter. The choice to tell the history of my fieldsite as a history of its rhetoric is one aspect that signals this as a project of rhetorical ethnography. Housing is only one lens through which the history of a neighborhood can be told, but in Uptown it is an important one because this history has continually generated arguments about the contradictory "rights" of citizens: the right to profit from a hot housing market; the right to decent, affordable housing; the right to inhabit public space as you see fit; the right to control how your property taxes are spent; and the right not to be displaced from your neighborhood through gentrification. In Uptown, even general battles over public space tend to lean on rhetoric that links housing to a citizen's rights (e.g., *She's a renter, so isn't invested in what happens. We, as homeowners, are the ones taking care of this place and we suffer the consequences of social dysfunction associated with building more affordable housing.* Or: *He is a loiterer, living in a shelter, bringing down our neighborhood, threatening our safety, and lowering property values. He doesn't even live here. Why should we vote for something that exacerbates this situation?* Or: *Renters are just as staked in the processes of gentrification as homeowners because it is renters who are priced out while homeowners reap benefits. So, resisting the onslaught of boutiques and condo projects, and supporting low-cost housing is in our interest.*) In short, studying Uptown's history of rhetorical wrangles over housing is a central heuristic for discovering the *places of invention* that have been historically significant to political contention and public formation in the neighborhood.

The Western rhetorical tradition is replete with heuristics designed specifically to help us locate ourselves within the economies of circulating rhetorical forces and to discover the places where the powers and tools of persuasion reside. When I say *places of invention*, I am evoking the rhetorical concept of the commonplace, or topos. While the term commonplace has several contested meanings, as I will discuss later, suffice it to say here that I mean those stock arguments, words, ideas, symbols, and discursive structures that circulate with force within a social space and that yoke the rhetorical, the ideological, and the material. The emphasis of *place* as it pertains to invention, therefore, is intended to: (1) capture the literal, concrete, material aspects of place that affect rhetorical invention and action and (2) highlight the competing rhetorical frames that circulate within and are tied to literal places. In short, examining the *places of invention* entails understanding how commonplaces (topoi) and literal places (concrete material spaces and spatial practices) enmesh, while also suggesting a method well-suited for field researchers whose sustained presence allows for a systematic study of the available means, modalities, and consequences of persuasion in specific places and times.

In 2008, I met Francis, who works at an Uptown affordable housing organization, and who had been involved in housing activism for two decades. I asked her to characterize Uptown's political history. One of the most striking aspects of this history, she said, is the way Uptown has been shaped by waves of "land speculation" in which housing has continually played a "central" role. Francis went on to say that at the "heart of our strife" lies a:

> *battle over land, which is why housing is so central to much of the heat in things taking place now. People have come hoping this neighborhood would be the next hot place, and they have dreamed and hoped and invested in those dreams. But the economic boom has been delayed and this is frustrating to people. We also have a lot of housing that keeps poor people and their plights in view. SROs, public housing, low-income housing, homeless shelters, affordable co-ops. And a longstanding dyed in the wool lefty Alderman who's been organizing here for a long time to protect those people and their housing. And there are a whole lot of people*

who support her. And a lot of people who don't. So, you might say that Uptown's history is one of land speculation and retaliation against that speculation.

While Francis's response merely hints at the contention that swirls around Uptown's history of land speculation, her focus on how competing visions of Uptown become implicated in "battles over land" and invested in housing is clear. Different types of housing (whether we are talking about vintage condos or public housing) become associated with certain people, particular demographics (race, class, aesthetics, and so on), and various ideologies and social dreams (of class mobility, luxury, stability, peace, and beauty—or of economic equality and radical diversity).

In Uptown, the material legacy of housing policies has led to everything from pernicious racial segregation to vibrant and diverse immigrant communities; from slum constructions to palatial Victorian homes; from public housing high-rises to upscale condo conversions, and from well-managed subsidized co-ops to atrocious flop houses. This legacy provides the material foundation that sustains the deeply contested publics in Uptown.[3] Another way of saying this, to return to the idea of invention, is that the brick-and-mortar material conditions of housing (given the broad contentious associations mentioned above) supply the literal places from which the rhetorical commonplaces about housing and democracy emerge and remain viscerally present. The examination of such relationships between places and commonplaces provides not only an opportunity to learn more about the rhetorical history that informs Uptown's contemporary politics, but also about the layered conception of the *places of invention*, as a way of conceiving and situating rhetoric-in-action. I continue by further developing this concept before offering a history of the housing commonplaces in Uptown that has informed contemporary debates in Uptown's everyday democracies.

On Commonplaces and the Places of Invention

The rhetorical concept of "invention" translates from the Greek word *heuresis* and from the Latin term *inventio*, meaning to "invent" or "discover." Aristotle famously defined rhetoric itself as the art of invention, or more precisely, as the "ability, in each particular case, to see the available means of persuasion" (Aristotle *Rhetoric* I.1.2). Over two thousand years later, contemporary rhetoricians Crowley and Hawhee similarly define invention as the "art of discovering all of the arguments made available by a given rhetorical situation" (51). To facilitate the capacity of invention, rhetoricians from the

Classical period forward have devised elaborate heuristics to help people locate, examine, and deploy the available means of persuasion. This heuristical sense of invention is captured by Corbett and Connors, who call "*inventio*" a "systematized way of turning up or generating ideas on some subject" (20), and by Consigny who calls rhetoric a "heuristic art" because it helps us "discover real issues in indeterminate situations" (180). Within the Aristotelian tradition alone, one encounters a complex schematic of proofs (*artistic* and *inartistic*), appeals (*ethos, logos, pathos*), and topoi (*general* and *special*), each designed to assist with invention.[4]

Within the Classical tradition, these inventional heuristics were referred to as commonplaces or topoi (sometimes the topics in English). Etymologically, "topoi" refers to "places" and, within the rhetorical tradition, the term generally references the places one goes to discover the available means of persuasion. While this seems like a rather unassuming definition, topoi have been defined variously and controversially throughout the history of Western rhetoric. As John Muckelbauer writes, "If there is any consensus that congeals around *topoi* it is quite simply that we are still not certain exactly what they are" (124). For Classical rhetoricians, the term was sometimes understood quite literally as the "places" on papyrus rolls where the topoi were written (Crowley and Hawhee 117). In this encyclopedia sense, the topoi acted as a "*place* or store or thesaurus" where one discovered stock ways to develop arguments, which might have included "lines of argument," lists of questions, or argument forms (such as compare and contrast, definition, possible or impossible) (Corbett and Connors 19).

But because Classical rhetoricians also understood invention as a deeply situated social act, rather than the labor of individual minds, commonplaces were also understood quite conceptually as publicly shared knowledge and ideological dispositions found "in the very language we speak and the symbols we rely on" (Crowley and Hawhee 133). In this sense, topoi are rhetorical structures that emerge from and guide the collectively held beliefs and practices within a community—and thus, topoi cannot not be fully known universally, but can only be found in the social, political, and material textures of places and times. Accordingly, one invents by immersing and orienting oneself within the rhetorics of particular places.

Part of these definitional variations, as Lanham notes, stems from the fact that topoi are seen as "both the stuff of which arguments are made and the form of those arguments" (152); in fact, Classical rhetoricians used the word interchangeably to refer to both the "stuff" and "form" of arguments (Crowley and Hawhee). Topoi have also been used to describe the methods and strategies one might deploy to discover arguments. As Lindquist writes, topoi "let speakers know 'where to go' to find the resources for a given argument," constituting a "system of knowledge *and* identif[ying] socially viable 'techniques' of persuasion" (73). Crowley and Hawhee separate the methodological functions of topoi from the content contained within them through distinct terms, using "*topic* to refer to any specific procedure that generates arguments" and "*commonplace* to refer to statements that circulate within ideologies" (118) or that "form bits or pieces of ideologies" (140), where "ideology" is defined as the "bodies of belief, doctrines, familiar ways of thinking that are characteristic of a group or culture" (128). Similar to their sense of the commonplace, Cintrón defines *topoi* as "storehouses of energy" that "organize our sentiments, beliefs, and actions in the lifeworld" ("Democracy" 100), including "verbal and nonverbal crystallizations that have sufficient umpf to actualize the body politic" (101).

Resonant with these latter two definitions, I use *topoi* and *commonplaces* interchangeably to refer to those bits of language, rhetorical structures, salient stock arguments, resonate symbols, and visual icons that emerge from and circulate with force within social spaces. However, I seek to expand this discursive/rhetorical/ideological conception of topoi and keep it in tension with a material sense of topoi. That is, I also understand topoi as the reified tools, material conditions and mechanisms (objects, spaces, genres, bodily habits, and other materialities) that constrain, enact, generate, circulate, and mobilize salient rhetorical structures. I am not alone in this inclination. For example, Bawarshi's theory of invention conceives of genre as a "place" where one might find resources for rhetorical invention, action, and intervention. Genres are "situated topoi within which invention takes place, habits as well as habitats for acting in language" (Bawarshi 13) and "within which individuals acquire, negotiate, and articulate desires, commitments, and methods of inquiry to help them act in a given situation" (113). In another view, object-oriented philosophers, such as Bennett, enable us to conceive of "vibrant matter" (things, objects, stuff) as vital nonhuman agents that emerge from and shape our social practices, participating in the formation of politics, persuasive forces, and our collective ways of knowing and doing.

Finally, while Debra Hawhee's scholarship on Kenneth Burke and the body does not explicitly reference topoi or invention, it helps us see how the body's dispositions, affects, and habits play a role "in shaping interpretation" (*Moving* 85) and collective "perspective" (103). Hawhee (and Burke) study the "bodily, affective processes that shape rational, and ultimately rhetorical associations" (*Moving* 85). These "bodily meaning-making" processes figure the body as a "vital, connective, mobile, and transformational force. . . . that exceeds—even as it bends and bends with—discourse" (7). If collectively held bodily knowledge and habits both shape and are informed by shared rhetorical and ideological dispositions—and if we understand topoi as the places where one goes to discover the resources of persuasion—then one begins to see how the body and its dispositions are part of those tools. In sum, while working in different fields, these scholars collectively point to a sense of topoi as those materialities that shape, condition, and order our bodies, activities, and rhetorical practices (and constitute rhetorical resources that cannot be reduced to symbolicity). This is all to say that the sense of topoi that I have in mind in this book, as well as the conception of invention that I am forwarding, necessarily keeps the production of symbolic persuasive forces tied to the means, modes, and material scaffolding of that production within specific places—thus, rhetorical structures are not perceived as universal, bloodless, or immaterial, but must be imagined in tension with the reified mechanisms, spaces, and bodily habits that reproduce and circulate rhetoric and within which rhetoric dwells.

If the clarity of what a topos is exactly is diminishing right about now (or sprawling out into the cosmos) rather than sharpening, it may be because, so far, topoi have been referred to as general, contentless argument structures (*topoi as stable-for-now argument forms*); as generic strategies for discovering arguments (*topoi as method, heuristic, or systematized process*); as the salient, capacious, circulating rhetorical structures specific to times and places that contain the contradictory meanings, ideologies, and political stuff that guide our everyday lives (*topoi as salient symbolic content, discursive "storehouses of energy," and concentrated "bits of ideology"*); and as the objects, tools, technologies, spaces, genres, and human/nonhuman mechanisms that organize social activity, help form bodily dispositions, enable particular relationships, and circulate argument (*topoi as materialities/material conditions that shape, enable, and constrain rhetorical forces, social energy, and activities*).

Muckelbauer suggests that the historical "confusion" about what topoi actually are might not be an "accidental gap" of understanding that "must be overcome" (127), but rather signal the "con-fusion of bodies and places" within which topoi reside as rhetorical powerhouses that occasion generative and immanent response (137).[5] The relationship between topoi and confusion, then, might best be seen as a "strategic style of movement akin to hunting," in which topoi, as the "'secret' places of argument," might be less concerned with "apprehension" than with prompting the capacities for grasping and responding to profoundly "immanent" rhetorical situations (127). In fact, he argues that topoi constitute the "very force that enables" such "grasping" and, therefore, "eludes that grasp" (132). Simply put, one cannot capture, comprehend, or mobilize topoi outside of the kairotic[6] social contexts of their circulation and use and without a capacity for "topoi hunting" (which we might boil down as robust rhetorical awareness). Attempts to reduce topoi to universal transportable heuristics or stable content might be useful pedagogically (as these things make topoi more seeable, graspable, teachable), but this move to universalize is also the move that extracts topoi from the particulars of the everyday immanence that constitute their power, and, thus precipitates the deflation of this power.

Immanence here resonates with Deleuze and Guattari's thinking on the matter, which locates the guiding powers of our world not in the transcendent realm of religions or gods, but rather in the vibrant forces that shape and are shaped by the mundane enmeshments of materialities, rhetorics, and ideologies that manifest in everyday, ordinary life. In plainer language, Muckelbauer's argument suggests that the power of topoi has to do with their responsiveness to and orientation within the dynamism of the everyday. Thus, part of the "inventive character" of topoi resides in their "capacity to respond immanently" (132), or rather to trigger such responses, to those enmeshments and dynamisms that they simultaneously constrain. If the power of *topoi* exists in the immanence and "con-fusions" of everyday life, then they teach, Muckelbauer insists, not by "promoting understanding or telling us what to do" but by "provoking an inhabitation" (137); therefore, in order to grasp what is "proper to rhetoric" or understand how to mobilize the "immanent variation" of *topoi*, one "would need to inhabit the particularity of place" (141). In fact, the "very question of what rhetoric *is* might provoke an inhabitation rather than demand an answer" (141).

The idea that comprehending rhetoric requires inhabitation begins to get to the nuance I am after in this concept of *places of invention*, which I will speak to momentarily. But for now, it should be clear that part of the difficulty of pinning down the definitions of rhetorical invention and commonplaces is the sheer complexity, variability, and dynamism of the situational textures that constitute rhetorical force, and thus affect rhetorical invention. Jeff Rice's call for rhetoric to be a "practice in the *very many*" is apt here—leaning on Bruno Latour, this practice includes the "very many things, people, ideas, concerns, and spaces that make up a given position, concept, and place" (*Digital* 5). For me, understanding this complexity means inhabiting and participating in the social, political, and ideological stuff of everyday life. If we take seriously the profound interrelatedness (or the "con-fusions") of rhetoric and its situations, then it makes sense to demand "inhabitation" as a requirement of understanding rhetoric-in-action. Simply, one must inhabit a place to grasp and understand how to use a commonplace in that place.[7] Miller also captures this requirement of inhabitation when she argues that the topos is a "conceptual space," a "region of productive uncertainty" that "rather than circumscribing or delimiting" and "rather than being a closed space or container *within* which one searches, it is a space, or a located perspective, *from* which one searches" (141). Miller's elegant description is steeped in metaphorical references to literal places—region, space, location, container—and implicates my insistence on investigating the available means of persuasion by examining topoi as conceptual spaces that are also intimately and immanently tied to places, locations, spaces, and materialities.

The primacy of inhabitation to understanding rhetoric brings to mind Lefebvre's work on social spaces, which helps us explore this precise question of how the materiality of everyday life constitutes the rhetorical and how the rhetorical constitutes the materiality of everyday life. This chiasmus is represented in Lefebvre's oft-quoted conception of social space as capable of generatively structuring and being structured by rhetoric (rather than simply as an inert container of objects): "Every language is located in space. Every discourse says something about space (places or sets of places); and every discourse is emitted from a space"[8] (132). Lefebvre's understanding of the production of social space provides a useful lens through which to look at how commonplaces become rooted in places—and at the relationship between this rootedness and the way arguments are used inventively to get things done.

As Ackerman writes, Lefebvre's work attunes us to the "spatial dimensions" of rhetorical situations and invention (85), reminding us that the "textures of. . . . language and activity would not exist apart from a specific location" (96). Reynolds's thoughtful crystallization of Lefebvre's spatial theories contributes a focus on how the body is implicated in how "spatial practices. . . . shape lifeworlds" (14). She insists that we "need to understand more about how spatialities become imprinted on a body and form a *habitus*, a set of embodied practices" that people "carry around with them—like skin, hair, clothing" (175). This all suggests that, given the reciprocal co-constitution of rhetorics and situations, studying the interaction and amalgamation of spatial practices, bodily habits, rhetorical commonplaces, materialities, and ideologies should be seen as the central act of rhetorical invention that not only requires inhabitation but also constitutes the *places of invention*.

Let me pause here to gather my threads and be more explicit about what I mean by *places of invention*. First, the term *place* constitutes the "available means of persuasion." *Place* draws on the concept of the commonplace (topos) structures (keywords, discursive forms, language, symbols, visual icons, etc.) that guide, organize, emerge from, and circulate within everyday life. *Place* also evokes the material places (and particularities of those places) that shape and are shaped by such rhetorical structures, which might include the objects, institutions, genres, tools, built and natural environments, and bodies, as well as the people, practices, conceptualizations, and competing ideologies, that constitute and are invested in those places. Second, engaging in acts of rhetorical invention, then, presumes that *rhetoric* (what it is, what it does, how it works) and *rhetorical situations* (the political, ideological, and material contexts, constraints, audiences, circulations, and consequences of rhetoric) cannot be separated. Therefore, referencing the *places of invention* foregrounds this idea that rhetorical invention requires an examination of the productive and profoundly situational enmeshments of rhetoric and materiality, words and things, bodies and symbols, commonplaces and literal places. Third, even if commonplaces exist prior to their uses, circulating in social spaces as potential energy awaiting activation, it is not enough to study them acontextually as one might study the periodic table and hope to unleash or understand their power. Since rhetoric is profoundly contextual and wed to materiality, such power is only fully discovered in concrete places and times. As Miller puts it, topoi cannot be "defined or specified beforehand" but "can be recognized and understood afterward" (141). Fourth, because the power of commonplaces cannot be known outside of the places and times in which they perform work, the act of invention, likewise, requires a thoroughly situational knowledge of places learned through the practices of "inhabitation." And, finally, above all, I seek in this term a way to keep rhetoric profoundly tethered to the material by playing on the double meaning of place (as enmeshments of commonplaces and material/literal places). To study the *places of invention*, then, is an attempt to keep in tow the rich, three-dimensional complexity of all that is involved in the act of invention, which is too often flattened out in the clean definition of rhetoric as the art of discovering what it is that moves people.

As a person who claims to be an ethnographer and a rhetorician, I believe that this term helps explain why I decided to go to something called a fieldsite to study rhetoric-in-action. Rhetorical ethnography not only offers a method that requires the researcher to inhabit the places of rhetorical production, but also provides a genre robust enough to represent the complexity of such places. While this section has set up general ideas about invention that resonate throughout the book, this chapter specifically asks what it means for a rhetorician to tell the history of a place. Telling the history of Uptown as a history of its places of invention is my response. Thus, the remainder of this chapter offers the history of housing as a central topos where democratic rhetoric and action come to a head, making housing topoi exemplary places for studying democratic persuasions in my fieldsite. In the sections that follow, I seek to historicize the rhetorical and material role of housing in historical cycles of investment and disinvestment as a foundation for understanding the ethnographic case studies that dominate the remainder of this book.

Housing as Commonplace

The antagonist relationship between land speculation and affordable housing initiatives has been a permanent feature of Uptown since the first organized movement for development under the federal urban renewal program in the mid-1950s was met by a countermovement of community organizers and disenfranchised Uptowners who were concerned that urban renewal would displace the poor.[9] The presence of affordable housing has provided the material foundation that not only enables low-income households to remain in the neighborhood, but also keeps commonplaces about poverty, structural injustice, and democracy as equality in view. In other words—to return to our earlier conversation on invention—affordable housing in tension with market-driven development (and, by extension, the people, politics, ideologies aesthetics, lifestyles, behaviors, and practices that come to be associated with each) underscores the rhetorical battleground maintained by Uptown's clashing publics. The key pivot points in these tensions generally spring forth from the following sets of questions, from which the commonplaces that link housing and democracy throughout Uptown's history emerge:[10]

> Is affordable housing a public good that democratic citizens have a right to and for which government should protect and provide, or is it an infringement on the rights of homeowners, taxpayers, and otherwise "responsible" citizens who not only subsidize it, but also live with the consequences of its presence?

> Should middle-class and affluent homeowners have more influence in the policies and practices that affect their neighborhoods, or should stakeholders also include renters, employees, transients, the homeless, and other nonproperty owners?

> Does affordable housing subsidized through government intervention interfere with the free market, burdening responsible taxpayers and sacrificing individual freedom, or does the free market create the conditions for radically unjust, systemic economic inequalities that require invention?

Does the presence of affordable housing perpetuate poverty, blight, moral depravity, and/or deviant public behavior, or does it correct widespread systemic injustice that is reinforced by the housing market?

In the context of a gentrifying neighborhood is urban development a positive energy that promises to boost safety, livability, conviviality, aesthetics, and property values for all or is it a pernicious force that threatens to displace the poor? Is market-driven development a "natural" or inevitable force that generally produces the best outcomes for the most, or one that systemically exacerbates inequality?

While people and their relationships to urban development are much more complex than the starkness of any particular topos they might wield in a given moment, below I isolate some of the most common topoi that such questions generate, that emerge from fieldwork, and that circulate in Uptown. Not every topos is present in every relevant rhetorical situation, and people who either oppose or support affordable housing in Uptown would never use (believe, support, operationalize) every topos of opposition or support. The various topoi that collectively constitute the available means of persuasion in either "category" listed below represent myriad conflicting reasons for opposing or supporting the housing that no one person holds in total.

Common Topoi Used to Oppose Affordable Housing:
—Poverty—and more precisely, the visible evidence of poverty as manifest through the presence of housing for the poor—is either the primary cause of Uptown's downslide or the roadblock to its renaissance.

—The literal architecture of affordable housing itself, by providing spaces of concentrated dwelling for the poor, "breeds" poverty. Eliminating low-cost housing or thwarting its further development will eliminate poverty (either totally or in a given area) and the social consequences/burdens associated with poverty.

—Affordable housing and/or the inhabitants of the housing are linked to (if not responsible for) the moral depravity, public safety concerns, poor aesthetics, damage to property values, blight, etc. You can eliminate such social ills and undesirable neighbors by eradicating their housing.

—Uptown has hit its quota of affordable housing, and no more should be built. I am not a NIMBY (Not In My Back Yard), but additional housing here is unfair/will further concentrate poverty, which is already past the tipping point.

—Subsidized affordable housing interferes with market logics, and unjustly redistributes private monies (via property taxes) for public projects that might harm property values and individual investments. Related: subsidized affordable housing evokes critiques of the welfare state, positing residents as lazy, irresponsible, failed citizens draining the public coffer on the backs of responsible, hardworking, taxpaying citizens.

—Affordable housing advocates (in Uptown) are renters or activists who do not live in the neighborhood. Since they aren't property owners, they aren't as staked in the future of the neighborhood. They neither pay for the affordable housing with their hard-earned dollars, nor live with the consequences once it's built. Related: housing advocates treat us (property owners) like bad guys, but I'm just a guy with a family and a mortgage, barely hanging on here, who just wants to live in a decent place.

—As a result of changes to national housing policy, the opposition to affordable housing is increasingly framed with rhetorics of empowerment that dovetail with affordable housing advocates. The most common topos: Rather than "stockpiling" poor people in substandard living conditions, we should provide the same safe, clean, and healthy homes that the middle-class expects. Anything short of this is an injustice to the poor.

Common Topoi Used to Support Affordable Housing:
—Capitalism produces and perpetuates systemic inequality, which is undemocratic. Intervention through intentional construction or preservation of affordable housing is an issue of social justice and necessary to counteract market forces. Related: the housing market will not produce enough units on its own, and thus requires intervention.

—Affordable housing is a democratic right that should be provided by the government. Everyone has a right to decent housing, and providing such is a democratic impulse from which everyone benefits.

—Property owners only care about property values. Property owners are merely "NIMBYs" who are selfish and not interested in social equality.

—Government subsidies and taxes are used to fund market-driven commercial development and infrastructure improvements; therefore, such public monies should also be used to ensure that people are not displaced through urban development so that they may also benefit from improvements to their neighborhood.

The moral starkness of these topoi, in particular, undercut the complex contexts that highlight why someone might need affordable housing in the first place, the myriad types of such housing, and the various reasons someone might oppose housing; and yet, these topoi abound in public discourse where they are sometimes wielded with crystal clarity. While the clear moral uprightness embedded in these topoi are mucked up in the messy ethnographic detail of Uptown's everyday democracies featured throughout the remainder of this book, I close this chapter with a history of how these housing topoi have manifested over time, enabled and abetted by the sustained tension between affordable housing and commercial development.

Roots of Contention

After its annexation to Chicago in 1889, and on through the Great Depression, Uptown's economic growth was driven by real estate speculation and commercial entrepreneurialism, which was to a large extent enabled by the extension of the Northwestern Elevated Railroad from downtown to Wilson Avenue in 1900.[11] During this period, Uptown became a port-of-entry for European immigrants arriving from Germany, Sweden, and Ireland, leading to an explosion in population from 44,562 to 89,552 between 1910 and 1920 (Siegel 30). The neighborhood also emerged as a booming shopping and entertainment destination that boasted a vibrant nightlife for the young, and a center of silent movie production, attracting big-name stars like Charlie Chaplin and Gloria Swanson. Many of Uptown's contemporary architectural landmarks were constructed in the 1920s, including upscale hotels, lavish movie theaters, and glamorous nightclubs, some of which are still in operation, such as the Aragon Ballroom and the Green Mill.[12]

While this time period is contemporarily heralded as a heyday from which the neighborhood fell, the perception is somewhat chimerical: during the 1920s and 1930s, for example, apartments were already being subdivided

5. Empty Uptown Theater in the Background in 2007. Photo by Author.

into cramped living spaces, and cheap hotels were constructed to accommodate the transient youth and iterant workers associated with the entertainment district. These practices of hasty overcrowding and shoddy construction predate the end of World War II, when the explosion of substandard living arrangements are associated in Uptown (Siegel 33; Lyden and Jakus 9). The stock of cheap housing provided a material foundation that catalyzed housing commonplaces. During the 1920s and 1930s, for example, the commonplaces that link poor people and low-cost housing and that identify such housing as an obstacle to neighborhood improvement was evoked by the Central Uptown Association (CUA), which sought to improve Uptown by ridding the neighborhood of "undesirables" (street merchants, peddlers, prostitutes, etc.). To do so, CUA targeted the buildings that housed such residents, arguing that razing their homes would eliminate their presence (and attendant social problems) from Uptown. In 1931, the president of CUA announced his organization's reasoning behind opposing Uptown's furnished boarding houses: "We have nothing against the better class transients," Wuehrmann said, "We believe, however, that the type of people attracted by unfurnished apartments is more profitable, both from the business and the civic points of view, than the type attracted by furnished rooms"

("Uptown Gains" D2). Although such business elites opposed housing "undesirable" tenants, these accommodations remained an ambivalent but lucrative real estate enterprise that contributed to the neighborhood's commercial success throughout the Depression Era (Siegel 35–37).

In the late-1920s, real estate speculation dovetailed with racist attitudes when housing policy became a means of controlling the racial character of the neighborhood. In Uptown, 1,500 white property owners organized a city-sanctioned restrictive racial covenant, agreeing not to sell properties to African Americans who were migrating by the hundreds into the city from the south (Siegel 47). For decades, this racial covenant "successfully" contained the growth of the African American population in Uptown to a few blocks between Winthrop and the Lake, Montrose and Lawrence. According to the U.S. Census, the African American population varied little for thirty years after the covenant, with 531 individuals in 1930 and 433 in 1960 (Siegel 51). Although the U.S. Supreme Court ruled such covenants unconstitutional in 1944, it wasn't until the 1960s that the black population grew in Uptown; between 1960 and 1970, for example, the population increased from 400 to 3,400, and by 1980 the population was at 9,700 (Siegel 167). In 2000, 21% of Uptown's population was African and African American, and the neighborhood currently has one of the few concentrations of black households on Chicago's North Side. The accessibility of affordable housing is a substantial factor in this presence.

During the postwar era, Uptown became a "port of entry," in part, because a Chicago-wide housing shortage prompted the lucrative conversion (e.g., cutting up) of single-family residences into substandard, overcrowded units that quickly dissolved into slum conditions. Despite a virtual freeze on city-wide construction, Uptown experienced a 33% increase in available housing units that resulted from such slum conversions (Haas et al. 10), and a population swell to almost 85,000 in 1950 (Maly 54) before steadily declining over the decades to around 56,000 in 2010 (which still felt like a dense urban neighborhood). From the 1950s forward, Uptown's affordable housing stock attracted waves of migrants and immigrants—serving as the material foundation of its radical diversity. Siegel locates the origin of Uptown's contemporary politics between 1930 and 1960, a period when immigrant, migrant, and refugee groups gravitated toward the area—creating a foundation of diverse and vulnerable stakeholders who were organized against the threat of displacement from urban renewal efforts that occurred in the 1960s and 1970s, and later from gentrification from the 1980s forward.

The diversity increased during the 1940s and 1950s, as Russian Jews migrated from the West Side of Chicago, along with Greek Americans. Up-

Foreign-Born Persons in Uptown 1970–2009[1]

Census	Number of Individuals	% of Uptown Population
1970	14,807	19.80
1980	20,431	31.70
1990	20,809	32.60
2000	20,982	33.00
2009	17,141	28.70

Table 1—Source: U.S. Census and Greater Chicago Housing and Community Development Website (1970–2000); Rob Paral and Associates (2009)

1. Excludes Puerto Rican and U.S. Island-born.

town was particularly desirable for these groups, and others to come, in part, because of its cheap housing and because it was hospitable to immigrants who did not fit easily into a city that was highly segregated into white and black neighborhoods. Throughout the 1950s and 1960s, tens of thousands of southern whites (from Kentucky, West Virginia, Alabama, and Tennessee) arrived searching for employment after the mechanization of the coal mining and agriculture industries. In the 1950s, Chicago was a destination for Puerto Ricans who immigrated to the US under "Operation Bootstraps." Originally settling in Lincoln Park and Lakeview, this population was displaced by urban renewal in the 1960s and 1970s to Humboldt Park, and to a lesser extent, Uptown. Between the 1960s and 1980s, the Latino population increased and consisted of immigrants from Chile, Cuba, Guatemala, Mexico, Puerto Rico, and El Salvador (Maly 63). In 1953, Native Americans began migrating to Chicago under the federal "Urban Indian Relocation Program," a failed strategy for dissolving the reservation system by providing incentive to move to cities. Hundreds of Native Americans, mostly from Minnesota, Oklahoma, and Wisconsin, settled in Uptown, and in 1963, the American Indian Center of Chicago opened in the neighborhood.

After World War II, Uptown attracted Japanese immigrants, some of who were leaving internment camps. The immigration spike shown in Table 1 also reflects a wave of immigrants and refugees from Southeast Asia (mostly Laos, Cambodia, and Vietnam) who concentrated around the Argyle-Broadway area in the 1970s and 1980s, as well as from African countries (especially Eritrea, Ethiopia, Haiti, Nigeria) in the 1980s and 1990s. Uptown's African American population also continued to grow in the 1970s and 1980s (Haas et al. 10). By 1990, a third of Uptown's population was foreign born (Maly and

Leachman 146), and non-white residents still comprised 50% of the population in 2014.

In addition to immigration patterns, in the 1970s, Illinois State policy led to the deinstitutionalization of individuals in psychiatric wards, hundreds of whom were reportedly bussed to or literally dumped in Uptown where there were social service agencies, affordable housing, and shelters to support these individuals, but which nonetheless caused an immediate spike in the homeless population (Bennett 43). Roberta, a longtime Uptown affordable housing and homeless provider, describes her experience with the "dumping" of humans during the 1970s and 80s:

> Roberta: *I remember this woman from DHS who drove the car. . . . she was the middle of the night person. You know, driving the emergency cars. And they would come and just drop people off [. . .] dumping people left and right. No files, no names, no money.*
> Candice: *DHS. This is the Department of. . . .*
> Roberta: *Human Services.*
> Candice: *Human Services? Wow.*
> Roberta: *The city had no idea what to do with the people. They were just dropping them off. With us. . . . outside our door.*
> Candice: *Just dumping people? From all over the city?*
> Roberta: *Yes.*

With increasing momentum after the 1950s, low-cost housing, which has consistently been pitted against Uptown's revitalization, took on central prominence when postwar federal Great Cities "urban renewal" practices hit their peak in the 1960s. In response to the conditions of decay, housing shortages, and disinvestment in U.S. cities, the Housing Act of 1949 was instituted to expand eminent domain for slum clearance, create development enticements, and offer provisions for relocating people displaced through development (Hirsch). In Uptown, federal urban renewal programs brought the contending discourses of development and displacement into clear view. The very definition of "urban renewal" was at stake. Would available funds be used to revitalize the commercial district, jump start the sagging real estate market, and attract middle class families, or would they be used to improve dire living conditions for the poor?

The prominent Uptown Chicago Commission (UCC) spearheaded the urban renewal efforts. UCC, an umbrella organization formed in 1955 by local businesspeople and civic leaders, focused on economic development, securing the middle class, reinvigorating the commercial and entertainment core, and upgrading Uptown's housing stock by tearing down dilapidated buildings and through the "deconversion" of subdivided apartments. Their claim was that housing had reached such a state of disinvestment that it "necessitates public intervention to prevent the engulfment of the community by blight" (*First Draft* 69). In 1960, UCC commissioned the *Meltzer Report*[13] to highlight their development goals; in it, Uptown's slum condition were revealed: "An estimated 40% to 50% of all existing housing units are the results of conversions; 50% of all housing units consist of one- and two-room units; and 27% of all units lack adequate plumbing facilities"(*First Draft* 2). As low-cost housing was linked to and responsible for urban blight, it had to be cleared out to make way for neighborhood improvements that would appeal to the middle class. In 1966, as a result of UCC's advocacy, Uptown become Chicago's fifth urban renewal site (Buck 3).

Beginning in the mid-1960s, a concentration of activists congregated in the neighborhood to protest urban renewal plans and fight for affordable housing (L. Bennett 1997; Guy 2013). The most prominent group was JOIN (Jobs Or Income Now), a radical leftist organization sponsored by the Students for a Democratic Society, whose mission was to "bring poor whites together to fight" for rights in "welfare policy, recreation, schools, decent housing" (Gitlin and Hollander xxii). During urban renewal, approximately 38% of Uptown's population consisted of poor Appalachian whites, earning the neighborhood titles such as "Hillbilly Ghetto" and "Hillbilly Jungle" (Guy 164–65). Starting in 1966, the JOIN newsletter encouraged these residents to join their movement with straightforward slogans such as "Urban Renewal is Poor People Removal." Thus, housing for the poor became the key battleground of urban renewal.

In 1967, Uptown's competing publics came to a head when two visions were proposed for how to use Model Cities funds.[14] The first, championed by UCC, favored placing the Truman City College of Chicago in the neighborhood's core to boost the economy and eliminate twenty-five "blighted" buildings. Although there was little disagreement that the college was welcomed, conflict arose around the eventual location, which displaced approximately 1,765 people, 90% of whom received government relief or were employed as "unskilled or semi-skilled" labor. The majority of the population was southern white, but there were also African Americans, Native Americans, Latinos, and Asians ("DUR" N10).

The second proposal, spearheaded by the Poor People's Coalition and Chuck Geary,[15] centered on the construction of a low-rent development called "The Hank Williams Village" that would have created a community for Uptown's poor. Rather than demolishing deteriorated buildings, this plan focused on rehabilitating existing structures, providing social services for residents, and developing retail and commercial opportunities. The proposal featured a community center for the eight thousand low-income people who would have lived in the "village." Opponents of Truman's placement argued that the people who qualified Uptown for urban renewal money should benefit from neighborhood upgrades rather than be displaced by them. This idea was passionately expressed by DeWitt Gilpin, who testified at city hall in 1969: "The poor people who helped qualify Uptown as a Model Cities target area, as they flee one step ahead of the bulldozer, at least will know that their poverty helped upgrade our area" ("Uptown Model" N1). By 1970, hopes for the Village were dashed when construction plans were finalized; in 1976, Truman College opened its doors to the public at the site where the Hank Williams Village had been proposed.

Uptown lost 25% of its housing stock under urban renewal (Guy 169; Haas et al. 10). In addition to setting the tone of Uptown politics as a divisive class war—which still resonates today—the urban renewal era provided the financial mechanism that led to the construction of ten HUD-subsidized high rise apartment buildings under the Section 221(d) program, which granted low-interest mortgages to developers willing to construct apartment buildings that would remain affordable for at least twenty-five years. So, while certain affordable housing initiatives, such as Hank Williams Village, failed, others, such as these ten buildings, succeeded, providing a material foundation for the presence of thousands of low-income households in Uptown. The construction of this affordable housing not only ensured an actual place for low-income residents to live as the neighborhood developed, but the tangible presence of the housing also provided the concrete place around which commonplaces about poverty, capitalism, rights to housing, and democracy remained salient.

These subsidized buildings, however, were a far cry from UCC's plans to "renovate existing buildings, reduce traffic, and deconcentrate the population" (L. Bennett 93). Rather than prompt commercial development, some of these buildings became "home to the kind of intensive social pathology usually associated with public housing" (93). The buildings were also a far cry from the vision for the Hank Williams Village, which had conviviality, supportive social services, and community spaces as central components of the plan. The ambivalence of affordable housing is punctuated by these HUD buildings, which continue to play a significant role in Uptown. However, the reality of what have, at times, been dire living conditions undercut the strength of affordable housing advocates' arguments decades later. The significance of these buildings reemerges in the 1990s and then 2000s, which

I will discuss presently.[16] Notably, the urban renewal money also funded an explosion of social service agencies created to serve Uptown's various disenfranchised populations (Maly 55). As Marciniak puts it, "Uptown's center of gravity shifted to welfare. That became the main business and the biggest source of jobs" (qtd. in Maly 55). The presence of these agencies—many of which are still in operation—increased the perception and reality of Uptown as a destination for the downtrodden.

In 1980, four years after the completion of Truman College, UCC's Executive Director, Herb Williams, argued against more "subsidized low-income housing," emphasizing his faith that the market would solve social problems in Uptown by attracting middle-class homeowners without threatening the neighborhood's "diversity":

> We ought to let the free market take care of itself, and it will do for the community what never has been done through tax dollars. . . . If we start drawing in middle-class property-owners, Uptown's diversity will continue. Already people of all racial and ethnic backgrounds have bought in. They won't be driven out by redevelopment. As I see it, if we can't make the community more middle-class, it is possible that we will go in the direction of a single racial area. Subsidized low-income buildings in Chicago are 90% black. (qtd. in Bennett 177)

Here, Williams's rhetoric contains several themes that repeat in Uptown's contemporary public discourse. First, Williams conflates poverty and "racial" diversity, which not only undermines the fact that a large percentage of Uptown's poor in 1980 was white, but also, by arguing that free market development will not eliminate the neighborhood's "racial and ethnic" diversity, he elides the class politics involved in gentrification. Although race and class are unfortunately closely linked in the United States—a connection glaringly apparent in Chicago's economic and racial segregation patterns—the argument for affordable housing in Uptown is first and foremost about responding to systemic class inequity not to the maintenance of racial diversity. Second, Williams valorizes the free market, believing it will "take care of itself." The free market generally does not "naturally" produce affordable housing in gentrifying neighborhoods, and there is no reason to believe it ever will without intervention. Third, the fear that "subsidized low-income housing" could become "a single racial area" carries dangerous racist undertones and was (and is) factually inaccurate in the case of many of Uptown's subsidized high rise buildings, such as 850 W. Eastwood, which includes households from India, Russia, Pakistan, Kenya, and Vietnam, to name a few.

These criticisms aside, Williams's comments must be seen in the context of the high poverty rates and levels of social dysfunction that were endemic in Uptown throughout the urban renewal period and have persisted into the present. In 1970, for example, 19% of Uptown's population lived below the poverty line, and 28% did in 1980. The neighborhood was, by all accounts, blighted—a perception and material reality that is reinforced by widespread descriptions of the neighborhood as an apocalyptic zombie wasteland. In 1979, for example, a reporter described the neighborhood in the following unflattering terms: "Take a spin through the heart of Uptown . . . and what do you see? People lurching down the street past burned-out tenements separated by vacant lots, dilapidated six-flats and deteriorating courtyard complexes. There is an occasional bright spot, a building being salvaged, but the dominant theme in this neighborhood is death and decay" (Hafferkamp 194). After reaching its economic nadir in the 1980s, Uptown's gradual gentrification picked up steam during the 1990s housing boom when redevelopment efforts escalated and narratives of progress abounded once again with rhetoric that portended the long-awaited resurrection of a once-great neighborhood. Uptown was suddenly back on the maps of real estate agents, who sought to market the neighborhood's "diversity" and historical attributes. In the 1990s and forward, the opposition to affordable housing grew into a critical mass of business owners, longtime homeowners, and new property owners whose interests in protecting their investments merged in exasperation with a neighborhood that continually stalls gentrification. While Uptown politics in 1960s and 1970s were consumed by urban renewal, the 1980s and 1990s saw a series of organizations form within the tensions of displacement and development, with housing remaining a core pivot.[17] The commonplace that posits Uptown's affordable housing stock as the major obstacle to development was increasingly evoked, as was the opposing topos that housing is a democratic right and displacement through market forces is unjust.

One of the definitive features of this era was the controversial work of the radical leftist alderman Helen Shiller, who remained in office from 1987 to 2011,[18] and served as a lightening rod for these movements and countermovements. Shiller, a native of Queens and once-member of the Students for a Democratic Society, moved to Chicago in the 1970s as an anti-poverty organizer. When Shiller took office, Uptown was ripe for real estate speculation after its southern neighbors—Old Town, Lincoln Park, and Wrigleyville—had already gentrified. While Uptown seemed next in line for development—given its easy access to transportation, the lake, and downtown, and its beautiful, vintage housing—the neighborhood has obstinately resisted full gentrification up to the present, thwarted (or aided, depending on whom you are talking with) by the large affordable housing stock, highly organized housing advocates, and many local organizations that represent the interests of the poor.

Throughout her twenty-four years in office, Shiller made affordable housing her legacy issue. In 1988, Shiller evoked the commonplace that housing was a "commodity" of speculation that would displace the poor: "Development is going through the North Side with a tremendous amount of displacement . . . The most speculative commodity is housing . . . Hot spots are being created . . . For the poor, it's a struggle for survival" (qtd. in McCarron). Shortly after her aldermanic win, the *Chicago Sun-Times* described her as a "60s-style power-to-the-people kind of activist" who is "doing just about everything in her power to put the skids on the wholesale gentrification of her ward. What others describe as the free market at work, she describes as a 'free for all.' Rather than unfettered gentrification, she wants to see government controlled 'planned development' that would leave no current Uptown resident without a home" (Sweet 10).

Within her first year, Shiller forwarded two affordable housing ordinances (both of which failed to pass): the first required landlords within "affordable housing" zones to pay a $2,000 relocation fee to tenants who couldn't afford rent increases of 15% or more, and the second proposed the creation of an "Affordable Housing Zone Commission" that would support housing projects through the taxation of condo conversions (McCarron 1). Shiller did, however, impede Randall Langer, a real estate speculator who purchased nearly five hundred Uptown properties in the 1980s. Shiller worked against his wide-scale rehabbing by refusing to grant zoning permits and fighting his attempts to buy vacant lots (Sweet 10). In 1988, the *Chicago Tribune* wrote that Shiller, who had "based her campaign on what she called the 'people's struggle' for affordable housing," rejected Langer's mall because it failed to accommodate "low- and moderate-income families struggling to survive rapid gentrification" (McCarron 1).[19] "The lot," Shiller said, "was better suited for 'affordable' housing" (1).[20] Although these are only a few examples of her housing work, several of the commonplaces mentioned earlier appear here. Market-driven development is pitted against the plight of the poor, and affordable housing is the bulwark against the displacement of low-income Uptowners.

Beginning in the late-1980s, but picking up steam in the 1990s forward, Uptown has experienced demographic changes that one would expect from a gentrifying neighborhood: decreases in the non-white population and increases in the Non-Hispanic white population, medium income, property values, homeownership, and education levels [see Tables 2 and 3]. Although

Uptown's Racial and Ethnic Composition by Percentage of
Total Population Compared to Chicago's, 1990–2010

	Chicago			Uptown		
Race/Ethnicity	1990	2000	2010	1990	2000	2010
White	37.9	31.3	31.7	38.3	42.10	51.63
Black[1]	38.6	36.4	32.9	24.6	21.1	20.00
Hispanic	19.6	26.0	28.9	22.6	19.9	14.21
Asian	3.5	4.3	5.5	14.0	12.9	11.38
Other	.04	2.0	1.0	8.2	3.90	2.78

Table 2—Source: U.S. Census and Greater Chicago Housing and Community Development Website (1990-2000); U.S. Census (Chicago, 2010); Rob Paral and Associates (Uptown, 2010)

1. Includes African American and African-born individuals.

Uptown Poverty Rates, 1970–2000

Census	Overall Population	Persons Living in Poverty	% of Uptown Population in Poverty*
1970	74,838	14,200	19.00%
1980	64,414	17,614	28.20%
1990	63,839	19,153	30.00%
2000	63,551	15,330	24.90%
2009	58,300	14,963	25.70%

Table 3—Sources: U.S. Census and Greater Chicago Housing and Community Development Website (1970–2000); Rob Paral and Associates (2009);

*percentages are rounded up.

the population is becoming more affluent, a relatively high concentration of poverty remains. Uptown's median income, still below the city average, rose from 75% to 84% of the Chicago's median household income of $38,625 in 2000 (Hass et al. 12). And, although Uptown had 531 Housing Choice Voucher (Section-8 voucher) households in 2003, the percentage of the general Uptown population that received any form of public assistance income fell from 16.2 to 7.5 from 1980 to 2000 ("Chicago Community Area").

The Census data cannot account for profound changes in the built environment resulting from the general transformation in housing characteristics accompanying the real estate condo boom of the 1990s and 2000s that is palpable when walking the streets. Between 1990 and 1999, parcels in Uptown with rental apartment buildings declined by 12%, while condominiums swelled by 102% from 273 to 555, compared to an average increase of 67% citywide (Haas et al. 14). Uptown's homeownership rates have increased from 15% in 1990 to 24% in 2000 ("Greater Chicago"). Further, the median price of single-family homes increased by nearly 95% from $190,000 to $370,000 between 1993 and 2003, and the number of owner-occupied units increased in percentages of all occupied units in Uptown from 5.5 in 1970 to 15.4 in 1990 to 24.5 in 2000 ("Greater Chicago").[21] This shift in housing has not only threatened Uptown's diversity, some would argue and the Census would support, but also energized the renaissance of activism that coalesces around two competing orientations that have, as I have demonstrated, resurfaced cyclically in Uptown for decades—one toward an interest in market-driven development, aesthetic upgrades, and safer streets; the other toward a commitment to halt and redirect market-driven development by intervening in the processes of gentrification on behalf of the disenfranchised.

During her time in office, Shiller was involved in countless initiatives to halt gentrification, earning her a love-hate response from supporters and dissenters. For nearly three decades, Shiller's opponents criticized her as divisive and anti-progress. In 1997, Ben Joravsky described the Uptown political divide as "good old-fashioned class warfare. Shiller's made it clear there will always be a place for the poor in Uptown and some people can't abide that. She says her cause is justice; her foes say she keeps the poor in Uptown so she can control their votes" ("Helen's" 8). Such criticisms have continued to resurface in contemporary politics. In 2007, an anonymous blogger claimed that Shiller "doesn't give a damn about the quality of life for our poor. She just wants them warehoused and under her control where she can use them for her own political purposes" ("Uptown Resident").

The fight for affordable housing remained pitted against the fight for market-driven urban development, catalyzing a new wave of community groups, block clubs, protests, and civic actions. The UCC remained one of the strongest voices pushing for commercial development, and the Organization of the NorthEast (ONE), founded in 1974 by Brooks Miller and Robert Thrasher, emerged as the most prominent organization working for affordable housing preservation and construction. Starting in the 1980s, ONE played an integral role in the fate of the ten HUD-subsidized buildings erected during urban renewal mentioned earlier.[22] While these buildings were contractually obligated to remain affordable for twenty-five years, a loophole was discovered in the federal law in 1980 that allowed owners to prepay their mortgages and sell or rent their property at market rate. Several owners announced their intentions to take advantage of this technicality.[23] ONE lobbied HUD and worked with the tenant organizations to preserve the affordability of these buildings. Although hundreds of affordable housing units were eventually lost in Uptown through "prepayment," some of the buildings were preserved as affordable. Buildings, such as 850 W. Eastwood and 4848 N. Winthrop, were preserved through their purchase by community economic development corporations committed to maintaining affordability.

ONE also successfully lobbied for the first tenant buyout of a HUD "prepayment" building in U.S. history in 1994, when the three-hundred-unit Carmen Marine apartment building was converted into a limited-equity cooperative under the short-lived federal Low Income Housing Preservation and Resident Homeownership Act (Nyden and Adams 13). Rooted in democratic principles of equality, limited-equity cooperatives provide community ownership for low-income households that sharply contrasts with the market-driven model staked in individual investments.[24] Both the co-op and CDC-managed buildings promote egalitarianism, and are explicit strategies for keeping housing out of the speculative hands of the market.

Although the housing stock in Uptown has generally improved since the 1950s as a result of widespread urban renewal "slum" clearance and as a consequence of the Chicago condominium boom that began in the 1990s, Uptown continues to sustain a significant concentration of affordable housing that includes single room occupancies (SRO), project-based public housing, low-income subsidized rentals, limited-equity cooperatives, and homeless shelters.[25] Not surprisingly, the rising pressure from the housing bubble re-invigorated Uptown's decades-old public contest over the fight for urban renewal, on the one hand, and the fight to halt or intervene in commercial development by securing more and better quality affordable housing, on the other.

The ethnographic content of this book deals with the continued tensions between development and displacement that occurred between 1997 and 2014. During this time, the most prominent place of invention was the dramatically controversial Wilson Yard redevelopment plan, which featured a community-driven process to determine what to build in an empty lot that would represent Uptown's diverse population. As one might suspect, the rhetorical floodgates opened, and the project became a battleground that re-energized the arguments discussed here. In the 2000s, the Wilson Yard development spawned several new organizations and energized older ones that either supported the subsidized housing (Queer to the Left, Organization of the NorthEast, COURAJ, Voice of the People, Catholic Worker House,

Stone Soup Co-op, and so on) or fought to block the housing (Buena Park Neighbors, Fix Wilson Yard, Uptown Neighborhood Council, Uptown Chicago Commission, and so on).

The project yielded a Target, retail space, and 178 units of affordable rental units for low-income seniors, individuals, and families (the latter of which fueled the controversy). The project required a staggeringly complex eighteen layers of financing, which included substantial monies from Tax Increment Financing, Low-Income Housing Tax Credits through the Illinois Housing Development Authority, and pre-development funds from Local Initiatives Support Corporation Chicago. The plan, featured in Chapter Two, serves as an ongoing touchstone throughout the book, so for now let me say only that this project inspired passionate contested publics that locked in bitter rhetorical battles, protests, civic action, and lawsuits for over ten years in the process of determining what was in the best interest of the neighborhood. The project served as another material place that produced potent commonplaces linking democracy and housing.

Shift the Places, Change the Commonplaces

During my time in the field, significant shifts in national housing policy affected the rhetoric used in Uptown disputes. In Chicago, these changes involved the massive restructuring of public housing through the Chicago Housing Authority's Plan for Transformation, in which nearly nineteen thousand units were lost through demolition. This loss occurred within the context of a woefully inadequate affordable housing market (Chicago received an F for its work on affordable housing construction and preservation in 2010).[26] Within the Chicago region, the affordable housing shortage comes with various dire overlapping issues, including the poor quality of the affordable housing stock, the concentration of affordable housing in poverty-stricken areas on the South and West Sides of the city, and the general stigma that affordable housing is undesirable and detrimental to market values (Lewis, Nyden, and Williams 3). Policy changes under the Plan from Transformation, which Jason Hackworth describes as the neoliberalization of public housing, were prompted by Congress's $5 billion HOPE VI program, initiated in 1992 to improve public housing.

The Plan for Transformation had two core strategies aimed to de-concentrate poverty and increase individual choice, both of which lean on democratic topoi. The first, focused on replacing high-rise public housing projects with low-density, mixed-income developments (where identical units are divided into 30% public housing, 30% affordable, and 30% market-rate). Mixed-income developments are justified with democratic commonplaces, such as equality and equal opportunity to decent housing. The second strategy advocated Housing Choice Vouchers,[27] which ostensibly increased flexibility and choice for public housing residents who were "empowered" to fend for themselves on the private rental market. The result has largely been the transformation of vertical ghettos into horizontal ones. The voucher program leans on the democratic topoi of freedom and individual autonomy and choice.

Hackworth argues that the these policy shifts make it more difficult for affordable housing advocates to make their cases because "on the surface" the policy "enjoys almost universal agreement," and because policymakers marshal language that "frame(s) the federal government as a 'savior' of sorts, who finally 'decided' to improve the lives of tenants by improving the design of their dwellings" (186). Marketing for the Plan for Transformation focused on improving living conditions and increasing individual freedom and choice, which sounds desirable, progressive, and remarkably similar to the arguments made by housing advocates. These topoi of empowerment, self-sufficiency, choice, and decentralized power are hallmarks of neoliberal discourse, as are the linking of these commonplaces to the democratic topoi of freedom and liberty.

These changes to public housing policies and practices has led to rather novel commonplaces in Uptown that deploy the language of best practices in urban design—stressing low density, quality construction, the deconcentration of poverty, and choice for affordable housing. The topoi look something like this: *I support affordable housing, but it should be as good as middle-class housing. It should allow for maximum choice and flexibility. It should be beautiful. It should not concentrate the poor in single buildings. Anything short of these guidelines is bad urban planning, undemocratic, insulting, and/or dangerous to the people who dwell in the housing and to the society at large.* While these topoi reflect ideals that are universally agreeable in the abstract, the extreme shortage of decent affordable housing in Chicago produces a gap between the desirable ideals expressed by these commonplaces and the material conditions working against their implementation. In other words, the policies fail to account for what urban planning theorist Janet Smith calls the "spatial features that have historically shaped where and how low income families live in the U.S, including racism and classism and a general aversion by the market to produce affordable rental units and mixed-income developments" (221). Within these gaps and omissions, Uptown stakeholders have discovered a lot of rhetorical play.

Uptown's controversial Wilson Yard development served as the prominent place in which these novel commonplaces circulated. Opponents of the proposed affordable housing at Wilson Yard commonly heralded HUD's mixed-income developments as an exemplar that should be universally applied. Although Wilson Yard's units are not public housing and the building is not a high-rise, it was common for opponents to argue against the housing on behalf of hypothetical future residents. In the following quotation, Uptown-homeowner Rob vehemently opposes affordable housing at Wilson Yard along these lines:

> *I think that families would be better served if it were a low rise, mixed-income building [. . .] because I believe that parents want to see their children play in the backyard. I believe parents don't want their children going up and down the elevators with strangers, and I also believe the building standards and maintenance are better and it would be better managed if it were mixed income. [. . .] I want it to be more conducive to supporting parents and the raising of their children [. . .] If I had a choice between a low rise, mixed-income building or a high rise, I would choose the low rise building. Which would you live in?*

This argument becomes more difficult to counter because it works through a rhetoric of empowerment, and, of course, no one is interested in arguing that low-income residents should be housed in shoddy housing that breeds social dysfunction. Affordable housing advocates must contend with the moral appeals of such empowerment rhetoric that promotes quality design and improved standards of living, but not the means to provide enough housing that adheres to these standards. This empowerment rhetoric establishes a set-class expectation (e.g., middle-class ones) for design, behavior guidelines, and aesthetics for subsidized affordable housing, rather than a protection from (the social consequences of poverty) or the basic opportunity for shelter and stability. Now we must talk about affordable housing in terms of meeting middle-class standards. These shifts in practices and discourse affect the terrain of invention.

Diane, a member of a group called Queer to the Left that supported affordable housing at Wilson Yard, critiques these logics:

> *I think another strand twisted around the poverty argument is the suggestion that poor people need to be around middle class people [. . .] otherwise their life was meaningless and not worthy. This completely negates the structural components of poverty. This suggests that if they can just rub up against some wealthy young children in school, that those poor people are going to be better. Rather than actually putting money into the fucking schools or making sure that people have jobs and health-*

care. Housing is a lens to through which to see the potential problems in our society. In that rhetoric there is a big assumption about who, about what the good life is about. [. . .] And that it is bad for poor people to live amongst poor people. That's incredible. It's incredibly racist. And it is incredibly classist.

Another novel topos, which has evolved from an older one that equates housing with depravity itself and which Diane is challenging, contains the claim that mixed-income developments work toward ending the "cycle of poverty" by locating low-income households in proximity to middle-class households—or more precisely, to their values, work ethic, and other resources, such as quality schools and job opportunities. This underlying argument that mixed-income housing will facilitate the upward mobility of the poor into upright, middle-class citizens, presumably through osmosis, is closely related to the idea that if low-income households are spread out, poverty will cease to exist, an idea that assumes that poverty is produced through poor architecture or attitudes, as opposed to the belief that it is systematically produced through capitalism.

Below I share a version of this commonplace in action, as evoked by Susan, an Uptown homeowner, who explained her reasoning for opposing affordable housing at Wilson Yard:

Susan: It is a culture of poverty that we have nurtured in this country and we have nurtured it in a way that disgusts me.
Candice: Do you feel comfortable talking more about that?
Susan: No I am totally cool talking about it because if you don't talk about things, you can't change things. [. . .] We have created these communities, and they started many years ago, when we created public housing, and we took all of the poor and we threw them into the neighborhoods and put them into high rises and they were very lovely high rises. And the mindset was, "You are only going to be here for awhile, until you get on your feet." [. . .] But then what happened is this culture of poverty festered and grew; it was an infection that just spread throughout our society.
Candice: What do you mean when you say culture of poverty?
Susan: It is the mentality and the beliefs and it is the people who live within this.
Candice: So, you are also taking about the policy makers and people who serve the poor?
Susan: Exactly because the one thing that nobody ever wants to say is . . .

> *The belief-systems we have is that you are poor, you are going to stay poor, and I am the person who is going to take care of you forever. That is truly the belief system that we have nurtured in this society. And so what happens is that we perpetuate that and now because you have all of these young girls who have children at 15, 16, or if they are lucky 17, they have their first baby. There are in an endless cycle, and we are probably in the 6th or 7th generation. [. . .]. This [idea of building affordable housing at Wilson Yard] is like a microcosm of what doesn't work. The words that were used [to justify affordable housing at Wilson Yard] just continue to foster it. And those words come from beliefs that we've continued to nurture.*

Susan critiqued what she perceived to be a paternalistic attitude toward caring for the poor, perpetuating poverty that is "nurtured" primarily through a "mentality" and a "belief system" that we are "going to take care of [the poor] forever." In this understanding, architecture that concentrates poverty coupled with the attitude that poverty is always going to exist are framed as the primary causes of poverty (or at least the cause of its perpetuation).

In the following, self-proclaimed leftist housing advocates Barbara and Edward discussed their ambivalence about arguing for more affordable housing in Uptown in a manner that resonates with some of Susan's concerns about maintaining a "culture of poverty":

> *Barbara: The reason I got involved in this Wilson Yard project is that I wanted to think about what it meant to keep this neighborhood diverse. Diverse. That word is used a lot and we don't really talk about what that word really means. People use it differently. For instance, one of the arguments [that we have used is] that we need to keep economic diversity, we need to keep poor people in the neighborhood, but in a larger context, it is also asking for keeping poverty alive. [. . .] People on the left don't address this. I have always been bothered by this notion of economic diversity because it says that we always need a certain proportion of poor people. So how do you then say that and also fight against a system that insists on poverty? [. . .] It bothers me that our main argument is to keep poor here because it completely erases the larger question.*
> *Candice: What is the larger question?*
> *Barbara: How do you the erase question! That is the larger question. Because if you want to keep poor people in the neighborhood, you are also saying that you want to keep them poor.*
> *Edward: Yes, but we can't erase poverty and so we want to know that there is a place in society for them.*

Barbara: I agree and I understand that, but we have gotten to the point where that is all we have to fight for. In the sense, that is all we have. I think that is one reason the fight is so polarized.

Albeit from different political orientations, both Barbara and Susan questioned the argument for maintaining economic diversity because they felt it necessitated a permanent underclass. However, while Barbara's critique revealed her desire to overcome structures of inequality rather than merely arguing for the permanent accommodation of those structures, Susan's position obscured the structural causes of poverty by locating the cause in the festering, infectious mentalities, rather than systemic material conditions, associated with our "culture of poverty."

In sum, the introduction of neoliberal housing practices that promote market-driven ideas through rhetorics of democracy and empowerment has led to shifts in the material practices of how affordable and public housing is done, as well as to the production of new arguments that make it harder to argue for building more affordable housing while simultaneously strengthening the moral force of opposing arguments. These shifts in housing policy and practice lead to the simple, yet profound, notion that when material conditions change, so, too, do the places of invention tethered to those places. As new arguments emerge in tension with changing practices, other arguments become less forceful, salient, or retreat completely from view. The leftist contingency in Uptown is uniquely challenged to counter the moralistic and universally agreeable language of the neoliberal housing practices discussed here, which are increasingly framed as moral appeals on behalf of the poor. While it is the material presence of affordable housing and its residents that has sustained the contested places of Uptown, and that keep arguments about systemic injustice in view, Barbara's concern about maintaining economic diversity by keeping a quota of affordable housing reveals an ambivalence that housing advocates face. By preserving housing, you retain a certain number of poor people in the neighborhood, but you might find yourself in the business of accommodating structural inequity and not fighting it, subjecting yourself to Susan's critique of nurturing a "culture of poverty." Yet failing to preserve housing leads to spatial changes that can erode the visible, tangible, visceral, material foundation that make arguments about housing as a democratic right relevant.

Conclusion

While I have generally been interested here in tracing the legacy of housing as a central place of invention in Uptown's contested publics (with the aim of providing a history of both the fieldsite and its salient rhetoric), I have also been interested in the narrower concern of how the materiality of affordable housing (its visceral existence, the presence of the people who dwell in the housing along with their everyday inhabitations of space) constitutes a place that keeps certain arguments alive, if you will. The contention between housing as a democratic right and housing as a commodity that began this chapter is chief among them. If you lose the material foundations that tether commonplaces to literal places, do these commonplaces disappear from the collective social imagination? If so, do they cease to be places of invention?

My inhabitations of the field indicate that the simple answer is yes. In Uptown, persistent battles over displacement and development hinge, in part, on the radically diverse and incompatible ways of knowing, believing, and living that are invested in and made possible by housing. As I have been saying, housing has historically been the place in Uptown where such incompatibilities play out in everyday rhetorical acts designed to define, stake claim in, and fight for Uptown's future. Without the presence of affordable housing, its occupants, and its advocates, it seems likely that certain arguments (about poverty, welfare rights, market injustices, and so on) would retreat as matters of public concern, as they have in nearby neighborhoods within which signs of poverty have all but vanished from view.

In Uptown, however, the pressures of gentrification could be felt everywhere in 2016 (materially speaking, in the form of condo conversions, increasing property values, new trendy restaurants, boutiques, vigilante tactics to police public space, and so on), just as starkly as the presence of poverty (in the form of subsidized affordable housing, homelessness, crime, drug trafficking, prostitution, loitering, and shoddy aesthetics). Not surprisingly, the debates between development and displacement remain strong in contemporary politics. The historically maintained affordable housing stock has provided a clear target for a well-organized and active array of activists, community organizations, and neighborhood groups that have pushed agendas of commercial and economic development, as well as an equally powerful group of stakeholders that share a vested interest in mobilizing against development that threatens to displace the poor. Such tensions have played out over and over again in everyday exchanges as well as throughout planning processes of major development projects where the paradoxes of democracy are revealed through radically incommensurable evocations of democratic rhetoric and practice.

Finally, I would like to bring this discussion back to rhetorical invention. As I mentioned much earlier, this chapter aimed to provide a history of salient rhetorical structures that have constituted the places of invention in Uptown with nods toward ethnographic context to come where the commonplaces presented here crop up in all manner of situations, twining themselves to local issues, broader ideologies, bodily affects, spatial practices, policy decisions, and various arguments about and inhabitations of contested public space in Uptown's everyday democracies. By amplifying the visibility of particular arguments that have evolved over time, my overall aim was to historicize the places of rhetorical invention on a macro level. The remainder of this book continues to ethnographically ground such places of invention in Uptown's everyday democracies. And so, into the field, we go.

2
Democratic Persuasions in Contested Publics

> The Rhetoric must lead us through the Scramble, the Wrangle of the Market Place, the flurries and flare-ups of the Human Barnyard, the Give and Take, the wavering line of pressure and counter pressure, the Logomachy, the onus of ownership, the Wars of Nerves, the War.
>
> Kenneth Burke, *A Rhetoric of Motives*

The rhetorics of democracy can be turned on their head, picked up, and used to support diametrically opposed agendas. Democratic rhetorics are comprised of myriad practices, incompatible ideological dispositions, and a tangled web of commonplace myths, symbols, stock tales, icons, and contradictory blueprints for the good life that we collectively associate with democracy. This includes the arsenal of topoi that embody democratic ideals, such as freedom, equality, and liberty. The flexible uses of democratic rhetoric are possible because their topoi function as persuasive rhetorical engines that proliferate meaning and mobilize action by activating discourse already circulating in the social imagination. Kenneth Burke referred to such topoi as "god-terms" because they do the work of gods, providing the "ground of all possibility; substance; nature; history; society; . . . truth . . . ideal . . . good" (*A Rhetoric* 298–301). In any such term, he writes, "We can posit a world . . . we can treat the world *in terms of it*, seeing all emanations, near or far, of its light" (*A Grammar* 105).

Theorists have attempted to make sense of the "worlds" that emerge from and adhere to "democracy" through various conceptualizations of the "public," such as via the "public sphere" metaphor, one of democracy's core topoi, which crystallizes the hopes and ideals, as well as the limits and contradictions, of liberal democracy. The public sphere is predicated on the powerful faith that rational deliberation among private citizens about matters of public concern will produce a more inclusive, empathetic, and just society. The sheer moral force of these promised public goods is capable of obscuring gaps between democratic ideals and material realities, eliding the inherent contradictions within the democratic project, and legitimizing arguments that make use of democratic rhetorics, regardless of content or social consequence. Democratic topoi can be used flexibly not because they are contentless but because they are capacious proliferators of content.

Whatever it is we imagine democracy to mean, we can be sure that our neighbors will have a very different understanding. That both conflicting claims, mine and my neighbor's, can be theoretically legitimate within a single democratic framework means that determining the content of "democracy" might be more a matter of raw power, material constraint, and rhetorical savvy, than about whose argument is more rational, just, or better equipped to secure public goods and increase neighborliness. Because democratic ideals can inspire action toward very different ends, it is dangerous to equate democracy with social justice or to presume that democracy alone can mitigate human suffering and violence, and further, this ambivalence of democracy suggests that democratic politics cannot be comprehended strictly from a god's-eye view.

In this chapter, I consider how Uptown stakeholders use democratic rhetorics to argue about their neighborhood's future. I begin by discussing the public sphere, as democracy's conceptual model, arguing that although the transcendent ideals represented in the model are capable of inspiring conviction and action, the substance of these ideals remains elusive until they are put to use in concrete situations. I then examine the uses of democratic rhetoric in debates over affordable housing in Uptown to consider how democratic rhetorics are used to support very different investments. Ultimately, the goal is to extend my examination of the places of invention within democracy, generally, and within Uptown disputes over a controversial affordable housing development, known as Wilson Yard, specifically.

In the heart of Uptown lies a five-acre lot called Wilson Yard, which stands literally at the crossroads of affluence and decay. There is nothing particularly striking about the lot: it sits sandwiched between the eL-train and a strip of hodge-podge businesses. Historically, Wilson Yard was a train repair shop built in 1901 at the terminus of the Northwest Elevated, which served as a central transportation hub that fueled Uptown's growth as a commercial and entertainment center at the turn of the twentieth century. The repair shop remained in continual operation for over ninety years, until a fire destroyed it in 1996, leaving behind a lot that remained empty for fourteen years. The controversial public debates over what to build here began in 1997, when Chicago Transit Authority sold the land to the city, prompting Uptown's former alderman Helen Shiller to initiate a community-driven, "democratic" planning process to collectively design a project at Wilson Yard.[1] The eventual outcome was to represent the will of the people and stand as a material monument to the ability of inclusive dialogue in the public sphere to pro-

6. Wilson Yard in 2004. Photo by Author.

duce the greatest good for all. While suggestions for how to develop the lot included everything from public gardens to community centers and from a movie theater to luxury condos, the plan quickly formed into a mix of commercial development and subsidized affordable housing that attempted to strike a balance between the competing publics splintered by desires to fuel gentrification and hopes to halt it.

The controversial Wilson Yard plan resulted in a Target, street-level retail (including Subway, Bedding Expert, Weight Watchers, etc.), and two ten-story subsidized affordable apartment buildings. One building includes ninety-eight units for low-income seniors, and the other—which lies at the center of this controversy—contains eighty units for households making no more than 60% of the area median income, which was $30,420 for one and $43,440 for a family of four in 2014 ("Area Medium"). In this latter building, 23% of the units are restricted to "extremely low income" earners, 56% for "very low income," and 21% for "low income"[2] ("Median Income"). Beginning in 1998, dozens of public meetings, plenaries, planning charrettes, protests, fundraisers, and town halls were hosted by the alderman, her supporters, and her critics to discuss the fate of this lot, gather community input, roll out and critique plans, and launch litigation against the Wilson Yard plan. Informally, many more were held behind closed doors, in living rooms, at bars, and in community organizations to plan for ways to push the affordable housing through or to thwart it. Numerous organizations and Uptown stake-

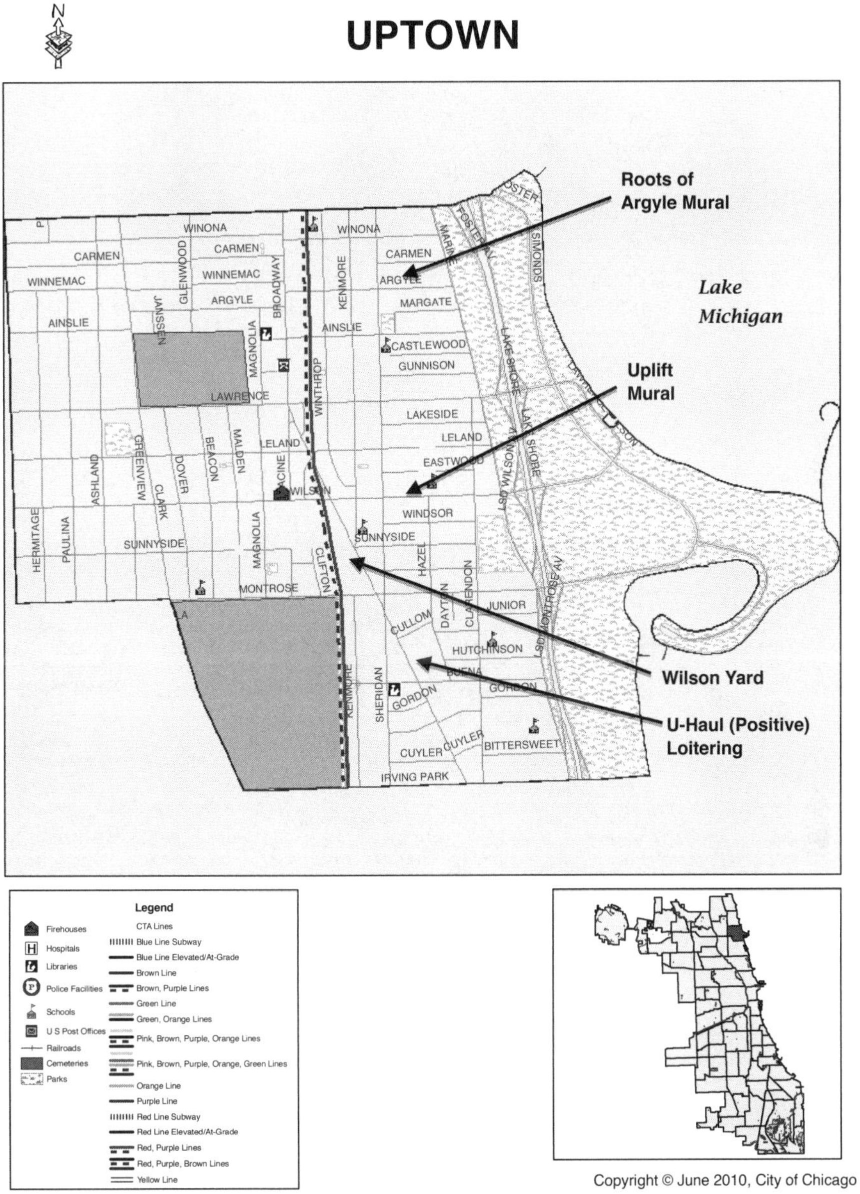

7. Map of Uptown Neighborhood Area. Courtesy of the City of Chicago

8. Target at Wilson Yard, 2010. Photo by Author.

9. Affordable Housing and Retail at Wilson Yard, Target on the far right, 2010. Photo by Author.

holders[3] have evoked democratic rhetoric in public discourse and at community meetings to justify and support arguments both for and against affordable housing at Wilson Yard; to both slander and support public officials; and to both legitimate and blast the processes of gentrification. Arguments that the creation of affordable housing is a democratic response to social inequity were met with counter-arguments that building more affordable housing is undemocratic because it threatens public safety, concentrates poverty, favors the poor, silences homeowners, and/or unjustly reappropriates property taxes. I'm interested here in how such radically different investments could all be supported using democratic rhetoric. Many people are invested in Uptown, just not in the same outcomes. To elucidate these investments, I turn to field descriptions of the contention at Wilson Yard, and to a consideration of how competing Uptown publics illustrate the theoretical and practical contradictions within the democratic project.

I learned straightaway that the subject of Wilson Yard provoked strong reactions. Gene, a longtime affordable housing activist and Uptown resident explained, in 2005, why his organization, Queer to the Left, took on Wilson Yard as one of its central issues, roughly between 2001–2006:

> *We were concerned with gentrification and affordable housing. We chose Wilson Yard because we wanted to create a concrete positive political platform that bridges gaps between class differences, race differences, cultural differences, sexual differences. We recognized that Wilson Yard was going to send out a message about what Uptown is about and what it will become. Wilson Yard was a big blank space.*

This insistence that Wilson Yard is a "blank space" waiting to be filled with symbolic content reveals much about why the lot became so significant. The emptiness of the lot became a rich resource for rhetorical invention that catalyzed all sorts of arguments about the city, democracy, and citizen participation, and about what the neighborhood should become. Despite the significant role that Wilson Yard played in Uptown politics, Seth, an Uptown native and lawyer who had "fought for social justice" for decades on behalf of Uptown's disenfranchised, stated in 2007, that the project was a gigantic waste of time:

> *Seth: Frankly, I think Wilson Yard is the most overblown, overrated project ever. I don't think it will make one bit of difference. We are talking about 200 units [of affordable housing] or so. Elsewhere in the city there are 10,000 units of affordable housing in one place. In the past 15 years, the private condo conversions must be like 15,000 in the surrounding area. I think the commercial development will make a big difference, but the housing will not.*
> *Candice: Why do you think it has become so overblown?*
> *Seth: It has been a convenient issue that is used for political purposes. Again, people organize around anger when it comes to Wilson Yard.*

> *The impact will be none. The commercial part should've been built five years ago. So, much wasted energy has gone into talking about it, writing about it, planning for it, contesting it, setting it up. Some are using it to push their affordable housing agenda, others, I don't know, are just being defensive or afraid. So, overblown. Frankly, I can't believe it.*

Although this informant is not alone in feeling that the Wilson Yard is overblown, the fact remains that this development project was at the forefront of the social imagination for well over a decade and was put to rhetorical use in a wide variety of political situations—including two aldermanic races in which candidates' stance on Wilson Yard was the central hot-button issue. It is precisely the "blankness" and its capacity for being "used for [various] political purposes" that made the lot such a powerful site for rhetorical invention by providing a material site (an empty lot of prime land to be filled up with something for everyone) and a process (planning charrettes, public hearings, protests, picketing, petitions, and so on) that served as a repository of concrete "places" and a storehouse for rhetorical commonplaces for arguments about democracy. The very "emptiness" and indeterminacy of the project is central to understanding why it became such a powerfully rich and resonate resource for rhetorical invention.

Democratic Theory, Power, and the Limits of the Public Sphere Trope

By analyzing Uptown's emergent public in action, one bears witness to what Chantal Mouffe calls the "paradox of democracy." Mouffe articulates this "paradox" as the incompatibility between political liberalism (which foregrounds a politics of liberty and individual rights) and democracy (which foregrounds a politics of equality). Arguing that this paradox is an inherent and valuable feature of democracy, she advocates "agonistic pluralism," a politic that secures contestation as a permanent and foundational condition of democracy. In rejecting the possibility of "establishing a consensus without exclusion," agonistic pluralism calls for the maintenance of democratic institutions and processes that keep "democratic contestations alive" (*Democratic* 105). Compelling in theory, "agonistic pluralism" presents serious limitations in the material world, where concrete, timely, and compromised decisions must finally be made. In Uptown, something had to be developed at Wilson Yard despite what could have been (and certainly felt like to many) an infinite debate over what should be built. There is much to be learned from the stalemate of competing rhetorics in Uptown, in that eventually, public policy must *act*, and often act in ways that some part of the constituency may deem "undemocratic."

Former alderman Shiller referred to Wilson Yard as a "virtual basket" because her plan attempted to capture the competing interests in her ward within the literal design of space. Rather than something like a public park, which would have been easier to claim as a universal public good, the development is a pastiche that represents a bit of everyone's interest while simultaneously fulfilling no one's. The logic of the basket metaphor works a lot like the "melting pot" metaphor, except, rather than different elements melding together into an indistinguishable and harmonious whole, the basket allows various ideas to co-exist despite incommensurable difference and contestation. With a Target, retail chains, a large parking structure, and two affordable apartment buildings jammed into a five-acre lot, one can see how Wilson Yard earned the name "Franken-development" from an Uptown dissenter.

Indeed, mocking Shiller's "virtual basket" metaphor, members of a dissenting group called Uptown Neighborhood Council (UNC), discussed shortly, gathered in October 2006 to mark the ten-year anniversary of the Wilson Yard fire and to challenge Shiller in an upcoming aldermanic race. They staged a New Orleans–style funeral parade, led by a black casket draped with a banner that read "Wilson Yard Virtual Basket of Broken Promises." Rather than a virtual basket, the protestors argued that Wilson Yard had become a "virtual casket" that, as one UNC member stated in her "eulogy" to vibrant mixed development, is:

> *dying a slow death [. . .] choking on a cock-eyed design that shuts out the community and creates what one urban planner called—A future slum in Uptown. It's suffocating under years of neglect, poor public policy, and misguided leaders who work against the residents, not with them. It's drowning in a sea of political abuse of our taxpayer dollars. We mourn the loss of sensible planning.*

The play on virtual baskets and caskets is but one of many examples that represent Uptown's political stalemates and democratic publics at odds. In the following ethnographic scene, to provide another brief example, Mouffe's "democratic paradox" can be empirically observed in the tension between stakeholders at the public unveiling of the Wilson Yard plan on September 8, 2004. A six-year "democratic" process preceded this meeting, including a community survey and planning charettes, where these and other adversarial positions about the future of the neighborhood were vetted.

Over six hundred Uptown stakeholders crowded into Truman College's cafeteria to hear about the Wilson Yard plan. The room was electric with tension. The sound of buzzing chatter and metal chair legs scraping on waxed linoleum punctuated the palpable anticipation of the homeowners, renters, community organizers, urban planners, city officials, business owners, religious leaders, and journalists who gathered there. It was visually apparent which side of the affordable housing controversy people stood on. Those who opposed it were primarily members of the Uptown Neighborhood Council (UNC), which was founded in 2003 as a grassroots group of residents and business owners who opposed subsidized affordable housing at Wilson Yard. These activists wore bright orange t-shirts that read "Unite Uptown" on the front, and "Build a Better Community through the Arts" on the back. The "Orange Shirts,"[4] as they came to be known, argued that if affordable housing must be built—and they'd prefer that it wasn't—it should be reserved for artists. UNC activists I spoke with were concerned about public safety, feeling that the housing would further concentrate poverty in the area, increasing crime and derelict public behavior. Artists, however, were presumed to be productive, value adders.

Those who favored affordable housing at Wilson Yard wore green stickers that read: "Uptown Supports Affordable Housing." This contingency represented a variety of political agendas that converged around the support of affordable housing as a pointed response to systemic inequality and to displacement caused by gentrification. The diverse housing advocates included longtime Uptown residents and members of an array of neighborhood organizations such as Jesus People, Queer to the Left, Organization of the North East, and Coalition of Uptown Residents for Affordability and Justice. Field informant and housing advocate, Gene, described this coalition as an example of "people with different agendas . . . mobilized around the opportunistic purpose" of fighting for affordable housing. Fellow Queer to the Left activist, Diane, concurring with Gene, noted the "amazing [. . .] cross-fertilization" that occurred in the fight for low-income housing at Wilson Yard (between groups as potentially contentious as the Jesus People, whom Diane felt had expressed anti-gay sentiments, and Queer to the Left). As Diane told me:

> *Community typically requires the suppression of difference, you know, and it didn't seem to be necessary. I think that was important in terms of not hiding any of the issues, and for me, it was very liberating to work with the Jesus People. We were all long-term social justice workers who cared about low-income people.*

Shouts and counter-shouts were blurted out throughout the meeting. Those in orange shouted things like: "This development will concentrate poverty. We have enough subsidized housing in Uptown!" "We don't want our tax money to be spent on this." "This isn't democracy. I didn't want this." Those in green shouted: "This represents all of our interests. We need affordable housing. Uptown needs to take care of all of its citizens!" After the formal presentation, things became so raucous that, at one point, the president of Truman College came to the microphone with great exasperation to tell the crowd to calm down or the meeting would end. The rather unruly "public" that emerged was a far cry from idealizations of citizens engaged in empathetic, rational deliberation about the common welfare. This public appeared nothing like John Rawls's model in which stakeholders bracket their private interests behind a "veil of ignorance" in order to derive universal principles of justice that ensure the greatest good for the all. On the contrary, Uptown stakeholders nakedly displayed their investments with visual flair—agendas boldly emblazoned on brightly colored stickers and t-shirts. Splintered by competing investments, this is a public incapable of deriving consensus.

This scene crystallizes some of the logomachy that underscores the uses of democracy in Uptown and exemplifies Julia Paley's argument that the "use of the word 'democracy' occurs neither alone, nor steadily, nor completely; it is, rather . . . ethnographically emergent. Therefore we must ask: Whose term is it? What does its usage in any particular case signify? Where does the term arise and where not?" (486). Democracy is "ethnographically emergent" because the indeterminate meanings of democratic topoi can only be understood within the concrete contexts within which they are evoked. Karen Tracy's "ordinary democracy" is also apt here. She offers a model of "actually existing democracy" that resists idealizations and is "empirically anchored" (4) in descriptions of situated uses of democracy (5).

By insisting that the solution to the problems of democracy does not reside in a more participatory or better-executed democracy, Barbara Cruikshank calls into question the large body of public sphere theory dedicated to conceptualizing an evermore robust, inclusive, and just civil society. Rather than accepting democracy as an a priori virtuous good, she understands democratic government, like all government, as "relations of power" that are "continually recreated" (18). It is not that we need a more accurate or finely grained model of the public, but a way to theorize how democratic politics produce subjectivities and sentiments that are reinforced and activated through "relations of power," in particular circumstances that make certain beliefs and actions seem more reasonable (and more "democratic").

In the unveiling of Wilson Yard, the core tensions within democratic subjectivity manifest through two pulls. Put too starkly for the moment: In the first, democracy is framed as individual liberty, which appears in the Orange Shirts's claim that the plan is undemocratic because their private interests are not being served (*This isn't democracy. I didn't want this.*), and that taxpayers should have control over how their money is spent (*We don't want our tax money to be spent on this.*). The second pull frames democracy in terms of social equality, which appears in the mobilization of affordable housing as a "public good" that should be made available to everyone (*We need affordable housing. Uptown needs to take care of all of its citizens!*). My concern here is not to determine which sentiment is morally superior, but to highlight that both pulls are always legitimately at play in liberal democracies. Rather than representing two distinct conceptions of democracy, these pulls signal contradictory tensions within a single theoretical framework. The liberal democratic subject circumscribes the desire for both liberty and equality, for both individual and social rights, and thus, encompasses the paradoxical stalemates to which these competing transcendent ideals point.

Indeed, these stalemates carried on for another six years of organizing after this 2004 unveiling, which included the creation of blogs, online message boards, and community groups, as well as numerous public protests, community information sessions, and fundraisers, sponsored by the alderman, city officials, and citizens. All of this, of course, does not account for the hundreds—if not thousands—of hours that individuals spent organizing at home, at bars, and in public; writing and reading letters to the editor, online comments, flyers, news articles, web copy, blog entries, and the like; and showing up time and time again to participate in these public events. Before further discussing these activities, I'll consider how we might regard the "public sphere" in light of these stalemates. Jürgen Habermas's public sphere model, rooted in Enlightenment rationality, catalyzed a body of criticism on the possibilities and limitations of democracy as a means of deriving a public that is both inclusive and radically diverse. For Habermas, the public sphere exists between private life and the state, and crystallizes the "people's public use of their reason" to determine through rational debate a consensus about matters of public concern (27). The public sphere as the conceptual model for liberal democracies rests on a morality that insists that civic engagement, inclusive and transparent politics, and institutionalized spaces for citizens to debate public matters offers our best hope of cooperating through discursive, nonviolent means. Theorists—including Nancy Fraser, David Fleming, and Gerard Hauser, among many others—have critiqued the Habermasian model as idealized, each driven by a similar impetus to conceive a public that more fully accounts for the political complexities that confound democratic deliberation.

In rhetorical studies, Hauser moves away from Habermas's idealism, offering what he calls the reticulate public sphere, which he defines as "A discursive space in which individuals and groups associate to discuss matters of mutual interest and . . . to reach a common judgment about them" (*Vernacular* 61). Hauser's insistence that "publics do not exist as entities but as processes" is predicated on the idea that "collective reasoning is not defined by abstract reflection but by practical judgment," and therefore, a public's "awareness of issues is not philosophical but eventful" (64). To say that a public is "eventful" is to suggest that it manifests, emergently, kairotically, contextually, locally, as action and activity that responds to exigencies in concrete spaces where people dwell. While Hauser notes that "rhetorically salient meanings are unstable," he also hopes that the physical proximity of agents in local publics might make contestation less volatile and more prone to the "formation of shared judgments" (63).

Similarly, Fleming pursues a public sphere that remains "open to hybridity, pluralism, and mobility" (34). He seeks a "commonplace" that is both material and conceptual, "where we can disclose our differences to one another but also solve our shared problems, where we can encounter conflict and opposition but still feel that we belong and matter" (34). He considers urban neighborhoods to be ideal sites where such publics might offer a "setting which is true to human diversity but still allows for 'commonality' and 'solidarity'" (52). While Fleming and Hauser have contributed much to our understanding of the rhetoricality of actually existing publics, I understand their projects—given their desire to accommodate social plurality without exclusion or violence—as reinvesting Habermas's idealism into miniaturized, competing, vernacular public spheres that may be more qualitatively grounded, but no less idealistic.[5]

I want to say, however, that tensions within democratic society are not a matter of scale, but rather, cut down to the very core, to the most local, to the most finite detail of social interaction and knowledge production: down to the production of the democratic subject itself. The irresolvable conflicts in Uptown emerge not from a lack of rhetorical competency, a dearth of material spaces for debate, or a disconnect from official power. Democratic publics do not fail simply because of misunderstanding, procedural distortion, or failure to achieve stasis. In Uptown, we see a radically diverse public engaged in deliberation, yet unable to agree on a collective vision of their neighborhood. Democratic participation abounds around the Wilson Yard development—in city hall, in neighborhood meeting rooms, in community organizations, on the streets, in public discourse, and in public oratorical performances. The impasse reached by this public has not resulted from procedural malfunction. The commitment to solving the problems of democracy by practicing "better" democracy requires one to hold onto a transcendent conception of democracy that does not exist. There is no available Platonic truth that Uptown stakeholders might discover through more refined dialectical practice.

Rather than understanding democratic politics as occurring "out there, in the public sphere," Cruikshank insists that we are better served by understanding how democracy works at the "very soul of subjectivity" (124). This points us to a concern with how democracy (its discourses, practices, institutions) activates particular sensibilities, dispositions, and practices that constitute a politics of the everyday. Cruikshank is particularly interested in how what Foucault calls *biopower* "operates to invest the citizen with a set of goals and self-understandings" (41). Foucault discusses power as a force that reproduces through social relations a "field" of possible actions: "Power . . . operates on the field of possibilities in which the behavior of active subjects is able to inscribe itself. It is a set of actions on possible actions; it incites, it induces, it seduces, it makes easier or more difficult" (340–41).

Biopower complicates the democratic subject defined as free and autonomous. As Cruikshank argues, the "citizen and subjects are not opposites," rather "citizens are made and therefore subject to power even as they become citizens" (20), and "although democratic citizens are formally free, their freedom is a condition of the operationalization of power" (22). In light of Cruikshank's rendering of democratic subjectivity, the question of how to better facilitate solidarity among autonomous, free citizens in the public sphere shifts to a concern with how "democracy" (its practices and rhetorics) leverages power unevenly through the active participation of citizens engaged in defining contested urban space. The preoccupation in public sphere theories with how to produce more effective persuasion is undermined by the limit written into the impossibility of rational deliberation to produce consensus, a shared sense of justice, or material force.[6] Moreover, the tendency in public sphere theory to cast rhetoric as a superhero is sorely challenged by this case study, which reveals the shakiness of democracy's moral foundation, in lieu of which sheer power typically bowls over rhetorical competency.

As such, ecological models of the public are more amenable to tracing how rhetorical power is leveraged and created in ongoing, dynamic processes. Within rhetorical studies, for example, Asen and Brouwer prefer the term "public modalities" in place of the "public sphere" because it emphasizes the "productive arts of crafting publicity" (3), and attunes our critical lenses to the "diverse range of processes through which individuals and groups engage each other, institutions, and their environment in creating, reformulating, and understanding social worlds" (16). Edbauer's work on rhetorical ecologies traces public rhetoric "as a process of distributed emergence and as an ongoing circulating process" (13) in which we study dynamic "intensities of encounter and interactions" (12). Fleckenstein et al. advocate an "ecological metaphor" because it foregrounds a complex account of "activities, actors, situations, and phenomenon as interdependent" (388). Dingo's "networking arguments" method observes "how and why rhetorics move and change" and "connect the relationships among persuasion, language, power, circulation, and contexts" (154). Such scholars help direct our attention to the processes of active crafting of rhetorical salience; to how democratic topoi circulate and evolve in various situations; and to the material agencies, ideological contours, and political textures of the rhetorical situation. Such attunements are the subject matter of the following section.

Into the Field: Uptown's Publics and the Rhetorical Uses of Democracy

The frenzied Chicago real estate market that began gathering momentum in the mid-1990s started showing signs of distress by 2006.[7] Beneath this boom loomed an affordable housing crisis characterized by gentrifying inner-city neighborhoods, an aging housing stock concentrated in poverty-stricken areas, a net loss of eleven thousand public housing units under Chicago's Plan for Transformation, and dwindling federal and state dollars. In 2006, approximately 30% of Chicago's households were rent-burdened (paying more than 30% of their income on rent), and of those households, 72% were classified as "extremely low-income" (earning $20,350 or less for a family of four) (*Affordable Housing Conditions* 2–4). Within the context of rising poverty rates—and with respect to a widening gap between income and housing affordability—Chicago housing advocates faced incredible challenges in their efforts. Part of this challenge can be said to be rhetorical, in the sense that advocates must make the case for affordable housing as a general public good that is in the interest of all, but such rhetorical work must be seen as inextricable from these material and economic realities.

Uptown was particularly affected by the housing bubble, given its access to Lake Michigan and downtown, abundance of public transportation, and ample stock of beautiful historic brownstones. Between 1990 and 2000, Uptown's median rent increased 38%, and the median home value nearly doubled from $139,000 to $270,000 (*Affordable Housing Conditions* 34). Although Uptown became less "affordable," it is critical to note that at the end of the 1990s, 18.2% of Uptown's housing stock was publicly subsidized through various city, state, and federal agencies (Haas et al. 18–19),[8] and in 2010, 25.7% of Uptown's population lived at or below poverty ("Chicago Community"). The concentration of poverty and subsidized affordable housing in Uptown has been the basis for some to reasonably argue that the neighborhood is already beyond the tipping point.

The national real estate bubble and its precipitous burst affected housing debates in Uptown (and Chicago more broadly), which had been pushed hard by real estate agents as a hot, "diverse," and up-and-coming neighborhood. By 2012, approximately 44.5% of homeowners were underwater in Cook County, of which is Chicago is the largest municipality (Podmolik). As the real exigency of underwater mortgages mounted, the fear of being stuck in an undesirable neighborhood grew, as did the animosity toward anything that appeared to threaten property values. Affordable housing activist, Diane, offered a pointed critique of the new Uptown homeowners who were surprised to encounter the disconnect between their desire to live in a "diverse" neighborhood and the class inequity that underscores Uptown's "diversity":

> One of the things that get said a lot is that I moved here because I wanted to live in a diverse neighborhood. So, that [. . .] the rhetoric of diversity operates in the way people talk about Uptown. People present themselves as being incredibly open, liberal, and wanting a diverse city because diversity is such a good thing. They always then mobilize the other rhetoric of concentrated poverty to say that to diversify the neighborhood that we need more market rate housing because we have too much of the other stuff, but there is on every corner market rate, housing going up.

Roberta, a housing and social service provider in Uptown, described her perception of a "bitterness" that set in when Uptown did not deliver as the vibrant "diverse" neighborhood that young homeowners were "sold" by their real estate agents:

> Condos were built up in this neighborhood everywhere you looked. Because there was easier financing before the great fall. [. . .] Young people probably pretty much saw a cheaper way and next to the lake [. . .] and they were told this by realtors. [. . .] I always get confused when they say, "We want to be in a diverse neighborhood," and I'm thinking, "Do you really want to be in a diverse neighborhood?" You know because they don't

think of class diversity [. . .] and I think they just were disappointed that things are a little bit more a class problem than racial diversity [. . .] they interpret that class thing as we're unsafe and in danger. [. . .] However, if you are a younger person who has moved in, got your condo, and when you walk down Wilson all of a sudden you see alcoholic people you know, you're like wait a minute . . . this is not fitting in with my viewpoint [. . .] Then there's a disappointment that comes along and then there's a bitterness and it just sort of snowballs.

Roberta's observation is critical. Emotional freight underscores Uptown politics that is partly informed by the housing boom and bust—some critiques of constructing additional affordable housing are unwritten by a profound sense of disappointment, anxiety over losing one's investment, fear of everyday encounters with crime and social dysfunction, and frustration with an alderman and strong leftist contingency that works against and often vilifies the perspective of middle-class homeowners. And, while it is certainly possible to locate "greedy capitalists" in my fieldwork who wanted only to buy cheap to flip their properties for profit, this attitude was not the norm among protestors of Wilson Yard I spoke with who were, by and large, middle-class professionals with varying politics, who found themselves living within the reality of structured debt in a sinking economy. It is also important to note that nearly all of the advocates of affordable housing that I spoke with—though deeply committed to Uptown, its people, its history, and its future—were renters. The currents underscoring what it means for me to say these things will be explored throughout the remainder of this chapter.

Chicago's Housing Affordability Research Consortium asserts, "One of the main obstacles to increasing public support for development of affordable housing is the perception that the free market will ultimately provide sufficient housing if left to do so" (Nyden, Lewis, and Williams 2). Uptown homeowner of over two decades, Michelle, who actively opposed Wilson Yard housing, forwarded an argument that reflects these sentiments about the free market:

I really believe that government needs to get out of orchestrating society and that we need to allow the freemarket to do what it needs to do and that everybody will benefit in the end. I'm very [. . .] in favor of letting the free market just work and if there's a need for affordable housing then somebody will find a way without the government intervening because when the government intervenes the cost of it probably increases hundred fold. And when the cost of it increases a hundred fold, then [. . .] the private market, can't do it.

The belief that affordable housing needs will be met through market demand, however, is untenable, in part, because the very idea of affordable housing necessitates selling or renting below market rate, which runs counter to market logic and tends to require government intervention to achieve.

Eleanor, who directed an Illinois affordable housing financing institution, discussed another obstacle to public support of affordable housing (namely that opponents have strong perceptions about the "type of people" that such housing will bring into a neighborhood):

One of the biggest obstacles, I think, historically is the NIMBYs—Not in my Back Yards—which is, you know, people in Wilson Yard didn't want it [the housing] because they say "we don't want that type of housing units because it will mess up the area." There's a perception of what affordable housing is and what type of people are going to come. [. . .] So there's that perception that I think people think that you've got people of low income they're going to mess up the area.

In response to such challenges, the Chicago Rehab Network frames affordable housing as a basic human right: "We believe we are better off with all people being better off—and having basic rights of food, clothing, and shelter. We believe it is in valuing affordability that we return to a core principle of democratic practice" (*Affordable Chicago* 2). Here, the "core principle of democratic practice" is construed as guaranteed equal rights to basic public goods for all citizens. By positing "housing" as one of these basic rights, the argument carries moral force. Counterarguments waged against affordable housing are most forceful when they respond with universal appeals for public goods that carry equal moral heft, such as public safety. The jockeying for moral high ground—abetted through the inventive use of democratic rhetoric—also underscores the arguments for and against housing discussed below.

For the remainder of this section, I analyze how democratic topoi are used flexibly in Uptown affordable housing debates to structure responses, mobilize action, establish ethos, and both support and blast competing understandings of what it means to live and act within democratic society. In so doing, I focus on the places of invention within which these topoi are evoked, circulated, and put to work. Rice's argument that topoi "create public discourse by offering a site around which to gather our talk" (*Distant* 84) is apt here, helping us conceive topoi as places that attract, house, and literally facilitate debate and that tether the material and the rhetorical. The four topoi I will examine (democracy as *inclusive and transparent deliberative process*, democracy as *justice*, democracy as the *mechanism for securing shared public goods*, and democracy and the *taxpayer/property owner*) are by no means exhaustive.

Topos One: Democracy as Inclusive and Transparent Deliberative Process

Attacking the credibility of a democratic process is one of the most effective rhetorical strategies for discrediting the outcome of that process, and Uptown residents who opposed affordable housing commonly resorted to this tactic. When asked to comment on the legitimacy of the Wilson Yard planning process, Alex, a homeowner who moved to Uptown in 2003 said,

> Ha! And, how good was that study . . . if we can even call it a survey? Number one: I believe the charrettes were done in the middle of the day, and most people [. . .] have full time jobs and couldn't attend. Number two: it was far and away not a scientific survey. [. . .] I mean how many people actually did the survey? 400?

That this is factually incorrect (1,762 completed the survey and charrettes were held on Saturday) is beside the point. The "truth" of the matter is less important than the way this speaker discredits the ethos of the process itself, thereby, discrediting the resulting plan.[9] It is important to note that Chicago aldermen, as democratically elected representatives, are generally under no obligation to gather extensive community input on development projects.[10] Although the survey yielded more community input than is typical, the survey did have credibility issues that support this resident's perception. For example, although "low cost housing" was ranked second behind "movie theater" in response to a question about most desired development, "retail" yielded more votes overall. Critics argue that this fact was obscured by the survey design, which diluted the retail results by asking people to check off very specific types of stores (such as Starbucks, Verizon, Target) as opposed to one general box for corporate chain. Wilson Yard critics commonly evoke this design feature as an intentional obfuscation to push the housing through under the guise of public will. Interesting to me is how the demand for transparency in democracies underscores this critique, and how what counts as transparency itself became a point of contention.

John, an Uptown homeowner, attacked the planning process for its lack of "transparency":

> John: Here it does not feel democratic, but she [former alderman Shiller] touts that [. . .]. But where's the documentation. Where's the sign in sheets for the meeting? You know, when did it happen, where did it happen, who was there? [. . .] The whole process is very sketchy and not transparent. That's the word [transparency] that a lot of people have used [. . .]
> Candice: What does transparency mean?
> John: Transparency doesn't just mean sharing information; it also means showing where you got the information. You name the 50 people who were in support and tell me the streets they live on. Don't just throw numbers around.

Another common criticism of the process is that not everyone was allowed to participate. Gary, a local storeowner, argued that although the process appeared "democratic and fair," it was not legitimate because not everyone had his or her "way":

> On paper, it was the most open, most community involved process for any kind of development. There were lots of community meetings to discuss what would be a part of the Wilson Yard process and in that sense it was very open and seemed democratic and fair. You have a lot of meetings, a lot of opportunities for different members of the community to give input. [. . .] But, the process was very much that I will create this structure that in theory let's you participation, but [. . .] you will not have your way.

In contrast, proponents of affordable housing stressed the inclusiveness and transparency of the community process as evidence of the democratic outcome. Diane, an Uptown renter who organized for affordable housing starting in 1998, celebrated the equitable and open planning process:

> The TIF did open a process for involvement. Our alderman opened the process for us. It helped to have a progressive alderman. I think in the Wilson Yard project, we all felt that there was a possibility of having a voice in the process. [. . .] getting into this in the first place was about caring about people, and who belonged here and who had the right to be here.

This resident established a moral ethos for both the process and its outcome by framing them as a consideration of people that "belonged" and "who had the right to be here."

Paul, a resident and employee of an affordable housing organization in Uptown, also commended the Wilson Yard planning process:

> Candice: Were you part of the Wilson Yard organizing and planning?
> Paul: I was. [. . .] I think it was visionary, in terms of getting people involved. Most developments get planned and pushed through and this was not the case. This was a real process and there were very large numbers of people involved. It isn't common in city politics for an alderman to open up a space like this. There were hundreds and hundreds of people sharing table space and talking about what the neighborhood might look like and what might be built there. That is something. I know the Orange Shirts complained that they didn't feel like they were part of the process or that Shiller was part of the machine politics and rolled over them with this project. It's a nice narrative to believe and convincing, I suppose, because in the U.S. we are used to hearing people protest political figures who block them out of the process or leave out their voice and that politicizes them.

Another affordable housing activist, Brian, offered further response to the common critique that we were not "part of the process":

> The Orange shirts always say they had no community input, which kills me because I was at many of the community input meetings. I was there and I thought I saw the community get together, and I thought I remembered that there was give and take on both ends, and that this [the Wilson Yard plan] was what came out. [. . .] You know, no matter what you do, the people who feel like they were left out are going to complain that they didn't have their voice and say, 'We want our voice in this, too. We are here now, and we feel like we're being shut out.' [. . .] It is a fantasy to say that the Wilson Yard didn't have community input.

As is clear, the perceived fairness and transparency of the democratic process has itself been an ongoing debate; discursive jabs around the virtue or corruption of the process have been endemic in public discourse and used to both justify and vilify the outcome of the process.

The following brief ethnographic scene, drawn from a field note, exemplifies what happens when the opposing perspectives on Wilson Yard and its planning process, came to head in a community meeting:

> It's 7:00 P.M. on April 4, 2006 and contention is in the air. I arrive at Jane Addams Hull House in Uptown for a community meeting to update

people on the Wilson Yard plan. The Uptown Neighborhood Council (the "Orange Shirts") sponsored the meeting. Outside, affordable housing activists from the Organization of the NorthEast handout green flyers, pre-emptively, in an attempt to set people "straight" before going in. The flyers read: "The Real Facts About Wilson Yard," stressing Wilson Yard as the "most comprehensive community planning process ever undertaken."

Inside, there's a crowd of 200 seated in rows of folding metal chairs, facing a large projection screen and three deliberately placed empty chairs with signs taped on the backs that read in bold black letters, "Alderman Helen Shiller, Peter Holstein [Wilson Yard's developer], and Lori Healy [former commissioner of Chicago's Department of Planning]." The moderator begins by pointing to the three chairs, "We've been requesting a meeting for 9 months, and as you see, our three guests have not arrived." The empty chairs are referenced throughout the evening as evidence of Shiller's perceived lack of care to hear her constituents.

During the slideshow, we are told: the plan changed several times without public approval, the affordable housing costs had increased and the movie theater slated for construction dropped out, leaving a hole in the project's finances. There were potential density and safety issues and the Target is iffy. We are told that the "community has been disrespected by those who are using our tax dollars to fund their development." Ideas for getting involved are aired. Near the end of the presentation, a slide titled, "Governmental Response to Community Needs and Concerns" is "left intentionally blank" and gets a hearty guffaw.

During the Q & A, a resident speculates that the movie theater was just a "Trojan Horse" used to push through the affordable housing. Another said angrily that the affordable housing has been "shoved down their throats" by the Alderman. Another laments the existence of poverty, but that "stockpiling people in towers of desperation" won't help anyone. Another exclaims: "This is our neighborhood. I don't know how many of us are staying here, but we're here now and we're paying taxes, and they are walking over us because they can. We're trying to develop the neighborhood. We want it to look like Lakeview [a more affluent neighborhood to the south] and it can be, it's got all the elements."

A dissenting voice booms from the back: "Why can't we have Uptown? Why can't we work towards an Uptown that includes all of us?" The woman, a housing activist, goes upfront and says, "I thought this was a community meeting, but many longtime members of the community wanted to speak and they have not been allowed to speak. Why? Why weren't we allowed to speak? What is your organization doing to support affordable housing?" Some audibly boo and grunt. Someone yells,

"Shut up and sit down!" The moderator gently asks her to please sit down and she does. A moment later, a well-known, longtime affordable housing activist stood up and said, "I just came to listen, not to speak, but the bullshit in this room stinks!" The raucousness continues for a bit before the energy is spent.

This scene is replete with the sort of democratic topoi I have been getting at here: the valorization of "comprehensive" democratic planning as a sign of justice served; the appeal to a politics that "includes all of us" and where nothing is "shoved down our throats"; the denigration of processes that exclude or that fail to be transparent—or worse yet—dubiously distract the public with "Trojan Horses" set to unleash harm; government that is "unresponsive" to the people, and so on. Everyone forwards the same complaint of not being able to speak, of not being heard, and of not being represented in the process as a calling out of injustice—different content, reasons, and ideological underpinnings, but the same basic logic and arguments at work in structuring how people engage politics. The desire to report the truth and root out the moral high ground devolves into another classic Uptown shouting match, again suggesting the limits of rational debate to resolve the contradictions within the democratic public sphere.

Indeed, the trump card in the Wilson Yard debates is often "democracy" itself. Below, affordable housing advocates and members of Queer to the Left discussed the tactical uses of democratic discourse in Uptown. Marie reflected on the Wilson Yard planning charrettes that took place between 1998 and 2000, and the others on the 2004 public unveiling described earlier:

> Marie: *There was a lot of criticism that there was not an extensive enough process at Wilson Yard. That brings up questions of democracy. You know, I found the notes from several of the charettes where people were invited to come and help design what the Wilson Yard would be. [. . .] Everyone was invited. It was held at Truman College. I mean what is not democratic. But not that many people came, so does that make it not democratic. I mean they had many of them, if you missed one, you could come to another.*
> Gene: *[. . .] One of the people who spoke at the last Wilson Yard meeting [in 2004], said that this process is not legitimate because this process has taken so long, you are basing the project on principles that were laid out in 1999–2000, but we are all different now, and we were left out and we should have a say in what gets built. Now, we want a voice. We're new and we were left out. That was the way they phrased it.*
> Diane: *You know there are problems with democracy that I can imagine*

us on that side. *This example makes that clear. We, I can image us organizing around this argument: "Well, but now we are here and we want to be consulted, and we live by that toxic dump (or whatever) and I think it should be moved." Or whatever. There is something about the whole thing that is fraught with indeterminacy.*
Gene: *The other side of it, though, is that the reason it has taken so long is because it is an open process. [. . .] Yeah, opening up dialogue has made the process longer. And then you have the issues that new people move into the neighborhood and want to redo the process because they weren't involved.*
Diane: *Right, but that doesn't mean that that the process is faulty. [. . .]*
Gene: *Right, and we could have a never-ending process, because we could do it all again, but you could all be gone before it is implemented, and then we'd need to do it all again.*

In sum, the most common inventive moves pertaining to the democratic process include: (1) *Attack the legitimacy of the process if you don't like the outcome*: Any indication of procedural problems in the democratic process (lack of transparency, questionable survey instruments, unfair facilitation of community discussions, formal or informal exclusions) becomes the grounds for discrediting the outcome; (2) *Stress the copious opportunities for debate and evidence of inclusion if you support the outcome*: By highlighting the openness, inclusiveness, and fairness of the process, you strengthen the claims that "democracy" has occurred; (3) *Emphasize biases and exclusions if you want to cry undemocratic*: The attempt to discredit the democratic process based on biases can be seen in all positions from UNC members feeling the "decks are stacked" to housing activists' sense that the Orange Shirts were only interested in private gain.

Topos Two: Democracy as Justice

One might argue that the substance of "justice" within a liberal-democratic framework becomes clearer as you move closer to interaction on the ground, but such is not the case in Uptown. Sometimes, as indicated above, justice is predicated on the inclusiveness of the "democratic" process, and sometimes it is defined as development that represents all interests. At times, justice is perceived as the satisfaction of individual preference, and at others times, as social and economic equality for all. For some, "consensus" signals justice, and for others, consensus is a form of violence that evacuates politics from public debate, which, for Mouffe, becomes the "very condition" for the "elimination of pluralism from the public sphere" (*Democratic* 49). The simplest reason used to argue against the affordable buildings at Wilson Yard is "I don't want them." As an argument for public policy, this statement rests on a perception of democracy as a system that protects private interests, and that legitimates planning decisions as "just" only if they represent everyone's interests and seem to favor no one's.

Former alderman Shiller supported affordable housing at Wilson Yard as a project that self-consciously intervenes in the housing market to correct material inequality, an arguably democratic impetus and social justice imperative. Likewise, affordable housing advocates tend to rest their arguments on the ideal of social equality, arguing that all citizens should have a *right to* decent, affordable housing; however, Shiller was often accused of both being undemocratic in favoring the poor and for general divisiveness. For example, UNC member and Uptown homeowner, Alex, expressed this latter perception that a "good leader" should foster "common ground":

> *I think that [Shiller] is a divisive figure [. . .]. She divides people and then galvanizes people on her side of the divide, and then laments that there is a division. A good leader would be someone who could bring people together. I would suggest that if you wanted to have no trash on the streets and a more functional eL station, then you [shouldn't be seen as] against the poor, hating them and wanting to kick them out. [. . .] That is inflammatory and divisive language. That's not the kind of language that fosters common ground.*

Susan, another UNC member, corroborated this sense that the goal of the community process was to gain consensus while challenging the legitimacy of the process:

> *I have the transcripts from all the Wilson Yard charettes, when you read them you can see at the end of them that they are not really charrettes [. . .] Charettes are supposed to be a process that is professionally moderated, and the goal is to gain community input and consensus around ideas for whatever it is that you are working to create.*

Susan and Alex's call for consensus is a common appeal in the discourse that discredits the process and its outcome as unjust because the Wilson Yard plan did not reflect common ground.

In the remainder of this subsection, I want to tease out how this call for justice as consensus comes to head within an extended field example from

2004, in which consensus is simultaneously heralded as a desirable goal and called out for hiding profound ideological differences and tacitly perpetuating material injustices. In a creative assent to the already-approved affordable housing in the Wilson Yard plan, UNC members issued a "compromise" position, signaling their willingness to build consensus around the issue of affordable housing, but only if units were reserved for Chicago's "struggling artists." Groups who lobbied for affordable housing as an explicit social justice call to counteract gentrification, such as Queer to the Left, ONE, and COURAJ, understood this compromise as a cheap ploy, and pointed out what they perceived as class and racist undertones of the artist requirement. Although Shiller didn't take the artist housing seriously, the debates around this proposal crystallize how consensus is heralded (or challenged) as the desired outcome of a democratic process and justice achieved. UNC member and local business owner, Gary, described the proposal for artist housing as such:

> *The process was stacked from the beginning. There was no hope for consensus. Shiller wanted affordable housing. The compromised solution that was proposed, and I supported this absolutely, was to have a lot of artists studios there so that way you are supporting lower income individuals that will be bringing back something to the neighborhood through their arts. I thought this was an excellent idea that would bring artists there and keep community discussion and cooperation alive, but the Alderman's attitude was, that's not what I mean by low income. And those were pretty much direct statements. So, the idea that the process would result in something we all agree with died right there.*

Arguments for the artist housing typically presented artists, matter-of-factly, as neutral, value-adding low-income residents.

In opposition to UNC's call for affordable artist housing at Wilson Yard, a group of Uptown artists staged a protest, donning black berets and signage as "artists protesting artist housing." Chicago artist Laurie Palmer was one of these protestors, and documented this action in *Trashing the Neoliberal City: Autonomous Cultural Practices in Chicago*. In this essay collection, Palmer's contribution features a picture of her holding a large white poster board with black block letters that read A.S.S.H.O.L.E. (Artists Seeking Solutions to Housing by Ousting Low-Income People From Everywhere!). Palmer's slogan targeted the proposed artist colony at Wilson Yard, which she summed up with the following words: "Organized gentrifiers introduced yet another twist. They decided to push for the idea that the affordable housing quotient still remained in the development plan be for artists housing because, they argued, artists too need subsidized space. It was a pathetic attempt to use artists—those supposedly class-less value-adders—to augment their property values" (Palmer 9). Two members of Queer to the Left, Barbara and Edward, also criticized the UNC's push for an artist colony at Wilson Yard as a position that relied on cultural, racial, and class-based assumptions about what constitutes a "good" poor person. Below, these QTL members reflected on actions that took place in 2004 around Wilson Yard in an interview with me:

> *Barbara: The Orange Shirts wanted artist housing at Wilson Yard. [. . .]*
> *Edward: Yeah, yeah, yeah, that was hilarious. That was their counterargument to affordable housing. If we have to have affordable housing in Wilson Yard, we can make it artist lofts and let's make it only for artists and it would be AFFORDABLE to artists and the artists would come in and give lessons for the community about art and provide culture. They said that Uptown has no art and no culture.*
> *Barbara: And they were also drawing on very cultural notions of what passes as a "good" poor person. A good poor person is an artist. There is a certain kind of good poor person.*
> *Edward: There are a lot of racial undertones in these conversations. I talked with one person who feared that the people who would come to Wilson Yard will be black and on welfare and former public housing residents. Some already have an image of what they see as the "bad" poor person. People are worried Wilson Yard is going to become Cabrini—Green.*[11]

Another longtime affordable housing advocate and Uptown resident, Paul, echoed a similar characterization of the arguments for artist housing at Wilson Yard:

> *Oh God, then there is the argument about the artist housing! Artists are good poor people was the unspoken. We don't mind living with them. We just don't want poor people of color. Of course, no one says that, except on online message boards, where people really let loose. The argument about Wilson Yard being like Cabrini—Green is bunk, just erroneous, as far as I am concerned. Cabrini—Green is code for poor, out of control black people and failed housing policy. It recalls the most nightmarish version of public housing. This is not that.*

The calls for justice or calling out of injustice become flexible persuasive strategies that mobilize the power of democratic rhetoric toward various ends.

This strategy is endemic to the Wilson Yard debates. What is not ubiquitous is stasis among the arguments. For example, to reach stasis, one could argue whether it is more or less just to reach consensus than not (therefore, compromising on the artist housing), or one might argue about whether it is more or less just to build low-income housing to counteract material inequity (therefore, not reserving it solely for value-adders with cultural capital). However, people clearly generate rhetorical power by strategically forwarding arguments with no desire to reach stasis.

Topos Three: Democracy as the Mechanism for Securing Shared Public Goods (such as Fair and "Sensible" Urban Development)

Uptown citizens do not agree on the terms of urban development projects in the context of gentrification. Here are four very different perceptions of gentrification in the neighborhood, for example, which implicate very different notions of what might constitute "sensible" development that results in public goods:

> One. *An Uptown housing activist described gentrification as a process by which "slowly but surely all the poor will be driven out of Uptown and [. . .] forced elsewhere." Building affordable housing is a "matter of social justice."*
>
> Two. *A homeowner expressed his dislike of the term gentrification and preferred "urban renewal."* He believed that gentrification has negative connotations and *"always suggests that people are being pushed out"* and implied that *"condo owners and wealthy people come in and kick out the poor"* in order to make the neighborhood what they want.
>
> Three. *A landlord, who had lived in Uptown since the 1970s, expressed his disdain of the term "gentrification," arguing that the leftists in the neighborhood "like to call it gentrify,"* but that *"We call it decriminalize. Civilize. [. . .] it is a term that they've [the leftists housing activists] come to use—GENTRIFY—gentrify, like when you hold up a cross at a vampire. 'Ooh, ooh, gentrify, gentrify. Oh, you're a gentrifier. Oooooh!'. . . . No, I'm a civilizer!"*
>
> Four. *An affordable housing tenant and activist expressed her anxiety about gentrification and its responsibility for "making it harder to get by if you don't have much."* More and more *"condos are popping up and places are getting so expensive to live. Our building owner is thinking of selling for profit and getting out of the HUD business."*

At heart, how one defines fair and sensible development, given the divergent politics represented above, gets to the matter of how public good is defined in relation to neighborhood change in Uptown. As the fieldwork revealed, affordable housing at Wilson Yard is seen by some as a democratic, just, and reasonable response to the processes of gentrification, and by others as an irresponsible contribution to the already-existing problem of concentrated poverty and public safety issues.

Advocates of affordable housing tend to rest their arguments on the ideal of social equality, arguing that all citizens should have a *right to* decent, affordable housing. Uptown affordable housing advocate, Paul, put it this way:

> *Candice: Then, do you see housing as a right that government should protect?*
> *Paul: I believe we have a social responsibility to provide affordable housing for everyone. I don't think this is a private issue. It is a public one. I do believe that it is something that the government should. . . . I think the government is a tool that enables us to carry out these responsibilities. I think housing is a right. I think it is a human responsibility. The notion that taxes are to be directed towards projects that individuals desire is irksome. I understand we don't all agree on where they should be directed, though.*

In the following, Annabelle, a longtime Uptown affordable housing tenant and community organizer, echoed Paul's assessment that housing should be viewed as a right and discussed arguments she used to support affordable housing preservation on the local and national level, as well as commonplace obstacles affordable housing activists face:

> *Candice: What were some of the most important arguments you all made for why preserving affordable housing is important?*
> *Annabelle: Housing is a human right. Everyone has the right to housing and to be able to live in a decent neighborhood. [. . .] The government had created the housing programs that we were fighting for, for a reason. To provide opportunities for people to live in good places they can afford. Almost everyone is just one check or two away from being homeless. This is a societal need. We all need housing that is decent and that we can pay for.*
> *Candice: Some people in Uptown have criticized public housing and subsidized housing on the grounds that the government or officials shouldn't use public money or tax dollars to provide "handouts" to people who become dependent on them. Or some argue that the housing market will take care of itself without intervention.*
> *Annabelle: Hah. Yeah. And, no! It won't! Unless, taking care of itself means poor people can only live in bad, nasty places. No poor people by the lake. No poor people in the Gold Coast.*

Annabelle's framing of affordable housing preservation and construction as a basic human right and public good to which democratic citizens should have a right is a commonplace.

In response to the argument that low-income renters and homeowners should have formally protected rights to remain in a gentrifying neighborhood, Uptown homeowner Alex argued:

There are no indigenous people in a neighborhood. It is a complete fallacy. Neighborhoods change and if they don't, they die. By that standard [. . .] Uptown used to be a playground for the wealthy and socialite in the 20s. Are those the indigenous people?!? It is a ridiculous statement. A complete fallacy. That pisses me off. It has no basis. [. . .] I don't agree with this idea that you have the right to live in any neighborhood that you want to live in. I don't have that right. You don't have that right. If I want to live in the Gold Coast [an affluent Chicago neighborhood], do I have that right? Does the government or someone have the obligation to subsidize my desire to live in the Gold Coast?"

This Uptowner suggested that no one has the right to demand that the government funds his or her preference to stay in a neighborhood and discredits housing at Wilson Yard by attacking the moral foundation that subsidized housing rests upon: namely, that people have a *right to* not be displaced by uneven market forces, that everyone has a *right to* decent housing, and that the government has an *obligation to* provide universal public goods. Further underscoring this argument is a perception of neighborhood change as natural, inevitable, and "good."

This sentiment of the naturalness of urban development can also be found in the following conversation, which elaborates upon what "balanced, sensible development" in Uptown is and is not according to the Uptown Neighborhood Council (the Orange shirts). UNC's mission is to "revitalize the Uptown community through balanced economic development, the arts and cultural enrichment and *sensible* community planning." In 2006, I interviewed Frank, a neighborhood business owner, and Susan, an Uptown homeowner since 2001. They responded to the charge that the UNC is "against poor people."

Frank: Well, I just want to say something about UNC. Something people say is that we are against the poor. Absolutely not true! That's absurd. It angers me to no end.
Susan: I don't even like that word. Poor.
Candice: What is the criticism [you have of Wilson Yard] then? Is it the concentration of poor?

Frank: On our side?
Candice: Yes.
Susan: I'll tell you. What we are talking about is the lack of vision. I'll give you a perfect example of where there is a vision going on versus where there isn't a vision here, and where there is a building of consensus versus keeping people polarized. [. . .] Bronzeville [a gentrifying, predominantly African American neighborhood on Chicago's South Side] is doing what we would like to do in this community, and that is using arts and culture as a jumpstart for building a healthy vibrant community. [. . .] That is what I call revitalization. [. . .]
Candice: What is the vision here?
Susan: There is no vision. The only vision is "bring us your poor, put in more low-income housing." All more of the same. The towers of subsidized housing where people are stockpiled . . . Uptown is the only place where they are building more of it, instead of tearing it down and giving people opportunity to live in low density, nice places where you can put your kids outside to play. [. . .]
Frank: We want to preserve the rich history and the culture, you know, we're not looking to get rid of that, but you know, unfortunately communities change over time. I mean every community changes.
Susan: The only community that never changes is a cemetery that is full.

Frank and Susan's concern about the further concentration of poverty and subsidized housing is not without cause. Uptown has a relatively high concentration of subsidized housing (18.2%), a large homeless population and visible street drug culture, a proliferation of social service agencies, and real public safety concerns. Further, the Wilson Yard TIF district encompasses two census tracts where 44.2% and 35.1% of the respective population is living at or below the poverty line ("Greater Chicago Housing").

While Susan's argument about further concentrating poverty has legs, her likening of the Wilson Yard housing to "towers" inaccurately evokes, according to housing advocates, failed public housing models that were being torn down in Chicago during this time, and replaced by low rise, mixed-income units and with individual housing vouchers that could be used on the open rental market. Uptown affordable housing advocate, Edward, spoke to the equation of Wilson Yard to "the projects" as fear driven:

> I can't tell you how many times people would stand up and refer to it [Wilson Yard] as "the projects." And they always used the word "project." And they always misused the terminology. . . . you know what I mean? It's affordable housing. It is not "THE PROJECTS." They don't see the

difference between affordable housing and Section 8 public housing. They constantly are saying we tore down "the projects," the high-rise projects, and now we're building a new one. [. . .] They feel they attract the same people and problems and this is really about fear. People are fearful and think the housing will make things worse.

The concern over "stockpiling" the poor into crime-ridden "projects" evokes the horrific conditions of Chicago's public housing complexes built during urban renewal that were racially and economically segregated, primarily in poor, black neighborhoods. Although Wilson Yard is not public housing, the fear that the housing will become gang- and drug-infested "towers of desperation" that breed poverty and social dysfunction runs rampant in commentary about the future of buildings, as Edward noted.[12] Wilson Yard's housing (which matches the height of surrounding apartment buildings) does not resemble the notorious public housing managed by Chicago Housing Authority (CHA) in the twentieth century, such as the infamous Cabrini–Green complex or Robert Taylor Homes, which housed fifteen thousand and twenty-seven thousand, respectively. So, whether one supports it or not, for good reason or not, likening it to CHA projects is hyperbolic.

Below, Sean, an Uptown condo-owner since 1999, also conflated affordable and public housing in his discussion of Wilson Yard:

It [Wilson Yard] is not designed for families and she [Shiller] says it is for families [. . .] But . . . we probably won't be able to attract the couples and singles with children because if they had a choice, they would go somewhere else. It will probably be mostly Section 8. My guess is that it will be all Section 8. [. . .] I don't want gentrification. I want good urban planning. It was lousy urban planning that put in too many shelters and too many mental ill facilities [in Uptown]. It was poor urban planning there. [. . .] I think a good neighborhood is a neighborhood that is an environment where the kids can prosper and blossom. The current set up will not allow children to blossom.

Given that contemporary public housing policies provide individuals with "Housing Choice Vouchers" to secure rental units on the open market and that Wilson Yard is reserved for low-income households, Wilson Yard will likely attract voucher-holders; however, even if the units were 100% filled with voucher holders, the scale of 178 units is radically different than Cabrini–Green's 3,607 units or Robert Taylor's 4,415 units. Further, in Sean's remarks above, the ultimate rhetorical trump card played is his universal appeal to children's safety. By framing Wilson Yard as detrimental to children, this rhetor forwards a powerful moral charge: namely, if you support the housing, you are not only against children prospering, but also a direct threat to them. Since there is virtually no one who would argue that protecting the safety of children is not important, this rhetor, for those he can convince, accomplishes a powerful case for the argument that affordable housing cannot be considered fair and "sensible planning."

Topos Four: Democracy and the Taxpayer/Property Owner

Yet another democratic topos that looms large in the discourse around Wilson Yard is the "property-owning taxpayer." The marriage of the burdened taxpayer to the upright property owner cuts a prominent figure as the model for citizenship. The core rhetorical moves of this topos are: (1) Taxpayers are personally invested, have sacrificed themselves, and should benefit from and have more say in how their taxes are spent (than renters, especially ones in subsidized housing); (2) Property owners are more responsible and likely contributors to the health of the community (and should, therefore, have more weight in urban development decisions); (3) Nonproperty owners are shiftless, careless, capable of being "bought out," or otherwise indifferent to local politics (thus, rendering their opinions suspect); (4) Those who have been "given government handouts" (in this case, affordable housing partly subsidized through property taxes) are enjoying public goods they didn't earn on the backs of hardworking citizens and are, therefore, perceived as economic burdens, undeserving, lazy, irresponsible, and/or unlikely to care for the property they have been "given." Although not all of these moves are expressed in every evocation of the taxpayer/property owner topos and many who evoke it would likely strongly oppose some of the moves, these logics accumulate as places of invention in Uptown, drawing on the long-standing equation of property and freedom, homeownership and stakeholding, citizenship and economic independence prevalent in U.S. democratic discourse.

The complaint by property-owning taxpayers that their hard-earned money is being used for something that "they do not want" and that they feel is potentially "harmful" to their investment is amplified by the funding for Wilson Yard through Tax Increment Financing (TIF), a widely used development tool that enables municipalities to capture and reinvest property tax dollars for development projects within designated geographic areas for twenty-three years.[13] TIFs justify leveraging private property taxes for public projects on the grounds that a blighted area would not improve "but for" incentives for developers. When an area is approved as a TIF district, the county assesses the base property value within the geographical area, and any subsequent increases to property taxes over this initial value are redirected each year to pay for TIF projects within the district. Such projects might include renovating schools, public parks, and infrastructure; funding daycare and job training initiatives; and subsidizing commercial development. TIF money cannot be used for "brick-and-mortar" housing construction, *except* in the case of building new affordable housing units (*Tax Increment*). Therefore, property owners who live within the Wilson Yard TIF district and oppose affordable housing will nevertheless help pay for over 30% of its projected cost of $151 million through property tax increases.

TIFs are commonly critiqued for bankrolling commercial developments that fuel gentrification and potentially displace longtime low-income residents. For all its controversy, however, the Wilson Yard pointedly inverses this equation by using TIF money to intervene in the housing market by redistributing incremental property tax increases to build affordable housing. However, some who oppose the housing at Wilson Yard do so on the grounds that their property taxes are being used for a project they oppose. In his discussion of the historical bias of property ownership in U.S. democracies, Krueckeberg highlights the role that property tax plays in symbolically entitling residents to have more voice than renters: "The implication is that some people do not pay property taxes and therefore have not earned respect. Ownership means privilege over non-ownership with reference to the thing owned" (11).

In their analysis of Minutemen discourses, rhetoricians Bleeden, Druschke, and Cintrón extend this sense of entitlement in their analysis of the taxpayer topos in liberal democracy. They write: "The *topos* of the beleaguered taxpayer complaining of wasteful government spending pervades the American imaginary, representing both left-leaning and right-leaning political philosophies" (184), as well as a "certain unassailable moral standing" (186). The taxpayer topos operates in two key ways: First, paying taxes represents a significant personal sacrifice, entitling taxpayers to "demand worth of those things for which [they] sacrifice," and, second, taxpayers, as Krueckeberg also insists of homeowners, "not only have made a genuine sacrifice of self but also have a more rightful claim on the state because they are authentic, moral citizens" (187). The entitlement of the taxpayer meets the moral standing of the property owner in public discourse about affordable housing at Wilson Yard, coalescing in a one-two rhetorical punch.

Let's turn to the field to see how this topos operates in everyday arguments. To begin, John, an Uptown homeowner, said the following in an interview:

> *As a taxpayer, I pay a crap load of taxes.[. . .] I think the people who are advocating for a TIF to use my tax dollars [. . .] should be bending over backwards to listen to what the homeowners and the property owners have to say who are within an earshot of this [Wilson Yard]. [. . .] And I don't think you use taxpayer money to build low-income housing—you just don't. Because you are never going to get that money back. I mean it's one thing if you put in a movie theater and stuff like that, that's going to generate tons of tax money.*

Gene, an Uptown renter and affordable housing activist, shared his thoughts with me on how tax dollars operate in consumer-driven democratic citizenship, which pushes back on John's sensibility:

> *You know it's interesting this thing about hearing people saying they don't want their tax dollars spent on this project. Trying to connect this to democracy is the idea that my tax dollars shouldn't be used for purposes that go against what I want. I mean we all sort of bemoan the fact that our tax dollars go to Iraq or whatever. It is more of a consumer ideal of citizenship; that I want to be able to direct my money wherever I think it will benefit me the most.*

Here, the "consumer ideal of citizenship" is defined through a conflation of individual preference with the right to demand of the social contract exactly what one wants. Within this model, anything that is funded with *my tax dollars* that *I don't want* is perceived as unjust. Some homeowners feel they are paying for something that is not only harmful to their investment, but also celebrated as a democratic decision, against which they had no opportunity to intervene. This concern about how affordable housing will affect property values is a powerful refrain.

Edward, a longtime Uptown renter and housing advocate, responded to concerns that the affordable rentals will harm property investments:

> *Property owners feel they should have more of a say. [. . .] They want to make sure that when they buy a property that a property is going to go up and they look at that as being the goal. I think they see that affordable housing is either going to plateau it or make it go down. Because it's going to make the neighborhood less desirable to people who are going to be homeowners.*

Embedded in the worry over how affordable housing will harm property investments lies an attendant concern about the presumed types of people that will occupy such housing. The housing at Wilson Yard is similar in height and style to surrounding noncontroversial apartment buildings, suggesting that it is not the housing per se but the demographics of potential residents that is "going to make the neighborhood less desirable to people who are going to be homeowners." Although blatant discussions of the race or ethnicity of potential residents are very rare in public discourse, what is commonplace, as I have mentioned, is the equation of Wilson Yard's housing and Chicago Public Housing Projects, the latter of which are overwhelmingly inhabited by poor, black Chicagoans on various forms of public welfare. Generally, Chicago residents know this and would be able to extrapolate without the need for explicit mention of race or class.

Below, affordable housing advocate Paul summarized and then critiqued his understanding of the ways these arguments about homeownership entitlement can sometimes function as "thinly veiled racism or classism":

> *Many of those who oppose the housing are anti-Shiller [. . .] Shiller has a long history of supporting balanced development and taking steps to preserve affordable housing. She has a very different vision than those who organize against her. [. . .] I think some people bought into the neighborhood hoping it would develop and become another Lincoln Park because it is close to the Lake and near transportation, and they see what Shiller supports as getting in the way of that vision. There is an entitlement that many newcomers have.*
>
> *And a lot of the arguments are thinly veiled racism or classism. For example, at one of the public meetings, I remember this guy saying, "I can't believe that when I go out for a cup of coffee that I have to step over a homeless man. Just because I can't afford to live in Lincoln Park shouldn't mean that I have to deal with that." There is clearly something very delusional there, a complete breakdown of perception. His life could not be more different than the homeless man's life. [. . .] They feel like they should have a say because they paid to be here and that tax money should go towards what they want. They are invested and public policies should all be bent towards supporting their investments. They feel they buy into the neighborhood and that gives them a particular entitlement to control their tax money.*

Although comments like "step[ping] over a homeless man" are very rare outside of online blog comments, the sense of homeowner and taxpayer entitlement to shape urban development decisions is familiar.

For example, below, we see the taxpaying homeowner topos tying together the discourse on taxpayers' right to control how their taxes are spent and on property owners as the model for the moral, responsible, self-sacrificing citizen. Alfonso, a multi-unit apartment building owner and landlord, demonstrated this twinning:

> Alfonso: We have more stake! I pay more taxes. I keep the neighborhood up. I keep the rents low because I have civilized people living in the building. No loud noise. No parties.
> Candice: So, do you feel that because property owners pay more tax that they should have more say in what happens in the neighborhood?
> Alfonso: [. . .] Well, yes.

Rick, an Uptown condo owner opposed to housing at Wilson Yard, provided another example:

> We have to pay for these developments with our tax dollars. OUR property taxes! And not only are our property taxes going up and up and up in Chicago, this thing is taking those dollars and rerouting them to something that is going to lower our property value. It is so frustrating! We are the ones who take care of things in this neighborhood and make it better.

In what follows, I share an extended conversation with Michelle, a self-proclaimed Orange Shirt and longtime homeowner, in which she talked about the role of property ownership and taxes in local politics:

> Michelle: But I have to say that the large proportion of people who really come out to CAPS [Chicago Alternative Policing Strategy] meetings, come out and clean up on neighborhood cleanup days, come out and plant in community gardens, work politically for the candidate of their choice. . . . I have to say a huge percentage of that is homeowners. [. . .]
> Candice: Why do you think that is?
> Michelle: Because when you. . . . well. . . . it's obvious. When you invest. . . . You want me to really say it?
> Candice: Yeah, well, I'm wondering. . . . If you don't mind. . . . ?
> Michelle: Because an investment always needs to be protected. You have worked hard to buy the investment and work for the investment to be able to. . . . I mean very, very few people are handed a lump sum of money to buy a home or condo. [. . .] You work for it. You realize that the only way that that work is going to be protected and that work will eventually. . . . pay dividends in the future is to put effort behind it. I mean it takes work to keep your property [. . .] you are continually going back and fixing and

repairing and making better. You're continually doing that on your property. So people realize that you have to continually do that in your neighborhood and your community. Your property, your neighbors, everything is interconnected.
Candice: Because of this, then, do you feel that property owners should have a larger stake in what happens with their tax dollars in the neighborhood? [. . .]
Michelle: I guess I'm thinking about how did we get to this point in democracy? Where every person gets a say regardless of the property that they own. [. . .] I understand that our democracy was set up on the fact that every person has an equal say in the process and I believe in that. [. . .] But after saying that, I think that. . . . well, maybe not in a horrible way, not a formal law that property owners have more votes than a non-property owner. . . . but I think that informally the representative of a community should take very, very careful consideration the views of the property owners because that is the health of the community. The views of the property owners and the needs of the property owners are not going to be counterproductive to a healthy community.

In this dialogue, Michelle equated property owners with model citizenship. It is the property owners who invest in the neighborhood through the purchase of their home and payment of property taxes, along with the everyday investment of time and money in property upkeep. Beyond these property-centric acts of civic duty, Michelle observed that it is property owners who participate in community events. Though Michelle had mixed feelings about whether these civic acts should translate to more voting power, her call for extra "consideration" of property owners as the prime contributors to "health of the community" is clear. I am not particularly interested in refuting or substantiating this claim, but in elucidating the way that the rhetorical moves of the taxpayer/homeowner topos are being picked up here and put to work.

In the following dialogue, Linda, a longtime Uptown affordable housing activist who has worked with ONE and COURAJ, recounted and responded to the logics of the taxpayer/property owner topos as she encountered it in Uptown politics. In her account, she verified this sense of political entitlement on the part of property owners, but also how the protection of property investments tends to trump and betray other political beliefs in local politics:

Linda: Well, there are a lot of fairly young people in the movement [against affordable housing], and many of them are left-leaning politically. We'd knock on their doors [. . .] and what we found like almost to

a person. . . . people were progressive in national politics you know? [. . .] they were all Democrats, they were all anti-war and blah blah blah, all that kind of good stuff but when it came to local Uptown things, they very much believed that it was all about their property values and that they, in fact, had an absolute right to buy into a low income neighborhood for cheap and in the course of a few years without any effort of their own [. . .] should be able to realize a huge profit. [. . .] they saw everything happening in Uptown through the lens of how this might affect my profit as if this wasn't people's place to live, that people hadn't struggled here to get better housing, to get better schools, but somehow they had just appeared here and it was their community.
Candice: So, did you have conversations with people where they actually expressed this? Where they said it was all about their property values?
Linda: Yes. I know a lot of people who weren't going to vote for Shiller because they did not see her as aligned with their property interests. Even though if I had been there about some very progressive national candidate they would have been fine with that, right? [. . .]
Candice: So, could we back up? Would you mind unpacking how you understand this logic driving the arguments about property?
Linda: Something like this: I am a responsible citizen. I own my home. It's an investment. I invest in this neighborhood through taking care of my property, through putting my dollars into my property, through whatever. Through spending money in this neighborhood, I am more responsible, because I am a property owner, than others because I am invested and I should have control over my tax dollars. I don't know.
Candice: Sounds familiar.
Linda: I mean that confounds various things though. So there's the assumption that because you own property you are, therefore, more responsible than people who don't. What would that be based on exactly? Some kind of prejudice right? That somehow property ownership equals greater responsibility and entitlement. That's almost like saying I'm a better or more important citizen or should have a larger voice because I own property.
Candice: Yes, that is precisely what some people say. [. . .]
Linda: A lot of us who are not so big on capitalism would say we're looking for that democracy that redistributes wealth and doesn't just say that [. . .] those who are already wealthy regardless of they acquired it, would have more say. I mean I think our democracy actually gives them more say. So they have already got that. So to say that we should reorient it so they get even more say and even more control? That's kind of a horrifying thought.

Although Linda's description of the logic of the property ownership topos aligned fairly closely to Michelle's accounting of it, she did not agree that "property ownership equals greater responsibility and entitlement." More importantly, she lamented how political investments are filtered through the "lens of how this might affect my profit," and was dismayed to find that so many progressive young people were protesting an ostensibly leftist housing project because it is perceived as being at odds with their property investment. Both Michelle and Linda represent positions that make claims to personal sacrifice and moral high grounds within democracy, but there is a sharp disagreement in where these commitments should reside. Whereas Michelle stressed a personal sacrifice of money, time, and energy in civic actions of caring for community through property upkeep and the participation of local events (like trash pick-ups), Linda sought a personal sacrifice of property interests in lieu of a commitment to the ideal of the "redistribution of wealth." In the former case, the prioritization of protecting property investments in local politics makes it difficult to support affordable housing because of the perceived harm to property value. In the latter case, the priority of achieving economic parity and in characterizing homeowners as profit-driven can mask the risk and social benefits of ownership.

From an abstract position, it might be easy to berate property owners for their preoccupation with private investments, but this moral position denies material reality. While I interviewed a few who did know people who bought cheaply only to their flip property, this tactic was relatively rare in my fieldwork, in part, because I don't think it was the flippers showing up at public meetings about the future of the neighborhood. As my time in the field extended, this rhetorical strategy of casting the homeowner in the crude role of the Mr. Bad Guy of capitalism seemed more facile. The purpose of this divergence is to raise questions such as these: if your aim is to critique capitalism and explicitly intervene in its systems (such as through securing subsidized affordable housing to counteract gentrification), how might this be done without dismissing the material circumstances of capitalism that extend to middle-class homeowners? Put more simply, is it possible to forward a traditionally leftist position without insisting on a moral high ground that creates greedy human counterparts, oversimplifying how capitalism shapes the material circumstances of those you oppose, or downplays your own complicity? Conversely, how might we reimagine the role that property ownership plays in determining our local political commitments? How do we resolve that property ownership places people in material opposition to a politic that supports affordable housing that may very well negatively affect property value? One could say: abolish property to avoid these ambivalences. But, this, too, seems facile.

Discussing the rights of property owners in the neighborhood, Herb hit on this ambivalence of being a homeowner with a family in a neighborhood with public safety issues:

> *I don't think that my rights as a property owner are any different than someone who rents . . . I think I have equivalent rights. But that's the problem, I feel like people try to diminish my voice . . . to assert . . . that the condo owners are bad and only interested in increasing our property values. I don't think of my property values. I think of where I could walk with my daughter and not expose her to bad things.*

This defense of homeowners is important. The dynamics in Uptown place individuals in contradictory positions; for example, a left-leaning, middle-class homeowner who believes in equal access to decent, affordable housing must come to terms with the reality that such housing might conflict with his desire for better schools, higher property values, and safer streets. Interestingly, the resident quoted above is concerned about being silenced; yet, he is, at least economically speaking, quite privileged in relation to citizens who would benefit from the *right to* affordable housing. Nevertheless, this claim of being silenced fits squarely into the democratic mythos, which claims both to protect private interests and to secure public goods. In attempting to protect the interests of those disenfranchised by gentrification, it would seem that Shiller and her supporters excluded the interests of those who opposed affordable housing. However, the inequities of redistribution within capitalism raise the question of what responsibilities democratic citizens, leaders, and institutions have to "correct" such inequity.

Conclusion

The city is commonly theorized as an ideal model of the liberal democratic public sphere. Iris Young describes the city as the "being together of strangers." She understands "city life" as "a vision of social relations affirming group difference" that "instantiates social relations of difference without exclusion" (227). This compelling vision of the city as a space for greater tolerance, radical diversity without exclusion, dynamism, and creativity has fueled wave after wave of urban planning schemes and community-based efforts designed to bring forth the "ideal city," which always seems just beyond reach. Despite its shortcomings, the public sphere remains a potent topos. The model might be better understood as a process that can be used to make claims for rights across wide-ranging ideologies; a heuristic for locating the foundational questions, contradictions, limitations, and possibilities of democratic life; and as a conceptual and material site for rhetorical invention, where arguments that inspire and justify a range of "democratic" actions and sentiments can be discovered and effectively mobilized in this or that fleeting moment of persuasion. Indeed, as a model for democracy, the public sphere provides rich ground for rhetorical invention that helps structure our arguments and actions on behalf of the "good life" and tether them to the situational contexts, material conditions, and resources available to us in our particular environs.

Democratic rhetorics have, historically, inspired some of the most courageous (and fraught) extensions of rights. It seems that concern over whether something is or is not democratic, obscures the more important question of whether various social investments do or do not produce desirable and just consequences. However, it is precisely the question of what constitutes the content of "desirable and just" action that democratic rhetorics cannot finally determine. For Marie, who lived in Uptown for years and fought with Queer to the Left for affordable housing at Wilson Yard, a deep nostalgia for the possibilities of collaboration underscored her understanding of what was meaningful about her activism:

> *I don't know how to think about concrete results. [. . .] At Wilson Yard, there is affordable housing and that is real, you know. We worked for that. Concrete. But, this experience of working with this group called COURAJ and then the kind of alliance that happened in Queer to the Left, there was a sense that there was a real possibility of organizing across space, across difference and it allowed housing to be an organizing principle. [. . .] You know there is this possibility of imagining working towards something. I'm not sure if you can easily translate the possibility to the next battle, but in a sense, I think it does translate. Gives you some strength and connection. That sounds fuzzy, I know. That sense of possibility, which is different from concrete results, still means something.*

Democratic topoi are generative; they structure hope, belief, and action. Just below the surface of democratic topoi are the messy and contradictory moral undercurrents of democracy. Marie's statement carries the moral charge of "possibility" that fuels the whole democratic project. However, that powerful hope for connection, for building coalitions, for working toward just social ends, can be inhabited by those who envision a very different Uptown than Marie.

For example, UNC member Michelle, discussed the "gift" of democracy that she felt obligated to honor through her activism to halt affordable housing at Wilson Yard. For Michelle, the hours spent protesting, attending meetings, letter writing, petitioning, engaging in legal actions, and emailing was evidence of her dedication to and participation in democracy:

> Michelle: I never felt linked to any kind of radical movement. Anything that we did, I always felt was the gift that democracy gives us. And that if we don't use it we are delinquent in our. . . . as a citizen. I really believe that. . . . I continually think about people who have made greater sacrifices. Humongous sacrifices of life, their own future. I think about them and I think they have preserved this gift for me, and I must use it or else I am slapping them in the face.
> Candice: And how do you understand the gift of democracy?
> Michelle: To me, the gift of democracy is to . . . well, it starts with educating yourself. Learn what it is that you are concerned about and then don't sit back with that knowledge but do the steps that are necessary to pass that knowledge on. Take action in a peaceable way.

Despite the deep contradictions within the public sphere, it is, ironically, the promised ideals reflected within the model that provide many with the courage, along with the rhetorical toolkit, to continually dream up and work toward new worlds that are more just and less cruel; worlds that we hope might transcend the horrors, contradictions, and suffering found within our material circumstances. And yet, here again, we hit the limit, the endgame: for democracy alone cannot ensure peace, dignified actions, material stability, or shared conceptions of justice.

For over a decade, the Wilson Yard remained empty and served as one of the core places (both material and symbolic) for people to locate and generate arguments for and against any number of local issues. In 2008, the UNC "Orange Shirts" morphed into a nonprofit group called "Fix Wilson Yard," which raised over $60,000 for a legal injunction waged against the City of Chicago and Holsten Real Estate Development (Wilson Yard's developer) to stop the project in the name of democracy. Their core claim was that Tax Increment Financing (TIF) was being used illegally to fund a project that was detrimental to the community and antithetical to the will of the citizens.[14] This claim was timely, as Chicagoans were growing weary of TIFs, particularly in the wake of the 2008 financial crash and in the face of spiking Chicago property taxes. Fix Wilson Yard phrased their mission as a citizen-led movement to correct the "failures and abuses of the current Wilson Yard TIF. . . . while protecting the rights and interests of Chicago's taxpayers" ("What").

Ultimately, while Fix Wilson Yard did not stop the project, the group proved to be a resilient, resourceful force to be reckoned with. The group held public meetings, enlisted members, held fundraisers, and produced a content-rich website (now defunct) aimed at educating the public about the Wilson Yard planning process (which they critiqued for its lack of transparency and community involvement). Perhaps most significantly, the Fix Wilson Yard activists launched one of the first and most public, citizen-led attacks on the city's use of TIFs. This is a remarkable feat considering the money, organizing, energy, community support, and citizen education required to launch the lawsuit. Ben Jorvasky—a writer for the *Chicago Reader*, longtime follower of Uptown politics, and stanch TIF critic—praised the Fix Wilson Yard lawsuit as a desperately needed citizen-led movement against the city's dubious TIF practices, but lamented, at "the risk of sounding ungrateful," that this "fight is against one of the few TIFs that might actually benefit someone other than the mayor and well-connected developers" ("The Right"). As already mentioned, TIFs should only be used in blighted areas that would not develop "but for" the TIF, but as the Fix Wilson Yard lawsuit argues, Wilson Yard was one of the largest parcels of undeveloped land on Chicago's North Side and would have assuredly developed on its own. Ambivalent in his position, Joravsky stated, "If Shiller's using the wrong tool to do the right thing, the residents are fighting the right battle for the wrong reasons."

In reaction to the lawsuit and perceived public slander, attorneys for Wilson Yard's developer, Peter Holsten, subpoenaed Google and Fix Wilson Yard for information that would unmask anonymous online critics who made biting comments about Shiller and Wilson Yard on several popular Uptown blogs and online community boards allegedly associated with Fix Wilson Yard (including What the Helen, Uptown Update, Buena Park Neighborhoods, and Uptown Neighborhood Council). The Electronic Frontier Foundation (EFF), a nonprofit that "defend[s] civil liberties in the digital world," provided legal support to Fix Wilson Yard and the anonymous commenters. Mark Zimmerman, an EFF attorney who worked on the case, framed the subpoena as a First Amendment violation, arguing that the "right to speak anonymously is a fundamental element of the First Amendment. Individuals need to know that they can express their views, and do so without fear of legal reprisal" (Electronic). It was unclear what was to be gained by this attack on citizens' right to make anonymous public critiques, but this subpoena was widely perceived as a radically undemocratic attempt by the powerful (developers and governmental officials) to thwart the voices and rights of disgruntled and vulnerable citizens.

This lawsuit and counter subpoena is particularly revealing of the paradoxes of democracy. There is murkiness and many inverses regarding who has power or justice on their side, whose political agenda is more democratic, where the moral highroad lies, and whose tactics are more transparent and just. Those in traditional roles of power in this case are ostensibly using their power to mitigate the systemic effects of capitalism on behalf of the disenfranchised, yet those feeling "shut out of politics" here are most commonly the "landed affluent." What appears to be the clear use of power to squash citizen dissent complicates the intentions of Shiller and her supporters; the lack of representation in Uptown politics and the vulnerable position of middle-class homeowners after the housing bust, complicates the dismissal of the Fix Wilson Yard's concerns. Indeed, my very brief sketch of these legal disputes represent just a few more rhetorical twists and turns of the public action catalyzed in response to the empty lot.

Fourteen years after the fire destroyed the Wilson train yard in 1996, Alderman Shiller and Mayor Daley gathered for Wilson Yard's ribbon-cutting ceremony in 2010, and with that the material indeterminism and rhetorical potency of the infamous lot were finally clamped down. From a rhetorical standpoint, the literal filling up of this "blank space" effectively emptied out much of its rhetorical force. Its flexibility, its potentiality, the capacity for people to latch all manner of hopes onto its future, to make moral claims, and to organize in favor of or against all sorts of causes were spent with the cutting of the ribbon, which signaled the shift from radical possibility to the opening of an ordinary and perfectly mundane Target, discount grocery, hodgepodge of retail stores, and 178 units of affordable housing. The prevailing emptiness of the lot provided both a tangible site for democratic practices and an imminently open place for people to locate their incommensurable democratic hopes, ideals, and desires. While I am not sure what it means to say that democracy is best studied (and, perhaps, practiced) when it is stuck in a seemingly endless wrangle over its own meaning, I can say that this lot provided an excellent case for testing the ultimate limits and possibilities of everyday democracy and a place for thousands of citizens to imagine and enact the practices and rhetorics of democracy.

3
Public Art and the Rhetorics of Diversity

> Recently, artists and critics eager to counteract the power exercised through neutralizing ideas of the public have sought to reappropriate the concept by defining public space as a realm of political debate and public art as work that helps create such a space.
>
> Deutsche 39

If you will, join me on Argyle Street at the northern edge of Uptown, amid passers-by hustling to get on the train headed downtown; spilling into eateries for shrimp cakes, bánh mì, and steaming bowls of Phở, or causally poking about in Southeast Asian import shops filled with tea cups, plastic Buddhas, and jars of spicy sauce. Home to a diverse population, the area—often referred to as Little Vietnam in Chicago—bears the mark of its history (and continued presence) as an immigration hub for Vietnamese, Thai, Cambodian, and Laotian immigrants and refugees who began arriving after the Vietnam War. As we direct our attention to the eastern wall of the Hoa Nam grocery store on Winthrop and Argyle, you'll notice a festive mural called "Roots of Argyle." Your eyes gravitate to the depiction of a central plaza where smiling citizens of various ethnicities mingle in convivial harmony. Three white kiosks flank the plaza, warmly greeting all who gather with the word "welcome" written in Chinese, Thai, Vietnamese, Japanese, German, English, Hebrew, and Swedish. Deep in the background, an auspicious seagoing ship evokes the immigrant's iconic hope for escape to the land of opportunity. Here, depicted in this allegory, lies the classical liberal dream of radical diversity without exclusion—the visual embodiment of the slogan: "Different but equal."

From here, follow me four blocks south and two east to another mural painted along a low brick wall that evokes a starkly different sense of diversity. The mural, known as the "Uplift Mural," flanks the entrance to Uplift High School on Wilson Avenue. This area is also bustling and home to a diverse citizenry, but most would agree, it's a bit "rough around the edges," with visible signs of extreme poverty, including a homeless population, pan handlers, and drug activity. High school students enrolled in a class on public

10. Roots of Argyle Mural, "Transition Area." Photo by Author.

art created this mural. It bears no graphic images other than universally appealing concepts—*Community, Truth, Respect, and (No) Social Justice*—styled in hip hop lettering in bold orange, yellow, turquoise, and magenta hues. You might like it, you might not; maybe you'd assume it was a community-sponsored mural, maybe you'd think it an amateurish eyesore. Whatever chord it struck, however, it is unlikely that you would suspect that it once stirred controversy. Two large, hastily painted black splotches at either end might cause an observant passerby to raise an eyebrow. Obliterated by those splotches are the iconic visages of the afro-wearing, Civil Rights–Era Black Panther leader Angela Davis and the bearded, beret-clad classic of revolutionary Che Guevara. The icons summon democracy's collective fight for equal representation—the struggles against systemic injustice, racism, and class discrimination by a marginalized people who must rail against the social machinery that excludes them. Here, in the political resonances of these images, we see the calling out of a lack of diversity or, perhaps, a calling attention to that which is silenced, absent, or pulverized in the peaceful image of diversity in the first mural. Behind both murals is a story of concerned citizens engaged in civic action on behalf of the public good.

These two murals, separated by only a few blocks, were created within months of one another in 2006 and 2005, respectively. The first mural,

11. Uplift Mural. The face of Che Guevara is painted over with the word "community." Photo by Author.

"Roots of Argyle," was initiated by the Uptown Chamber of Commerce, local businesses, and citizen-led block clubs. The Roots mural depicts one hundred years of Uptown history by celebrating the ethnic, cultural, and artistic diversity of the neighborhood. The Roots theme of multiculturalism has received praise from the general community. Such diversity exists peaceably, theoretically or otherwise, however, only to the extent that diverse groups (ideologies, races, ethnicities, cultures) are perceived as different but equal—as opposed to inhabiting incommensurable, adversarial, and unequal positions in relation to power. The second mural, which took up adversarial politics as its explicit content, was a collaborative effort by nonprofit Kuumba Lynx and Uplift High School teachers and students. The use of the icons of Guevara and Davis ignited public outrage. While some citizens supported the mural, felt it represented social justice themes applicable to the largely underserved student body, and sought to defend the contentious mural themes in a public forum, others rejected the content as inappropriate because it espoused dangerous ideology and provoked violence. The latter group, which felt school children were being used as "political pawns" by the school's ideologues, spearheaded a petition that led to a revision of the mural, which retains only universal values scrolled over the now-absent images of Davis and Guevara.

These mural projects, I will argue, are sutured by tensions within the diversity topos that encapsulate broader contradictions within the liberal democratic project itself. The topoi of liberal democracy include the contradictory blueprints for what freedom, citizenship, equality, rights, and collective public life might mean in everyday democracies. And, democratic rhetoric—like all powerful rhetorics—offers a rich ground for rhetorical invention precisely because it has this capacity to stitch together wide-ranging vectors of meaning across space and time, and for smoothing over the contradictions and incommensurability between democratic ideals and its lived practice. In this chapter, I analyze the contested spaces of public art production and reception in Uptown as a lens through which to study the diversity topos as a particularly powerful commonplace in liberal democracies.

My reasons for attending to the diversity topos are two-fold. First, "diversity" plays a starring role in liberal democracy's dream of radical diversity without exclusion. While history teaches us that democracies do not require heterogeneity, in contemporary American liberal democratic society, the presence of diversity, in all of its potential formulations, has serious implications. The lack of "diversity" suggests exclusion, and any exclusion in liberal democracies can be called out as decidedly undemocratic. Although the Civil Rights Era inspired important arguments against formal legal exclusions rooted in discrimination against identity-based categories (race, gender, age, sexuality, religion, disability, etc.), such arguments can work at the expense of questions about the role that economics and material inequities play in reinforcing such exclusions, as well as ways that racism now operates more insidiously and informally.

Second, Uptown is diverse, and talk of this diversity is ubiquitous. In fact, Uptown's "diversity" is one of the most common ways the neighborhood is characterized; however, what "diversity" means and the ways it is mobilized vary greatly. For example, real estate agents used the rhetorics of "diversity" as a hard selling point during the condo boom of the 1990s and 2000s to highlight the exotic variety of eateries and attractions in the area (as in "This north side neighborhood has become a port of entry . . . Its diverse cultures have earned Uptown the reputation as Chicago's United Nations. Its shops, restaurants and cultural facilities reflect the diversity") ("Around the City"); or "diversity" might be heralded as voyeuristic play (as in, "The diversity here is a tremendous amount of fun. You can be what you want to be") (Freemon). Some celebrate the neighborhood's racial and cultural diversity without addressing the economic disparity underscoring it, while others explicitly highlight economic inequity in their arguments for maintaining a diverse Uptown through, for example, deliberate intervention in the gentrifying housing market to secure affordable units for those ("diverse" individuals) who would otherwise be displaced. Diversity is seen as an asset (as in, "I am proud to live in such a diverse community where so many different kinds of people interact daily"); it can be used as a pejorative (as in, "Bah! Our neighborhood certainly is 'colorful,' isn't it?").

My continuing interest in tracing the places of democratic invention appears here as a concern about sight—by which I mean, the ability to see and then make visible the range of arguments about a given issue. Because we are attuned to public art and visual rhetorics here, this capacity of sight includes discovering arguments through literal ocular sensory perception of those arguments in concrete images (seeing persuasive images about diversity in public art); the imaginative and conceptual abilities to grasp the range of arguments and their impacts (comprehending the arguments that circulate about diversity and democracy, their stakes, their contradictions, their consequences); and a perception of how to make use of arguments (a knack for using the diversity topos for kairotic rhetorical intervention). In studying the places of invention, I take an ecological approach—one that entails, among other things, tracing how rhetorical structures morph across various contexts, social spaces, and times; analyzing the mechanisms, images, material vehicles, and agents that mediate and enable the circulation of and our encounters with rhetoric; examining the dynamic interconnectedness of various elements of the rhetorical situation; and contemplating the consequences, constraints, and affordances of rhetoric.

In looking at the mural projects described above, I seek to examine how the diversity topos facilitates the rendering of particular arguments invisible and how it boosts the salience of others; to understand the relationship between visual and discursive representations of diversity; and to trace the ways that rhetorics of diversity organize and motor the dynamic practices and processes that constitute everyday democracies. In other words, my use of "sight" here is getting at how rhetorics (language, discourse, symbols, icons) in tension with the material qualities of places deeply shape not only *what* one sees or doesn't see, but also *how* and *whether* one is capable of "seeing" to begin with. This sense of sight is closely linked to what Blair, Dickinson, and Ott call "public memories," which they perceive as rooted in collective exigencies; shared histories, identities, ideologies, affective currents, "senses of communal belonging"; and bolstered/brought into being through "material and symbolic supports" (6). While public memories are actively "invented" and "constructed of rhetorical resources," they are always beholden to the "more-or-less-limited confines of a set of available resources for representation and circulation within a specific cultural confluence" (13). Murals as "memory places" (27) both generate and reflect the "available resources" within public memory and provide material places to house, inhabit, and enact the places of invention.

Public Art, Places of Invention, and the Diversity Topos

In examining the diversity topos, I follow the lead of art and political theorists, such as Lucy Lippard, Rosalyn Deutsche, Martha Rosler, Pamela Lee, and Chantal Mouffe, who have argued that public art (even when privately funded) ignites contest over what is worth publicly remembering; whose tales are represented and in what manner; and whose experiences, perspectives, and histories are omitted. Public art and its contradictory purposes bring to the fore a series of productive tensions that exist in the liberal democratic public, more broadly. In the context of urban renewal, public art has just as commonly been critiqued for supporting the aims of global capitalism by creating aesthetically beautiful city spaces that facilitate economic regeneration as it has been attributed to providing the means for resisting the commodification of art for such purposes. Public art has been both attacked for promoting sanitized images of democratic conviviality, and celebrated for "giving voice" to people who have been marginalized through such images. Public art is sometimes a top-down initiative funded by city governments and sometimes emerges through community-led processes. Public art might be equally valorized or demonized for either fostering cohesion and consensus—or dissensus and debate.

Art theorist Rosalyn Deutsche contends that the concept of public space—which evokes ideas such as open accessibility, inclusiveness, universality, participation, contestation, diversity, and the civic—is "inextricably linked to democratic ideals" (35), and accordingly, she argues that public art, as an extension of the public sphere itself, should reveal, rather than smooth over, the incommensurability and antagonism inherent to democratic life. Public art is public (and democratic), for her, when it resists unified, coherent narratives that evacuate politics by "expelling conflicts" that transform the antagonism of the democratic public into private "spaces of exclusion" (Deutsche 43). In kind, Chantal Mouffe argues that public art should challenge visions of consensus, and foster permanent spaces of agonism that facilitate ongoing debates that constitute robust liberal democratic practice. The function of agonistic public space (and, therefore, public art) is to "foment dissensus," making "visible what the dominant consensus tends to obscure and obliterate," and giving "voice to all those who are silenced within the framework of the existing hegemony" ("Art" 12). To this end, Mouffe argues that the radical incommensurability and plurality of democratic politics need to be made "visible so that they can enter the terrain of contestation" ("Politics and Passions" 149). This call for public art to represent ongoing political contestation—rather than convivial narratives of democratic life—runs contrary to what we might commonly understand as public art's epideictic function of praising or blaming particular moral or social values through its artistic content. The shift in focus is from inserting coherent, value-laden political arguments into the public sphere to a postponement of assigning praise and blame in order to represent the strife, textures, contradictions, and nuances of political wrangle in democracies as such. (Or, if you prefer, we could say that the epideictic function remains intact with the moral disposition simply shifting to one that valorizes radical incommensurability, diversity, and perpetual debate.)

The work of rhetoricians Finnegan and Kang on the circulation of visual icons in the public sphere is influential in this discussion. Like Mouffe and Deutsche, they hope to avoid rarifying political positions represented in the public by shifting their focus from advocating and lambasting specific images (and the politics that underscore them) to tracing the rhetorical work of circulating icons. As they understand it, their work counters the iconoclasm present in public sphere theories that tend to dismiss image culture wholesale for its pacifying reinforcement of capitalist ideologies only to advocate ostensibly "good images" that bolster visions of robust democratic values. Within the humanities, these "good" images tend to be predictable leftist critiques of capitalism and power. Their concept of "circulation" is an alternative to such iconoclastic critiques of visual cultural, and is an "iconophilic, or image friendly, public sphere theory" (390) that "depend(s) neither on the denigration of images, nor the valorization of particular modes of vision to sustain itself" (390). A fixation on circulation embraces the "movement of images rather than images themselves," and "frees us from the paradox of 'good' and 'bad' images, from the will to cherish them and the will to destroy them" (396).

Finnegan and Kang draw on Bruno Latour, who argues that an image morphs as it moves through social spaces and is mediated (or, we might say, as it is activated, carried, circulated) by human and nonhuman agents, creating a "history of its own circulation" that is "often concealed or inaccessible" in order to "be perceived as 'the truth'" (395). And, central to our conversation, it is the attunement to the circulations of images, as opposed to an assessment of their moral status that "liberates us from the need to see images as true or false" and "from the binaries of love and hate.... because it embraces mediation" (395). Brouwer and Asen also insist that we resist restricting our study of publics "only to sympathetic cases" (21), even if it means "losing the secure normative ground that would come with placing [one's] project at a specific point along an ideological continuum" (21). As Brouwer and Asen warn, aiming your critical arrows at arguments across the political spectrum is risky. You might find yourself highlighting the wisdom of "unsavory" politics or undoing positions you hold dear. The labor of the iconophilic is to keep an eye on the circulations of images and on the material vehicles, channels, technologies, ideologies, genres, and so on that enable and facilitate circulation as such. Such a focus asks us to postpone a desire to speak truth to power so that we might attend to the role that our rhetorics, our images, our bodies, and our labors play in ever-emergent processes of the making of everyday life.

The work of Hariman and Lucaites on the visual icons of liberal democracy helps clarify the stakes of studying circulation in this manner. Specifically, such icons are "important resources for political action" and for living collectively as a radically diverse democratic public (48) because icons provide tools for accessing the contested arguments about what constitutes democracy, civil rights, social justice, and citizenship. The commonplace visual icons of liberal democracies help citizens "negotiate the self-understanding of a democratic society amidst historical change," to "work out public opinion and personal attitudes about specific political actors, polices, and practices," and to resolve the tensions between the "aura of transcendent representation and repeated refashioning in the vaudeville show of democratic public culture" (38–39). While Hariman and Lucaites are focused on iconic photographs, I find their discussion useful for thinking about the more abstract, yet equally recognizable, visual iconography of democracy, such as ports-of-entry, melting pots, multicultural "rainbows," Civil Rights leaders, and so on. Such visual icons of democracy, like democratic topoi generally, allow for the co-existence within publics of both democratic ideals and vernacular variance, of both universal abstract ideals and situated contradictions, of both dominant narratives and the seeds of critique of those narratives.

In this sense, icons, like topoi and rhetorical structures more generally, are such powerful tools in everyday democracies because while people can access them within their idiosyncratic and situated contexts of everyday life, they are also tools that transcend the details of those contexts, which means—among other things—that they can resonate broadly, forcefully, and flexibly across social spaces and political positions. As such, the visual icons of liberal democracies "model normative behavior," but also provide the resources for "satiric mimicry to challenge those norms, strategic improvisation to change them, and other forms of artistic invention for purposes both serious and silly" (Hariman and Lucaites 39). From here, I trace the work and circulation of the diversity topos as a central commonplace of liberal democracies within the two public murals in Uptown that I introduced in the opening. In attending to the diversity commonplace as a place of invention, moreover, I attune to the dynamic and varied entwinements of rhetorical structures (arguments, symbols, logics, visual icons, discursive bits of ideology) and materialities (literal mural surfaces emplaced within the spatial, historical, and political textures of Uptown, its people, and its streets). And now, having discussed some theories of public art, circulation, and invention, let me return to the field to substantiate them within the production of the "Uplift" and "Roots of Argyle" murals, respectively.

Consensus, Dissensus, and Diversity in Public Art—The Uplift Mural

In 2005, a group of teenagers at Uplift High School gathered for a workshop on muralism that resulted in the creation of the mural featured below. Kuumba Lynx, a Chicago youth organization located in Uptown, led the workshop. Founded in 1996, Kuumba Lynx's mission is to "empower youth and their communities utilizing arts and education." It offers "edutainment" workshops on dance, "turntablism," performance, muralism, and writing in collaboration with schools and local organizations. The Uplift School (grades 6–12) opened in September 2005 under the Chicago Renaissance 2010 initiative, replacing the failing Joan Arai School. In 2012, 93.9% of the 446 students enrolled at Uplift were reported as living at or below the poverty line, and the ethnic/racial composition of this student body was .9% caucasian, 82.7% black, .2% Native Americans, 3.8% Asian, 10.5% Hispanic, and 1.6% multiracial (Illinois State). Uplift School's mission centers on providing a "relevant student centered curriculum of the highest standards with the theme of social justice embedded in all areas" as a way to cultivate citizens who are "anti-bias, give voice to the unheard, promote responsible action to eliminate oppression in all forms and build community consciousness" (Vision).

I asked Nathan, an Uplift school representative, to speak more about the school's social justice mission; he responded:

> *Social justice means so many things. Ask 30 people and you'll get 30 answers, especially in Uptown. Some people say social justice is seeing something from both sides of an argument and then stepping back and letting kids decide. Some people say you should mobilize people towards some-*

12. Uplift Mural. Photo by Author.

thing more concrete. Some think that the market brings social justice and some people think that it does not. So much depends on the context and someone's background. We try to avoid giving students an answer to that question, but feel that it is important to bring issues to light for them and to help them see why they are important.

Engaged in a curricular unit on social justice, the teens created the Uplift Mural that featured Guevara and Davis described in the opening, in collaboration with Kuumba Lynx. Sarah, a young high school teacher on the South Side of Chicago and a founding member of Kuumba Lynx, was a core recipient of and respondent to public criticism of the mural. Sarah had attended high school in Uptown and performed spoken word poetry with Kuumba Lynx since it started in 1996. She flashed a smile when I met her, which turned into an exasperated sigh and headshake when I started asking about the Uplift Mural. Sarah described the Uplift Mural controversy in the following terms:

Why was it controversial? The man who wrote me [Sean, see below] is a notorious agitator in the neighborhood. [. . .] I think his primary concern was that we were brainwashing the children to be communists and militant. He said that they were violent images [Davis and Guevara] and that we were being anti-American and unpatriotic in a post-911 world. He didn't think it was appropriate for teenagers who he kept saying aren't capable of making decisions about which role models are safe and which are not. I feel there's a big problem with assuming kids aren't capable of making decisions. [. . .] The idea [for the mural] came out of the graffiti workshop, so participants were given the history of muralism. Some kids have previous knowledge and experience in painting or graffiti or tagging and others don't. Students had their own visions and we also participated.

Nathan, of Uplift, elaborated on this process and on the purpose of the original mural:

We wanted to involve the kids in a mural project that had historical significance [. . .]. It was done the summer before we opened. [. . .] The wall belongs to the Jesus People and they were ok with us doing the mural and they approved a mural with words like Respect, Truth, Social Justice and the like. Then a group of people protested the images of Che and Davis. They said that Davis was involved in bombing and was inappropriate and Che was linked to violence, but obviously we weren't trying to encourage kids to think that those actions were ok, just that they were certain types of heroes given the social context they were in. The histories and issues they were involved with are important and relevant to the kids' lives.

As Nathan suggests, the Uplift students, given their demographics, face a range of struggles that he felt coincided with the issues that Guevara and Davis took up: namely, various structural, systemic forms of inequity and exclusion. Many Uplift students come from families that live in public or affordable housing developments. Both Nathan and Sarah, among others, stressed that the choice to evoke the icons of Guevara and Davis was not intended to encourage violent acts but to engage students in the struggle against social injustices that they were already intimately aware of in their lives. Sarah brushed off the protests of the mural with the following comment: "These kids already know about violence. This is not about protecting them from something they don't already know about. These kids already knew about these revolutionary figures."

Critiques of the mural content surfaced immediately after the mural was completed. In 2005, an Uptown homeowner since 1999 walked down Wilson Avenue, and was alarmed by the new mural outside of Uplift. In particular, the concerned Uptowner, Sean, was disturbed by the representations of Davis and Guevara, whom he considered violent, dangerous, and unpatriotic role models for Uptown's troubled youth. Sean also felt that the mural's lettering-style resembled gang tagging, which he felt was a problem in Uptown. He believed this imagery condoned graffiti and might influence students at Uplift to join local gangs. Sean explained his core objections to the use of Guevara and Davis in the Uplift Mural:

> I objected to them because that area is the dividing line for three different gangs. [. . .] Both Che and Angela are involved in social justice, which I think is very important, but these two people used a lot of violence to fulfill their mission, and given the rate of violence in that area [near Uplift school], my belief was that parents would not want to see their adolescents have Che Guevara and Angela Davis as role models. Maybe MLK. Someone a little more peaceful. And it got into an argument about hip hop and that I was not respecting adolescents in their need to express themselves, and again, it was portrayed as "us versus them." They had some good arguments. My response to them that through my dealings with CAPS, they were [. . .] gravely concerned that their children were being coaxed into gangs, and given the violence in that area, parents are protective of their children and we need to provide role models that are more supportive in their endeavor as parents.

In my time in Uptown, I have known Sean to be very earnest and active in a wide variety of community events, including positive loitering initiatives, trash cleanup events, and public hearings on urban development in the neighborhood. While his critics often aligned his ideology with the interests of affluent homeowners who opposed the development of additional affordable housing and former alderman Shiller's leftist politics, his position, as he expresses it, was always more nuanced and balanced, emerging from a serious interest in building consensus and avoiding contestation. In public, he has commonly expressed his desire to dismantle the "us versus them" mentality in Uptown out of a desire to work toward resolutions that satisfy everyone's interests.

One of the things that I am focused on here is this tension within the democratic framework between political consensus and dissensus represented in the "us versus them" political dynamic in Uptown. Regarding the mural case, the diversity topos is staked in this tension, which is played out within morally charged debates about censorship. On the one hand, mural supporters contend that the original mural offers a social justice message that is appropriate—given the largely disenfranchised student body—and that erasing it due to its political nature is censorship and an eradication of diverse perspectives. On the other hand, mural dissenters argue that overt ideology is a poor choice for a public school, which should remain politically neutral; that adults should not use children as "political pawns"; and that the welfare of children trumps censorship concerns. The former position is a moral argument that sees censorship as an undemocratic exclusion of diverse perspectives; it favors robust debates among competing publics that expose structural inequities and represent marginal voices at the expense of peace, agreement, and consensus. The latter position is voiced as a concern for the "welfare of children" and perceives noncontroversial, nonideological themes as most appropriate in public spaces; this position favors conviviality, cooperation, and consensus as the mark of democracy at the expense of freedom and diversity of expression.

In both cases, the flexibility of the democratic topos is tested through the imagery and rhetorics of diversity. The protection of radical diversity drives Chantal Mouffe's refutation of consensus as democracy's aim. As Mouffe puts it, within liberal democratic politics, ongoing contestation should not be seen as an obstacle to be overcome en route to harmonious consensus, but as the "guarantee that democracy is alive and inhabited by pluralism" ("Politics and Passions" 149). She assigns public art the role of challenging and disrupting, rather than constituting, the "smooth image" ("Art" 13) of consensus, which she understands as a dangerous winnowing of liberal democracy. In the Uplift Mural controversy, the desire to foster consensus and avoid political contest, which resulted in the annihilation of Guevara's and Davis's visages, is an example of such a threat to liberal democracy.

In a conversation that resonates with Mouffe about the Uplift Mural, three Uptown affordable housing activists—Marie, Gene, and Diane—discussed what a unifying mural image might entail and whether a unifying image is even appropriate:

> *Gene: Well, to go back to the issue of democracy, and what that represents, and the idea that there would be some unifying symbol that would work for a mural. I mean because these images divide, they must therefore be undemocratic [to the dissenters] and [. . .] literally whited out. Unification versus division. I mean, regarding Che, the image is so all over the place. It is used for marketing.*
> *Marie: Yeah, it's used by Blockbuster. [. . .]*
> *Diane: But it reveals an anxiety over a history that Uptown shared. The Black Panther Party was grounded in Uptown, I mean not solely, but had an offshoot here, and distributed the paper here. And an important*

coalition was made between the Black Panther Party and the poor whites from Appalachia in Uptown. Maybe there is some concern that these kids will become politicized from learning history, not only from their own contributions, but also learning the history of others.

These housing activists challenged the argument that "democratic" public art must forward a "unifying" theme rooted in consensus, and suggested that the desire for such imagery might express an "anxiety" over Uptown's radically contentious political history, which, as this book makes clear, has been a heated battleground of clashing words, ideologies, and built environments for decades.

In contrast, Sean forwarded his own desire for a universal image for the mural that addresses racial inequity but that does not promote divisiveness:

> Sean: I'm not here to say that Marxism is wrong. I am a democrat and I should not be teaching or persuading children about my political ideology and they should not be teaching theirs.
> Candice: What would a politically neutral role model be?
> Sean: Rosa Parks, who just died.

With respect to consensus and dissensus, the tipping point of the mural debate was whether the public, public art, and public schools should promote consensus, unification, and harmony, thus representing everyone and alienating no one, or promote dissensus, debate, and radical diversity, thus highlighting myriad political perspectives, marginal voices, and contest. Should consensus be most preciously guarded at the price of radical diversity? Or should the diversity of incommensurable political positions be protected and represented at the expense of social harmony and cohesion? Such questions reside at the crux of the mural debate, generating the core lines of argument, and, thus, offering the primary tools of rhetorical invention.

Not surprisingly, they were also the core topics in a firestorm of commentary that erupted in a public online message board sponsored by the Buena Park Neighbors, a block club comprised primarily of homeowners who live in the affluent Buena Park area, about a half mile from the Uplift Mural on the southern border of Uptown. On this message board, most everyone donned generic screen names like Uptown Gal, Dog Lover, Uptown Dude.[1] The board served as a central hub where news about the neighborhood was disseminated, until its primary functions were supplanted by a more popular neighborhood blog called Uptown Update.[2] Although the opinions expressed on any topic do not reflect the range of opinions present in Uptown and can deteriorate into blatant inflammatory discourse (as is commonplace in such venues), the message board nevertheless served as a social node that connected hundreds of people on a daily basis. Without any desire of romanticizing this board as democracy incarnate, it was, nevertheless, a place where doxa was generated and where citizens gathered to discuss public matters affecting their lives. This online public provides a space where particular ways of relating are created and where publicly salient arguments are solidified, challenged, and circulated.

Below is an exchange that took place on the Buena Park message board, which begins to capture how the diversity topos works in censorship debates. The conversation focuses on whether the public/public schools should promote images that unite or divide people, promote agreement or spurn debate, or depict conviviality or the underbelly of democracy:

> UptownVoice: I don't think that children need to be Shielded from Che Guevara (and I will admit that I have less of a problem with Angela Davis). However, when you display a mural at a school you are GLORYFYING [sic] these figures and presenting them to children as something they should look up to. This is not a balanced view that should be expected at a PUBLIC school. [. . .] If there are parents in Uptown who want to indoctrinate a bunch of young Communist revolutionaries, they should form their own private school with as many revolutionary murals and red flags as they want.
>
> UptownUnderdog: [. . .] Your imagined role to keep children safe from themselves and the lessons of their teachers is at best an excuse for not being able to affect meaningful change in these children's lives. In the wake of such powerlessness you would rather do away with impressive attempts to diversify our political dialog than have them exposed to something with which you do not agree.
>
> UptownVoice: Your arguments don't hold any water. It's one thing to expose children to controversial figures, and another thing entirely to glorify them and condone their views. These images border on propaganda, and they don't belong in public schools [. . .]
>
> UptownUnderdog: I don't believe your arguments hold water either. Assuming control over children doesn't make your aesthetic opinions any more poignant than mine. You are condoning, nay, promoting censorship and bleating, 'Think of the Children' as if it is some sort of justification. Well, I'm thinking of the children too.
>
> UptownVoice: . . . . you are simply stating a knee-jerk reaction against all censorship. This mural barely qualifies as art in the first place. [. . .]

No, it's not pushing any artistic paradigms, but it is almost entirely a political statement, and a radical political statement at that. There IS a place for radical political statements in society, but that place isn't on the wall of a public school. Period!

I would like to highlight two key aspects of this exchange that have implications for the diversity topos. First, is the demand that public opinion be universal, nonbiased, balanced, and rational, which Habermas's early work forwarded as an official requirement for participating in the bourgeois public sphere. We see this "demand" appear in UptownVoice's arguments against the mural, such as: *"This is not a balanced view that should be expected at a PUBLIC school,"* and *"it is almost entirely a political statement [. . .]. There IS a place for radical political statements in society, but that place isn't on the wall of a public school."* Second, the arguments by UptownUnderdog respond to these nonbiased, universal demands of the public as censorship and as threats to diverse, political debate: *"you would rather do away with impressive attempts to diversify our political dialog than have them exposed to something with which you disagree,"* and *"you are condoning, nay promoting censorship."* While UptownVoice, as a mural dissenter, stresses that his or her concern was not one of personal taste or aesthetics, but about the inappropriateness of violent and politically charged mural content for children at *public* schools, UptownUnderdog dismisses the argument as censorship and attacks to the diverse public "dialog."

In another online thread about the mural, concern for children adopts a starker moral tone as it is once again pitted against concerns over freedom of speech, whereby teachers and artists are accused of using children as "pawns" to forward an ideological agenda that divided the Uptown community. ConcernedUptownNeighbor wrote: "Some adults used these children as pawns to promote their own political agenda. [. . .] We won't allow you to use children as pawns. We won't allow you to place your aesthetic needs ahead of the needs of children. We're not going to take it anymore."

In contrast, some voices that challenged the mural dissenters did so by asserting that the critics were censoring the content through a thinly veiled argument about the welfare of Uptown's children that had more to do with their aesthetic and moral values (and perhaps property values) than any genuine concern for children.

> As MuralSupporter put it: "You can get a mural painted over by sending a few outraged letters—but where's your outraged letters about how inner city schools have been shafted all these years, man? Broken

down buildings, crappy teachers, not enough books—the list is a damn mile long, man. [. . .] why aren't you marching in the streets about that? I say YEAH if its 'the welfare of the children' you're so damned concerned about, why aren't you witing [sic] letters about that? [. . .] I'm not buying this 'concern for the children' bullshit. This mural dogoodism is as thin as paper."

UptownUnderdog wrote: "I said that the underdog in this context is the censored and those you presume are incapable of interpreting art intelligently. [. . .] I am encouraging free-speech. I am discouraging censorship."

In a final example from an interview I conducted with Cynthia, an Uptown resident, renter, and educator, who supported the original mural, the mural dissenters' argument about the "welfare for the children" was critiqued as erasing the grounds for argument because no one is against the welfare of children:

They [the dissenters] claimed to be working on behalf of the students, and they said that we used graffiti lettering, which is one of the hottest urban art styles, and that because we have too many gangs in Uptown that this lettering would influence kids to join gangs or to send the message that gangs were ok. [. . .] There were a lot of negative things said on the [online] message boards. I do remember that one argument was about the welfare for children, and, of course, that strategy can really be hard to oppose. I mean, obviously no one is going to argue that they want to do something that is against the welfare of children. The moral high ground can leave no ground and it isn't that simple.

The arguments for revising the mural were almost always couched in such moral terms that centered on the claim that diverse perspectives and freedom of speech were trumped by the welfare of the children and/or by the demand that the public/public schools remain politically neutral. On the flip, arguments made in support of the original mural were couched in equally moral terms that valued a diversity of opinions and the inclusion of marginalized voices at the expense of the consensus and ideologically neutral imagery.

The Uplift School agreed to revise the mural, in the end, without extensive protest, in part, because the wall that the mural was painted on belonged to the Jesus People Organization, an evangelical group next door that expressed reservations about the mural after the controversy surfaced. James Sprugeon, the local artist and Uptown native who worked with Uplift and Kuumba Lynx to create the mural, agreed to revise the work. He was the one who roughly painted over the images of Guevara and Davis in black; where Guevara was, the word "community" was scrolled, and replacing Davis's face, "truth."

Given Uplift's social justice imperative and curricular theme, some teachers were outraged that the figures were painted over without a public discussion. Nathan, the school representative mentioned above, talked about the push by school stakeholders to stage a democratic public forum to air the positions and determine the fate of the mural:

Candice: Could you tell me about the democratic forum that your school tried to stage to talk about the mural controversy?
Nathan: We had thought it would be a good opportunity to have the people opposed come in and talk with the students and that this would be like an open forum and discussion that would be productive and good for the students. The neighbors could meet with students and talk with them about why they supported the mural or the neighbors could talk about why the images were a problem. That seems more democratic. A discussion. But that didn't happen.

Eventually, the explicit references to revolutionary leftist politics and the structural class and race inequities implicated by the icons were erased from the mural in the name of the welfare of children, demands for ideological neutrality in public schools, and desire for consensus. The violence from which children were supposedly being shielded from through the revision of the mural stands in stark contrast to more subtle, diffuse, and everyday violence that the same children experience in their everyday lives to varying degrees, which we might define as the violence of the Chicago housing market, the violence of capitalism, or the violence of a public school system that synonymizes quality education with affluence. In the end, representations of structural inequity and political strife in Uptown were removed from the Uplift Mural and never discussed as a possibility in the planning process for the "Roots of Argyle" mural, as I discuss next. The longing for consensus and what I will call a "palatable diversity" are both driven by a formation of the diversity topos that functions as shorthand for democracy while obscuring political incommensurability and class-based justice claims in order to achieve peace and "agreement."

Palatable Diversity, Violences of Omission, and Rhetorical Invention

While the visages of Guevara and Davis were being blacked out, on another street, a brick wall was being prepped for "The Roots of Argyle" mural, which celebrates Uptown's unique cultural diversity and depicts one hundred years of Uptown's history—from 1900 to the present. The mural was spearheaded by the Argyle Kenmore Block Club and funded largely by the contributions of local businesses and the Uptown Chamber of Commerce, which won a $10,000 grant from J. P. Morgan Chase Foundation to complete the project. "The Roots of Argyle" is located on the eastern side of the Hoa Nam grocery store. Argyle Street, the site of the mural, and the surrounding area, is a commercial and residential hodge-podge of convenience stores, restaurants, senior high-rise apartments, boutiques, SROs, polished brownstones, subsidized affordable housing, psychiatric nursing homes, and beautiful rehabbed Victorian single-family homes.

The mural is approximately one hundred feet long and eighteen feet high. The impetus for the mural emerged from a "beautification" initiative led by members of the Argyle Kenmore Block Club who were concerned with the poor aesthetics and safety of the neighborhood. The mural depicts a series of time portals marked in twenty-year intervals that feature significant historical moments. The mural's central image features a plaza through which immigrants arrive from a seafaring ship into what the artist calls the "transitional area." The mural brochure identifies these figures with generic ethnic descriptors, such as Asian female, Native American, European and Japanese immigrants, and anonymous Hungarian Jew. The "transitional area," as I mentioned at the start of this chapter, evokes the liberal democratic dream of the possibility of radical diversity without exclusion or strife. All are, as the mural reads in multiple languages, welcome. The mural's official website confirms this aim: "People often portray the . . . Uptown community . . . as an example of diversity and gentrification without replacing lower income residents. Different groups in the community are now engaged in a long-term process of sharing space instead of replacing one another" (Portal website). This ideal of gentrification without displacement is a dangerous phantasm that has little to do with material reality in Uptown.

Mark Elder, the muralist who created "The Roots of Argyle," described the initial resistance that he experienced from Uptown's former alderman Mary Ann Smith [48th ward; northern section of the neighborhood],[3] who, according to Elder, wanted to avoid a political depiction of Uptown: "I [Mark] said, 'What do you have against murals?' She said, 'They're always about

13. Roots of Argyle Mural. Photo by Author.

14. Argyle Street in Uptown. Photo by Author.

these social justice things. We've been social-justiced to death [here in Uptown]'" (Terry). Unlike the Uplift Mural, "The Roots of Argyle," which was added to the list of sanctioned attractions on a Chicago bus tour, is widely celebrated as a "positive" and "beautiful" representation of Uptown's multicultural diversity. The mural could also be charged, however, with evacuating the neighborhood's ongoing political struggles from the public narrative. The overriding theme of jovial multiculturalism leaves much out of Uptown's history. Diversity is depicted as a celebration of difference, which itself is used to promote beauty and commercial development in the neighborhood. Giles Gunn argues that "diversity" often becomes merely a source of drama and diversion in the city. "Diversity exists," he writes, "more and more in contemporary life, not as a heuristic instrument but merely as a theatrical entertainment or source of diversion" (166).

The difference in reception of the Uplift and the Roots murals by Uptown residents illuminates how certain forms of social violence are explicitly and tacitly delegitimated and how others come to be accepted and tolerated. The more subtle and difficult-to-pinpoint systemic violences can remain hidden behind the classical liberal call for rational consensus, tolerance, and universal values. The call for consensus can obscure the mechanisms of exclusion (and, in fact, that exclusions even occur), (as in "we just wanted a positive mural") or tucked behind transcendent moral authority (as in "we care about the youth and those revolutionary leaders are dangerous to them"). The elision of class in what Stanley Fish calls "boutique multiculturalism" is evidence of a more general tendency within the liberal democratic model of the public sphere to obscure the intractable contradictions, shortcomings, and antagonistic core of democracy. The rhetoric of diversity is just one mechanism that enables such obscuring. While we may or may not agree on the appropriateness or effectiveness of the Uplift Mural, we will likely agree that the one thing it did not do was obscure concerns about structural inequity in its appeals to social justice through the politics of Che Guevara and Angela Davis.

But, let's turn our attention back to how diversity operates in the Roots of Argyle mural. Although the official mural website claims that it celebrates the neighborhood's history, "diversity and cultural richness," there is a lot missing from this historical narrative about the less pleasant histories of Uptown. Where democracy's underbelly was front and center in the Uplift Mural, it was absent from the planning process for and the content of the Roots mural. Throughout the community process, stakeholders perceived values, such as beauty and harmonious cultural diversity, as endearing, positive, and economically beneficial to local businesses, and the "negative" aspects of Uptown's history were quickly dismissed as damaging to commercial development or simply as overdone in the neighborhood. These "negative" aspects are ignored in the flattering portrait of Uptown as a colorful port of entry where everyone is welcomed into a diverse group of neighbors. This depiction of Uptown's immigration history (see Chapter One) hides the violences that underscore the conditions under which people relocated behind a representation of the dream of equality and inclusion across difference. In Roots, a rainbow of people enter this dream through the motif of "doors of opportunity" modeled after the Essanay Movie Studio's.[4] Each of the six doors represents increments in Uptown's history, starting with the 1900–1920 portal, which features Uptown's history as a mecca of early moving picture production at Essanay, as well as the explosion of immigrants from Germany and Sweden. The 1920–1940 portal contains a nameless apple seller to signify Depression-Era poverty, and an "anonymous Hungarian Jew" to represent the ongoing European immigrant and religious diversity.

The 1940–1960 portal represents what was a tumultuous time in Uptown. While the historical framing essay for this portal mentions the slum-like conditions that housed postinternment Japanese immigrants, an explosion of homeless mentally ill people who were literally "dumped" in the social service–rich neighborhood after being released from Illinois wards, and the emigration of poor Appalachians dislocated due to the mechanization of coal mining, none of these realities is depicted in the mural. Instead, we see musicians Charlie Parker and Miles Davis (whose only claim to neighborhood is a couple of performances), traditionally dressed Japanese immigrants politely bowing to each other, and Joan Arai, a famous education reformer in Uptown. The 1960–1980 portal fails to represent the political volatility of the time, choosing instead to showcase an African American "blues guitarist" plunking away his tunes, two prominent Chinese businessmen, and Alderman Volini, a community activist turned city politician. The histories of Civil Rights protests, urban renewal battles, and deteriorating social conditions—among other things—are absent. The 1980–2000 portal features a nameless "Asian woman," two community leaders, and a Vietnamese man named Roc who was honored because he brought the muralists refreshments. The mural ends with "the future portal" that depicts a Native American man dressed in traditional plains garb staring off into the undetermined future.

The Native American figure, as Elder described it in an interview with me, represents the "spiritual figure, a seer looking into the future. I wanted to get the sense of the indigenous and that they were the first to occupy the land, and he is a seer looking into the future and he is a link. There is a sense of continuation from the past into the future." The nostalgia that

15. Roots of Argyle Mural, Native American figure as "spiritual guide." Photo by Author.

drives this stereotypical depiction of Native Americans as spiritual guides—as well as the mural's general portrayal of the American dream of the melting pot—is palpable. From Uptown's glitzy jazz age and stint as the silent movie capital of the world in the 1920s to its reign as a music, theater, and dancing center throughout the 20s, 30s, and 40s, the mural spotlights cultural hits and moments of immigration that add to the rich diversity of the area, while submerging the dire situations that drove the immigration or the deplorable conditions many found themselves in upon arrival. Neil Smith's argument that the past is often reinvented in gentrifying neighborhoods in service of market-driven development is apt: "Slum tenements become historic brownstones, and exterior facades are sandblasted to reveal a future past.... Physical effacement of original structures effaces social history and geography; if the past is not entirely demolished it is at least reinvented—its class and race contours rubbed smooth—in the refurbishment of a palatable past" (27).

In our case, the mural's depiction of a "palatable past" comes in the form of what we might also call a "palatable diversity." Palatable diversity features a rainbow of cultures and ethnicities that co-exist without exclusion, strife, or inequity. Uptown's ethnic and economic diversity is somewhat of an anomaly in Chicago, one of the most segregated cities in the US. If one took a comparative look at two demographic maps, one would see a clear correspondence between race and class in Chicago. A map representing "racial" groups would show a predominantly African American population on the South and West Side, a concentrated Latino population also on the West Side of Chicago, and a primarily non-Hispanic white population on the North Side. A map representing household income would show that the lowest economic quintillion corresponded with Latino or African American neighborhoods, and the highest quintillion with Caucasian ones. The extent to which racial and economic segregation literally map onto one another is as stark as it is disturbing, especially considering housing policies that have historically shored up this segregation. It is not surprising given these spatial arrangements that one might conclude that racial segregation is responsible for perpetuating poverty.

Although it would be dangerous to ignore the connections between racial and class discrimination, Uptown cannot explain away poverty due to a lack of diversity or segregation in the built environment, making it is a case study that helps illuminate how the "rhetorics of diversity" can distract from systemic class inequity with a vision of a palatable diversity. Because Uptown does not fit into Chicago's pattern of segregation, it is, in fact, sometimes heralded as a successful counter-example of racial/ethnic integration, and therefore, the achievement of social justice. For example, in 2006, a *Chicago Reporter* writer said of Uptown: "Were [Martin Luther] King [Jr.] alive today and visiting Chicago, 40 years after the Chicago Freedom Movement, the civil rights leader might take an initial look at the North Side's Uptown neighborhood and conclude that his vision had materialized . . . Signs of Uptown's mixed character abound" (Lowenstein). The evocation of King and the suggestion that cultural and racial diversity in Uptown would signal a "mission accomplished" for Civil Rights leaders provides an example of how diversity can become disassociated from material inequity, which elides class inequities as well as persistent forms of racism. Although Uptown is indeed one of the most diverse neighborhoods in the city, if not the country, it is a far cry from a romanticized image of a rational democratic public defined by radical diversity without exclusion.

The way American democracy tends to equate identity-based diversity (gender, race, cultural, linguistic, etc.) with evidence of greater social justice, at the expense of systemic class inequity, is what Walter Benn Michaels identifies as the "trouble with diversity." With the Civil Rights Movement, Michaels argues, the struggle against racism became increasingly synonymous with identity-based diversity such that increasing such diversity became the primary vehicle for fighting racism on the left and for avoiding class politics on the right. In either case, "diversity" can evacuate class politics from the scene, and in some cases, politics as such by transforming questions of social justice into a matter of respecting difference and eliminating prejudice, as opposed to questioning the redistribution of wealth. To this end, Nancy Fraser and Axel Honneth stress the importance of the relationship between redistribution (which is concerned with economic equality) and recognition (which is concerned with identity-based or symbolic equality). They recognize that the "decoupling" of redistribution and recognition in capitalist politics is "not the result of a simple mistake," but is rather "built into the structure of modern capitalist society" (69). The diversity topos is one rhetorical engine that facilitates this "decoupling" within liberal democracies—a divide that becomes apparent in the scene described below of planning meetings for the Roots mural whereby stakeholders embrace diversity as a mural theme, but only to the extent that its representation is perceived as "welcoming," "comforting," "peaceful," "positive," "consensual," and "beautiful."

Three community meetings were held beginning in April 2004 to collectively determine the mural content. Mark Elder,[5] Roots's lead artist and a prominent Chicago muralist, described the community process to me as "open meetings" in which "everyone's input was taken into account." I met with Elder to discuss the mural in 2007. He sported a salt-and-pepper beard and wore the kind of broad-rimmed brown hat you'd expect an anthropologist to wear in the field. Despite the community involvement in the process, Elder shared that certain types of content were dismissed early on out of a concern that political messages might "detract" from economic investments. As Elder put it: "Some people did have concerns about their real estate and their businesses, and wanted to make sure that the mural didn't harm or detract from their success. People didn't want something political. People wanted to see something positive. They wanted to see something positive about Uptown." On April 7, 2004, at the Bridgeview Uptown Bank, the first meeting was held to gather public input on the mural. The minutes from this meeting reflect an overall desire for a unifying, historical theme: "It [the mural] should give the feelings of COMFORT and PEACEFULNESS. They should also show DIVERSITY, a WELCOMING feeling and HARMONY."[6] In response to the idea for a central port-of-entry image, the minutes reflect that people "like" this imagery and suggested to "maybe add a BOAT to the scene . . . It should be a PORTAL TO SECURITY" (*Argyle*; emphasis in original). Both the port-of-entry and boat elements, as I have described, reflect the melting pot theme, a palatable diversity that made it into the final version.

Elder told me that former alderman Smith was initially "worried and "skeptical about the mural," and concerned that the mural would

> stir up trouble and be political and that not everybody would like it. That it would be more like graffiti. [. . .] So, I showed her some of my sketches and told her that we could have community meetings to get community input and approval. The process needed to be consensual. Something needed to be created that everyone could agree with. So, we had a series of community meetings. There were three of them where people came [. . .]. These were open meetings and everyone's input was taken into account as much as possible. [. . .] the driving question was, "How do people want to represent Uptown? What do people feel is important? Who might be represented? Which historical facts do we represent?"

Fred, a representative of former alderman Smith, who helped facilitate the mural's planning process, confirms this sense that people involved in the process, many of whom were local homeowners or business owners, preferred a universal theme and wanted to avoid an overtly political message. "People," Fred told me, in an interview,

> did not want the traditional peace and justice type of mural because social justice has already been overdone in people's opinion, and besides, [. . .] they are not always considered beautiful from the constituents' point of view. They are more about making a political statement, rather than pure beauty . . . They wanted something different, something that was more classic [. . .] something [. . .] with values that were universal [. . .] but that also included that sense of beauty, the element of beauty.

The desired themes expressed in the Roots process, then, were similar to ones the Uplift Mural dissenters called for: universal, beautiful, and nonpolitical imagery that reflect consensus, not contest. Moreover, in the conversation about how to represent Uptown in Roots, any conceptualization of the neighborhood's political or contentious history was very quickly dismissed and never brought up again because block club members felt "social-justiced to death" or that social justice had "already been overdone."

Compared to the original Uplift Mural, the Roots mural offers a peaceful representation of Uptown's history, populated with diverse smiling people. While there is much left out of this depiction, there is nothing blatantly false. If the most common critique of the Uplift Mural had to do with its valorization of radical ideology and political violence, the Roots mural might be critiqued for its violence of omission, for what is not seen in order to see the story being told. We might call this a form of narrative violence. For urban theorist Robert Beauregard, public discourse contains narratives that are "not merely an objective reporting of an incontestable reality but a collection of contentious interpretations," which are often "grounded only tenuously in an empirical reality" (21). The stories about the city that are represented in public discourse (and I would include public art in this category) comprise the collective interpretations of material conditions that form the imaginary entity we call the city. Because these stories help us make sense of the fragmented, contradictory, and sometimes-senseless events of everyday life, they play a powerful role in the production of public opinion (or doxa, as I'll refer to it in a moment).

The relationship between public discourse and public opinion is recursive in the sense that public opinion helps shape discourse that shapes public opinion. Beauregard argues that public discourse could be used to draw powerful connections that reveal, rather than obscure, the way that dominant ideologies and private interests influence urban policy, as well as reveal, rather than obscure, the "injustices and inequalities of urban America" (244). Public narratives always insert a claim for which social practices, histories, meanings are legitimate; therefore, to exert narrative control is to have a hand in shaping the social imagination, which also means shaping the range of visible arguments available for rhetorical invention and intervention.

Rosalyn Deutsche understands "coherence" in public art as a form of narrative violence because it implies a closed, and therefore private, representation of experience that excludes, rather than invites, participation and space for agonistic perspectives. As she argues, "Once an essential basis of coherence is attributed to public space . . . that space is converted, and not in an economic sense alone, into private property" (38), which entails eradicating the ongoing political debate that resides at the heart of democracy. Pamela Lee agrees with Deutsche, arguing that public art should "serve less to resolve the conflicts underlying social space than to expose them. Rather than consolidate some ideal vision of the public sphere, it should acknowledge the anti-idealizing foundations of radical democracy" (85). In the case of Roots, this tendency toward feeling "social-justiced" to death in Uptown indicates a point of exhaustion, and a moment in which members of the demos retreat from the democratic paradox to simply appease intractable political tensions with a positive message that negates conflicts. The diversity topos is so effective in facilitating this appeasement because it can stand in for democracy (see, we are all, in our diverse forms, included in the demos), while also closing down dialogue, papering over conflict, and eliding exclusions.

This narrative conflation of identity-based diversity and social justice in a democracy (such as represented in the melting pot depiction in Roots) performs a kind of violence through the omission of the history and continuation of material inequality. While I do not want to suggest that all public art should be expected to represent contentious, undervalued, or absent perspectives and histories; serve as a political platform for the disenfranchised; or elucidate the deep contradictions and violence present within our society, I do believe that these two mural projects help us think through the consequences of public work that does not do these things, especially in projects used as development tools in gentrifying neighborhoods. While simply recognizing material inequality (past or present) does nothing to rectify such inequality, maintaining the visibility of systemic class inequity in the social imagination is a critical foundation for the rhetorical invention of arguments and action geared toward addressing particularly pernicious systemic inequalities. Here are the rhetorical stakes: The rhetorics of diversity are particularly powerful within democracies. As discursive motors that can call attention to (or away from) various claims for social justice, they can either foment or thin out the available means of persuasion from which we make arguments about and within democracies.

Rhetorical invention, in this sense, is partly a matter of visibility—or, as I suggested earlier, *sight*. One must have the capacity to perceive (and a knack for leveraging) the range of salient arguments that are already in circulation within doxa, a rhetorical term most commonly translated as public opinion. Sharon Crowley defines doxa as the "current and local beliefs that circulate communally" (47). The "violence" of erasing class inequity from public representations reduces the arguments that circulate in (Uptown's) doxa that are available (or rather see-able) for counteracting class-based inequity within gentrification.

In the following, Mark Elder, the muralist, discussed his choice to avoid representing the political aspects of Uptown's history:

Candice: So, I have question about something you were quoted as saying. In an article for the News-Star, Angela Caputo quotes you as saying that "the mural brings in a message of pride and equality." I'm wondering if you can speak more about how the mural does this.
Mark: "Equality?" Well, I think it was a free exchange of ideas in the planning stage. There was equal input from everyone, and all kinds of people are represented and involved; there is a balance of history, ethnicity, past and present
Candice: Uptown has pretty heated battles over public space, gentrification and so on, and I wonder how you understand what it might mean to represent political strife in a mural.

> Mark: [. . .] things might have been different if I were making the mural in the 70s or 80s [. . .]. I think people would have been more accepting of politically charged images, but now, I don't think it would be ok with everyone. The portal on the far left (1960–1980) certainly represents a time of intense political struggle. A lot of things could have been done to represent this struggle. But it's a tightrope, you know. Balancing the politics. [. . .] There was tremendous political tension in Uptown in the 70s, 80s, 90s. I made the decision not to represent this because I thought people would not like this. [. . .] I did consider showing this struggle in a more subtle way by showing a decayed portal, to show that time period with a look of decay, but I decided not to do this. I didn't think it would make people happy to draw attention to this. The mural was supposed to be positive. Make people happy.

Elder's view confirms the opinions of many supporters of Roots about how best to represent the contemporary situation in Uptown. We see the deliberate choice not to represent the difficult history of class and political struggle, and we see how "diversity" is used in service of such a choice. Furthermore, Elder's discussion of "equality" reveals the way that "equality," when articulated in terms of equal representation of different racial groups, can completely sidestep discussions about class inequities.[7]

Below, Sarah, the founding member of Kuumba Lynx introduced earlier, responded to the depiction of harmonious diversity in the Roots mural in relation to the fate of the Uplift Mural:

> Do you know the book Our America?[8] At the end, the boys say that we have two Americas. Yours and mine, and there are things about mine that you don't want to know about. That mural that you mentioned on the north part of Uptown. There's a view of history that is whitewashed. People want harmony and don't want to acknowledge that there is another history. They chalk it off to people like myself causing problems or creating obstacles, rather than telling another part of the story, they say things like "just get over it" and "let it go." They treat someone talking about inequality like that person is just holding a grudge that they need to let go of.

I have attempted to show here some of the ways that the "diversity" topos can obscure the contradictions within democratic society, and how particular public representations of history, as Sarah suggested, simply do not "acknowledge that there is another history." According to Sarah, there is much at stake in keeping arguments about inequality visible.

Before we leave our two murals, there is a little more to say about doxa as it relates to places of invention. Doxa, or public opinion, stresses the situatedness of invention. One invents from within rhetorical ecologies that are invested with political, rhetorical, material, and spatial histories that come to bear on the rhetorical situation within which one attempts to persuade. Sharon Crowley draws attention to two meanings of doxa: the first, as "expectation," which "lends a temporal cast to doxa, implying something previously constructed that can . . . be met or thwarted" and, second, as "communal," which "lends it an affinity to ethos (character)" (47). Rhetorical invention, then, is dependent on a deep, situated, and timely knowledge of the doxa alive within the communities one seeks to persuade. The "function of the topos," as Carolyn Miller contends, is an "aid to pattern recognition, specifically as a region that permits or invites the connection between abstract and the concrete, between a pattern and the material in which it is instantiated" (142).

This is all to say that invention doesn't happen as hocus pocus whereby we pull something new from thin air: we invent, rather, from the weighty stuff (material, rhetorical, bodily, historical, ideological) that already exists around and resonates among us. Doxic knowledge, as Bruce McComiskey argues, parallels the sophistic understanding of eidô, a form of knowledge "that is derived empirically from a situation" with an etymology *"related to sight"* (24–25, my emphasis). If one hopes to be effective, he or she must have doxic knowledge: the capacity to see and make strategic use of rhetorical forces that are tethered to commonplace arguments, bodily habits, ideological valences, cultural practices, and histories of place that already exist in social spaces. And when the public discourses circulating in doxa become anemic, our lines of sight for invention and intervention do so as well.

For this reason, I would ultimately argue that both murals perform narrative violence in that they do not represent the democratic paradoxes as they manifest in or might relate to Uptown, nor do they indicate how exactly one might act within them. Moreover, both murals assume a morally virtuous stance (whether it be the sanctity of the melting pot or the righteous cause of leftist revolutionaries who speak truth to power) that floats above material circumstances, doing more to obscure than to illuminate the lines of sight for rhetorical invention and action aimed to redress the most devastating systemic problems in Uptown, and broader contexts. And both murals perform the dimming of "sight" made available through eidô (situated, timely knowledge) for kairotic action in the present. To discover the means for invention is also to locate, in the exigencies of our everyday situations, the tools for intervention. Here I think of Thomas Rickert's notion of invention as a disposition toward understanding situation and "local environs" as "active player[s]" in how the "world reveals itself" to us and, thus, as profound shaping forces of our capacities to both perceive the world and act within it (29). In the end, both murals fail to increase the stuff of invention. Despite what might be good intentions all around, the evocation of revolutionary leftist rhetoric divorced from the nuanced political textures of Uptown in the Uplift Mural rings just as empty, perhaps, as the palatable diversity depicted in the Roots mural. But, then, where does this leave us? What might be preferable mural content that draws from eidô and enhances our capacities for salient, situated rhetorical invention and intervention?

At heart, these questions are about rhetorical technê, production, and action. If rhetorical invention is partly staked in thoughtful and rigorous analysis and critique of the available means, it is equally driven by the question of how—given the radical ambivalence, complicity, and partiality of all human action and thought—we might craft symbols that help us act from within the thicket. With respect to the Uplift Mural, my tendency was to read citizens' desire for "positive" images and "pure beauty" quite critically—as an exclusionary evacuation of politics and dire material conditions. That is, to read these citizens' yearning for harmony as a desire that necessitates blotting out the experiences of others and obscuring the pernicious operations of power. (And, certainly, whether intentional or not, the mural blots and obscures in this way.) Yet, as a collaborative effort of people who share space and seek to live and work together, it seems problematic to simply dismiss these human labors outright. The collective yearning for something shared and "positive" also points to the rhetorical work of people crafting symbols to inspire action and social cohesion. I linger here to consider if it is not a perversity to strictly inhabit spaces of perpetual critique where the sole motivation is unmasking symbols or denuding power, rather than crafting productive symbols that might intervene and motivate. And, with respect to the Uplift Mural, I wonder what symbols the students might have crafted if they had begun with the goal of producing "positive" images to rally around that relied neither on leftist critiques of power nor on papering over political realities. What I am getting at is a wondering about what it would mean to think of creative labor that is positively productive, aimed at building and expanding whom we consider "one of us" and that also somehow works in response to systemic injustices.

Conclusion

Diversity is but one subject of this chapter, but in dealing with it, I aimed to trace ways that the democratic project is hinged to the topos. It was my intention to practice iconophilia, as Kang and Finnegan propose, postponing epideictic critical judgment of the Uptown murals in order to focus on how the diversity topos circulates in public discourse and through everyday practices to leverage and obscure a range of arguments about and actions within democracies. In so doing, I have sought to illuminate the places of invention within which "diversity" lives in democracies (as a rhetorical resource, as a powerful visual icon, as a rhetoric that both reveals and obscures, and as a topos that webs all manner of arguments, ideologies, ways of relating, social memories, and moral imperatives).

But, having spent some time now postponing the epideictic function, let me contradict myself entirely to consider this question of what mural content might uphold the ideals of radical democracy. I am interested not only in the representation of the democratic paradox and incommensurable public debates, but also in the depiction of people acting in the thick of such ambivalences. Such mural content that draws from eidô and enhances our capacities for salient, situated rhetorical invention and intervention might emerge from questions such as: How do the abstract ideals of democracy matter here, *in this place*? How have *we defined and operationalized democracy*, and *how have we dealt with the contradictions* that arise within democratic society? What is the history of our own uses of democracy? How do we wade through competing interests and ideologies within our democratic social imagination in order to act *here* in meaningful, "democratic" ways?

So, the matter would be how to design a mural that resists palatable diversity (as well as the righteous speaking of truth to power) and that neither casts aside democratic ideals, nor denies systemic inequities that thwart such ideals. Beyond the call for representing the democratic paradox as an ongoing debate, I am compelled by the rich history in Uptown of people using their energies to intervene in these paradoxes, across the political spectrum. Were it my mural to paint, I would be partial to the depiction of such people who tactically redirected the processes of urban development and gentrification in very fleeting and local ways that stare dead on into the paradoxes of democracy.[9] Why choose content rooted in urban development, housing policy, and battles over contested public spaces? Because that is what has mattered *here*, and what has propelled and catalyzed politics, protests, and civic engagement *here*. The goal of such a mural would be to increase rhetorical visibility, to amplify arguments that have become increasingly more difficult to see, to showcase intractable conflicts of democracy and myriad ways people have acted within them *in this place*. This would all be driven by the idea that by increasing sight, one expands the grounds for both rhetorical invention and intervention.

Given the complex theoretical demands I'm proposing, it is probably clear that I am no artist. I recognize the impracticality of these demands, and that a mural driven by them might be abysmal and incoherent. But let me provide a single example, nonetheless. The history of the three hundred–unit Carmen Marine co-op contains many threads of Uptown's politics. The building was constructed under federal housing policy of the 1970s, which arranged private-public partnerships through incentives to developers who would build apartments reserved for low-income residents for at least twenty-five years. The initiative—which was intended as an alternative to the failure of public housing "projects" that plagued Chicago and other urban cores for decades—led to the construction of ten affordable buildings in Uptown. Through legal loopholes, building owners were able to prepay their mortgages early for profit, resulting in the loss of affordable units and the relocation of the people who dwelled in them.

In the early 1990s, one of these HUD apartment buildings—the Carmen Marine—was spared as affordable through the extraordinary effort of a group of low-income and incredibly diverse tenants, community organizers, activists, and politicians that organized the first national tenant buyout of a HUD prepayment building in U.S. history. In 1994, the tenant association at the three hundred–unit Carmen Marine, which is just a few blocks from the Roots mural, transformed its building into a limited equity co-op,[10] which is a form of collective homeownership rooted in democratic impulses. Uptown experienced protests for and against the building's initial construction, its potential sellout for profit, and its ultimate establishment as an affordable co-op. This co-op is upheld in contemporary politics as both a sign of successful civic action and the perpetuation of a failed housing model that concentrates poverty. Such a historical mural depiction is desirable not because it is somehow above contradiction or because it points to a transcendent sense of social justice, but precisely because it avoids such a claim by rendering visible a highly contextualized instance of the democratic paradox and multiple avenues for rhetorical invention (and for action) that are situated, historicized, and cognizant of the social consequences of urban development in Uptown. It provides the grounds for us to think through the complexity of the salient arguments and actions available to us, and perhaps, to craft novel responses to them within the mired, complicity of everyday democracies.

4
Positive Loitering and the Ambivalence of Democracy

> Loitering with your neighbors is just one way to connect and make sure a strong sense of community binds the stakeholders in a neighborhood.
> Kay Severinsen, "First Step to Safe Neighborhoods"

I open with a field tale about ordinary citizens working together to improve their collective lives—by taking it to the street—which can tell us much about everyday democracies and the ambivalence that cuts through the core of the democratic project.

In August 2007, on a steamy summer evening in Uptown, approximately twenty-five activists staged a public protest to reclaim their streets. They called themselves "positive loiterers." Their target was an informal day labor market that had operated for decades on a sidewalk across from a U-Haul, where men gather daily looking for moving jobs. Most of the positive loiterers arrived right before the event's designated 7:00 PM start time, still dressed in business causal. The majority of positive loiters appeared Caucasian aged thirty to sixty, but the group included Asian and African American members. Some sipped Starbucks, pushed strollers, or came with leashed dogs. They formed themselves into a restrained tribunal around the seven African and African American men who were deemed "the (negative) loiterers." One positive loiterer asked, "Why don't you get a job? Why would you want to do this?" A laborer replied, "This is our bread and butter. What are we supposed to do?" A second positive loiterer blurted out, "Find a real job." A third awkwardly stepped forward, earnestly adding, "There is an alternative. Permanent employment." He insisted, "You need social work. You need help. We want you to stabilize your lives. The whole reason we are out here today is to help you stabilize your lives."

Cued by this response, the police officer in charge of maintaining order, a petite woman in her thirties, straightforwardly explained to the laborers that the "community" is worried and feels intimidated by their presence. The officer remarked, "The community says that you can't be here." One laborer replied, "But some of us live here. We are the community." The officer then held up a clipboard and a pen. Put your name on this piece of paper, she said, and we will get you help with jobs and housing.

A couple of men put their names down; others waved their arms in exasperation or simply sighed and rolled their eyes. After twenty minutes of such verbal exchanges, all of the energy of the event was spent. All parties milled about for a bit and then dispersed. Within an hour, several of the laborers had returned to the sidewalk to try, once again, to make their daily "bread and butter."[1]

While this anecdote may seem to have little to do with the study of rhetoric —let alone the study of democracy—I will argue that it can help us see and understand the work that rhetoric—and, in this case, democratic rhetoric— does in constituting, ordering, and enacting everyday life. Although I will consider appeals to democratic ideals within the practices of positive loitering, I am more concerned here with the everyday performances of democracy that not only evoke those ideals, but also catalyze, challenge, complicate, contradict, and upend them as they manifest in local acts of community policing. I also examine aspects of persuasion that exceed the discursive to include the persuasiveness of bodies and materials, as well as the nuanced circulations of democratic rhetoric as it moves across situations. This chapter is also concerned, in other words, with how the built environment and material objects work as agents, and with how democratic rhetoric tethers to other discourses and logics (in our case, neoliberal discourse), and along with them, to circulating emotional frames, affective forces, and bodily habits.

This chapter, in more specific terms, traces an exemplary community policing strategy—"positive loitering"—a citizen-led public formation that automatically designates its obverse, "negative" uses of public space, thus drawing stark lines that delineate upright community members from dangerous derelicts. By analyzing the everyday rhetorics and practices around "positive loitering" protests, I focus on the multifarious and nuanced channels by which the material inequities of the neoliberal state are remade through the active energies of citizens struggling to define contested public spaces and secure the future of their neighborhood. In Uptown, positive loitering was introduced by the Chicago Alternative Policing Strategy (CAPS) as a way for community members to combat gang presence, loitering, public drinking, criminal behavior, and drug activity. Piloted in 1993 and institutionalized citywide in 1994, CAPS is one of the most comprehensive community policing programs in the United States and an international model

16. Sidewalk Across from U-Haul. Photo by Author.

for successful police reform. Monthly CAPS meetings are held throughout the city where local constituents and beat officers gather to dialogue about neighborhood-specific crime-fighting strategies and develop ways to practice "assertive vigilance" (Garnett 8). Positive loitering, one such tactic invented through CAPS collaborations with Chicagoans, extends the reach and effectiveness of the Chicago Police Department through the active participation of citizens. The tactic emerged within the context of gentrification and decades worth of heated contestation over competing visions of urban development in Uptown.

Nearly everyday during warm months, men work the sidewalk along Broadway Street, hoping to pick up informal moving gigs that may pay handsomely compared to minimum-wage employment. Men might be offered $50 for a job; they might make $300. Most of the laborers are poor African and African American men in their thirties, forties, and fifties who live or have lived in Uptown, though some commute from Chicago's economically devastated South and West Sides. While some men are homeless or tenuously housed, many are not. Many movers admit to having criminal records (some for felonies, mostly not), which make livable wage employment difficult to find. Quite a few men have done this intermittently for ten, fifteen, even twenty years. Despite the relative stability of this tertiary economic activity, it has increasingly become viewed as a source of social disorganization and an obstacle to neighborhood development, especially as more upscale residents have targeted the district and associated commercial interests. In this changing local environment, new strategies of community control have emerged that illustrate the shifting terms of legitimate uses of spaces and the sources of local entitlement in determining what gets to count as acceptable versus deviant market activity.

Positive loitering, as I contend in this chapter, is one such strategy. Understood by participants as "community involvement" and civic participation aimed to improve the neighborhood for everyone, positive loiterers take their collective cause to the streets in the form of passive-aggressive flash mob actions where people simply show up and hangout where the laborers gather. The "street," as a rich democratic topos, leverages substantial rhetorical and moral force. Though portrayed at times as dangerous, disorderly, and hostile, the street also connotes open access, diversity, and tolerance. As a commonplace metaphor for the demos, the "street" is the place where citizens seek refuge from and recognition by systems of power that exclude them and where political will finds material expression. While the street comes equipped with its own topoi (citizen action, public good, community will, democratic participation) and a stock repertoire of material practices (marches, slogans, megaphones, picket signs, media stunts), the act is not equipped with preordained ideological content. Yet, the idea of vulnerable citizens gathered to collectively work on behalf of the public good—a sentiment that resides at the heart of the democratic affect—goes far to hallow any action that can be deemed democratic, regardless of substance or consequence. Positive loitering, I will argue, is driven by such a rhetorical engine that, at its heart, is taken by proponents as the will of the people who have banded together to fight crime, improve quality of life for everyone, and take back control of the street from riffraff.

My field research here illuminates both the discursive and practical performance of these contested conceptions of legitimate civic participation and uses of public space in Uptown, Chicago. Between 2005 and 2008, I observed dozens of monthly CAPS meetings in Uptown. This chapter focuses on fieldwork conducted in police Beat 2322 (which contains the sidewalk across from U-Haul).[2] In addition to beat meetings, I observed positive loitering events outside the U-Haul, and interviewed positive loiterers about their experiences in the neighborhood and the rationale behind their activism. All of the positive loiterers I interviewed were homeowners who were active in CAPS and all but two had lived in Uptown for less than ten years; several of these informants were active in other hot-button issues, including campaigns to protest proposals for affordable housing developments and a legal day labor business elsewhere in the neighborhood. I also interviewed Uptown's U-Haul store manager and the U-Haul positive loitering taskforce leader for their accounts of the street market and the evolution of the community-driven movement to eradicate it. Finally, I observed the interactions that occurred on the sidewalk throughout my time in the field, talking informally with a dozen or so regular laborers about their work, and formally with three men.

In this chapter, I describe positive loitering as a practice that is heavily influenced by broken windows theory, both of which have the effect of sharply delimiting the legitimate uses of public space by expanding the range of behaviors deemed disruptive of social order. I situate these arguments within field descriptions of positive loitering events in Uptown. In doing so, I claim that positive loitering crystallizes how democratic and neoliberal rhetoric can dovetail in local practices that obscure systemic inequality, vilify informal labor practices, and stigmatize individuals who have not achieved economic independence. Positive loitering also offers an example of how a priori conceptions of civic participation as virtuous can eclipse the recognition of how such participation—even when productive and resulting in social benefits—can obscure exclusionary dimensions of contemporary policing practices and performances of democracy and citizenship at the neighborhood level.

Positive Loitering in Uptown, Chicago

Lester and Melvin have worked on the sidewalk for twenty and thirteen years, respectively. Lester is nearly fifty, married with five children, and has been doing moving jobs in Uptown since 1987 to help make ends meet. He left the neighborhood for several years, but after his house on Chicago's West Side was foreclosed in 2000, he started coming back to Uptown to make extra money. Melvin, who is in his forties and married with seven children, reported that he struggles with bipolar disorder. He has worked the sidewalk more frequently in recent years to help keep food on the table. He and his family have lived in Uptown off and on but currently live on Chicago's South Side. Both have self-reported criminal records for a variety of misdemeanors. I asked the men for an explanation of why they come here for work:

> *Melvin: I do this because I have children. I want people to know that everyone out here isn't bad. You know what I'm saying. There are a lot of us out there who really need this here, need this money to make a living [. . .] We are not bad people. We are just trying to survive out here.*

> *Lester: Just like everybody else, we're going to work. Some guys get up in the morning and come down here like it is a regular job. I look at it like a training process for these guys. He's not doing anything bad, he's getting into the moving work, and when he do get a real job, he'll keep it because he's trained himself to get up every morning coming down here.*

Although Melvin and Lester are arguably engaged in practices that are amenable to the restructuring of the postindustrial city, with its characteristic forms of contingent and disorganized labor, their labor is not state-sanctioned and their presence on the street is framed as an obstacle to neighborhood improvement by the positive loiterers. Here we see contradictory forces of urban restructuring at work. Deindustrialization in Chicago and elsewhere, along with the retrenchment of the welfare state, produces a materially deprived surplus labor force. The informal day labor offers a tenuous solution to the problem of economic redundancy, while also interfering with emergent processes of market-led regeneration. Although this informal labor market has operated for over two decades in Uptown, the pressure to eradicate the laborers from public view has increased along with advancing gentrification. The visible signs of poverty in Uptown are perceived as threats to public safety, urban development, and property values. Within gentrifying districts, the presence of informal labor markets collides with property market interests and with the quality-of-life concerns of an increasingly privileged population.

The historical roots of contestation over public space and urban development in Uptown, however, date back to the 1950s (see Chapter One). At that time, the first concerted effort by affluent residents to commercially develop the neighborhood through the federal urban renewal program was met with vehement opposition by Uptown's poor residents and the myriad organizations representing them. A striking level of civic participation has been endemic in the neighborhood across the political spectrum ever since. Politically left-leaning former alderman Helen Shiller (1987–2011) was consistently criticized by her opponents as divisive, anti-development, and anti-progress; some went as far as calling her work to maintain affordable housing a completely self-interested means of maintaining a voting block and powerbase in the neighborhood's poor. One positive loiterer expressed the common frustration to me over feeling that his concerns fell on "deaf ears" at the alderman's office; he said, "I don't think that it is any secret that our alderman is an advocate of the poor, and a lot of this negative stuff she sees as tolerable because people are unfortunate and they need to be cared for." Encountering an alderman whom they felt was less than sympathetic, positive loiterers turned to the Chicago Alternative Policing Strategy (CAPS) to voice and act on their concerns.

Positive loitering was introduced by an officer at a CAPS meeting in July 2006, as a way to address the U-Haul loitering. Positive loitering, the officer told the small crowd of Uptown citizens in attendance, was a way to "send a message" that the community will not tolerate deviant public behavior. Because Chicago has no anti-loitering laws[3]—which means that it is perfectly legal for the laborers to gather on the sidewalk provided they do not block it—CAPS officers encouraged residents to devise ways to deter such "deviant" behavior by occupying the spaces where loitering occurs and publicly demonstrating "appropriate" behavior in them. At this meeting, the officer explained that positive loitering simply entails "showing up where the men gather, bringing your dogs, your strollers, and just standing around and talking." The point is to make the men feel uncomfortable and embarrassed. Positive loitering is an activity that "Takes the Police Beat to the Street," she said. A community member replied, "I like this. This sends out a message that this is our neighborhood and we won't stand for it." There were unanimous nods of support among the twenty or so people present.

It is important to place the U-Haul (positive) loitering case in the context of Uptown's relative crime rates. Uptown is located in the 20th and 23rd districts, two contiguous police districts that include other Chicago community areas, such as Edgewater, Andersonville, Lake View, and Lincoln Park. Although the district statistics in Table 4 include areas outside of Uptown, it is helpful to see the relative stability of crime for the police districts within which Uptown is located to demonstrate that crime has been neither exploding (a common perception) nor receding. While these numbers may seem high to readers, they must be read within a broader context. As is clear from Table 5, the 20th and 23rd police districts were ranked among the lowest for both violent and property crimes in Chicago during the time that I gathered fieldwork.

Finally, I include Table 6 because police districts 20 and 23 include neighborhoods outside of Uptown, which are more affluent and widely perceived as "nicer." I thought it critical, therefore, to separate out the crime stats in each neighborhood area, as well as in the specific beat (a smaller yet police unit within a district) where the positive loitering took place. Doing so makes it more difficult to dismiss the low crime rating in Table 4 as a result of the inclusion of the affluent neighborhoods. The Edgewater neighborhood is directly north of Uptown and Lake View is directly south; Lincoln Park is below Lake View, approximately two miles south of Uptown. As indicated by Table 6, in 2009–2010,[4] Uptown had marginally less violent crime than

Index Crime Statistics* for Districts 20 and 23

Police District	2005 Violent Crimes/ Property Crimes	2006 Violent Crimes/ Property Crimes	2007 Violent Crimes/ Property Crimes	2008 Violent Crimes/ Property Crimes	2009 Violent Crimes/ Property Crimes
20	474/2915	383/2703	365/2340	416/2461	418/2500
23	544/3199	441/3127	428/2909	495/3319	498/3358

Table 4— Source: Chicago Police Department (CPD), Index Crime Statistics

* Property crimes include burglary, theft, motor vehicle theft, and arson. Violent crimes include homicide, robbery, criminal sexual assault, and aggravated assault/battery. The Chicago Police Department (CPD) defines drug abuse as the "violation of laws prohibiting the production, distribution, and/or use of certain controlled substances."

Lowest Crime Statistics Rankings
(1 = district ranked with lowest crime stats; 25 = highest crime stats)

Police District	2005 Violent Crimes/ Property Crimes	2006 Violent Crimes/ Property Crimes	2007 Violent Crimes/ Property Crimes	2008 Violent Crimes/ Property Crimes	2009 Violent Crimes/ Property Crimes
20	2 of 25/ 1 of 25	1 of 25/1 of 25	1 of 25/1 of 25	1 of 25/1 of 25	1 of 25/1 of 25
23	4 of 25/ 4 of 25	3 of 25/3 of 25	3 of 25/3 of 25	4 of 25/5 of 25	2 of 25/4 of 25

Table 5—Source: Chicago Police Department (CPD), District Rank.

Lake View and somewhat higher rates than Edgewater and Lincoln Park, but Uptown had approximately half the property crime incidents of Lake View and Lincoln Park. While Uptown had lower overall crime numbers than its "nicer" neighbors to the south, drug abuse reports were significantly higher. However, Uptown's Beat 2322, which contains the sidewalk in question, had a relatively low number of the drug abuse and violent crime reports.

Although social conditions associated with this sidewalk have improved

Comparison of Reported Crimes in
Uptown and Surrounding Lakefront Neighborhoods
August 2009–August 2010

Neighborhood	Violent Crimes	Property Crimes	Homicide	Drug Abuse	All Crime
Uptown	332	1522	3	610	4870
Uptown Beat 2322	36	259	0	26	565
Lake View	367	3606	0	260	7320
Edgewater	267	1293	5	211	3608
Lincoln Park	222	3154	2	105	5496

Table 6— Source: Chicago Police Department (CPD), ClearMap Crime Summary.[1]

1. The Chicago Police Department qualifies this data as "preliminary information supplied to the Police Department by the reporting parties and have not all been verified." The complete disclaimer can be found at http://gis.chicagopolice.org/CLEARMap_crime_sums/startPage.htm#

dramatically by everyone's account, it is also important to note that serious public safety issues have included prostitution, drug and gun activity, public defecation and urination, drinking, littering, and harassment. While public drinking persists, the gravity of associated crimes has comparatively lessened. During more recent summers, one will typically find a group of three to ten men sitting on folding chairs or standing around against the side of the building across from U-Haul, shooting the breeze, often smoking, sometimes drinking, sometimes laughing, and talking very loudly, but who are otherwise relatively innocuous. However, according to the positive loiterers, their very presence on the street—regardless of whether they commit serious offenses—projects a significant negative symbolic force that, to them, is far from harmless.

Broken Windows Theory and the Rhetorics of Decline

Although positive loitering has become a nationwide community policing strategy, its center of gravity spun out from Chicago. The earliest references to "positive loitering" appear in 1993–1994 and are direct collaborations between CAPS police officers and Chicago community members. For example, Whelan mentions positive loitering as a tactic used in Englewood starting in April 1993 (2–3)—immediately after the South Side Chicago neighborhood was chosen as a CAPS pilot area. Skogan and Hartnett describe a positive loitering "march" in 1994 to combat gang activity that was called Operation Beat Feet—led by sixty Chicago residents and CAPS officers from the Rogers Park neighborhood (173).

At monthly CAPS meetings in Uptown (Beat 2322), anywhere from twelve to forty residents and five to ten officers typically crowd into a room at 7:00 P.M. at the Buena Park Public Library. One of the topics that dominated conversations throughout my fieldwork was U-Haul loitering. Residents complained about litter on the sidewalk and felt intimidated walking down the street. There was typically a moment in the meetings when participants recited a litany of eyewitness accounts of the goings-on there. A woman was whistled at. A man was seen drinking out of a brown paper bag. A community member once brought in pictures of a man passed out along the curb as evidence of the problem. The presence of the laborers was continually voiced as a public nuisance, and the residents wanted help from the police, who had also grown weary of the persistent loitering. These conversations catalyzed the formation of the citizen-led "Uptown U-Haul taskforce" in collaboration with CAPS in 2006. In the beginning, the taskforce met monthly out on the sidewalk—a tactic recommended by a CAPS officer who suggested, as one positive loiterer reported, that doing so would "make a more visual impact."

John, a neighborhood homeowner and member of the taskforce, discussed what positive loitering meant to him and others:

Positive loitering is simply using behavior [. . .] that you find impacts the area in a negative way, and using almost the exact same behavior to call attention to it and to make those that are doing things [. . .] feel uncomfortable by putting the spotlight directly on them. I think a lot of times when people are loitering, we put our blinders up and just ignore it and just walk past it, and this is the exact opposite. This is walking up to it and looking it in the face, and saying you know, "I can't believe that you are doing this here." You don't even have to be physically or verbally confrontational. Often times just the presence of community members and their kids and their dogs, showing up in a place is uncomfortable for them. They are used to being ignored and they are used to making people feel uncomfortable, and when you're clearly not uncomfortable being there, it kinda turns the tables. [. . .]

John shared with me that the taskforce was directly influenced by broken windows crime prevention theory. Kelling and Wilson, who originated the theory in 1982, argue that communities that do not repair broken windows—

a metaphor for any sign of negligence, indifference, or social decay that can be read in an environment—broadcast a vulnerability to criminals that can lead to more broken windows. The theory is underscored by four assumptions: first, that the environment communicates messages about a neighborhood's susceptibility to crime; second, that strong, healthy neighborhoods demonstrate control over criminal behavior by "fixing broken windows"; third, that social divisions between insiders and outsiders, upright citizens and deviants, should be reinforced by the built environment; and fourth, that crime is best addressed through the everyday practices of concerned citizens (Herbert and Brown 758).

Positive loiterer John summarized the broken windows theory, as it pertained to protesting the U-Haul loitering:

> *My understanding of it is when you give an appearance of a property that you live in, people assume a lot. If your lawn is overgrown and your windows are broken and your front door is off its hinges, you give the impression that [. . .] you really don't care about what's going on in your neighborhood. If you manicure your lawn and you pick up trash when it accumulates on your lawn; if something breaks, you fix it right away, if somebody spray paints it, you take it off right away, you give the impression that you are not going to tolerate those things on your property. You're not physically stopping anyone from doing anything, but the research shows that when you do that, people kinda resist doing those things to your property because they know it is going to get fixed [. . .] When it is an apartment building [. . .] and no one really takes ownership of anything, those are the buildings that tend to have trash around them. That's our mentality [as property owners]. You know, I live here and someone else lives there, and we're trying to spread that out to encompass and blanket that area with all of us watching and paying attention and taking some ownership of what goes on there, and trying to get the businesses to join us with that and kinda of blanket this little corner of Uptown with the message that we are not going to tolerate this here anymore.*

John draws a line between legitimate, upstanding community members who safeguard the public welfare and those who threaten it by inviting crime, which is consistent with the logic of broken windows theory. Also consistent with the theory is the role of property owners as bulwarks against urban decay in their collective fight for public safety through the everyday maintenance of their property—actions that publicly and aesthetically communicate their care for the neighborhood. For positive loiterers, it is a civic and moral imperative to "manicure your lawn" and "pick up trash" because this type of self-regulating behavior contributes to the common good. These everyday acts of caring for oneself and one's property have become an important way to enact citizenship and work toward collective goals. Aesthetics become paramount because, within this logic, physical order is directly linked to social order. As such, the visual signs of urban decline became tethered to affective frames and socially structured ways of feeling in ways that played a critical role in catalyzing the positive loitering campaign. The social theory of broken windows relies on such a linking of psychological, rhetorical, and embodied responses to tangible evidence of distress that can be read in the built environment.

Thus, a broken window (or a passed out man, empty liquor bottle, scattering of trash) takes on extreme rhetorical force in a neighborhood like Uptown. A broken window is not merely a temporary inconvenience for the property owner to deal with, and a pile of litter signifies much more than its literal components of greasy food sack, gum wrapper, and cigarette butt. These objects become symbols that resonate beyond their sheer materiality. Namely such symbols of urban decline are lethal to community health, according to the theory, because they publicly communicate something akin to this: *this is a place where we tolerate crime, where we allow riffraff to have their way, where we have given up, where no one cares, where bad things happen, where we are scared, where you, too, should be afraid, where we are on the verge of sliding into even worse states of criminality and decay.* Within broken windows theory, the antidote to crime is to reverse the rhetorical force of these messages through the active labor of citizens who fix broken windows, clean the streets, prune the bushes, and, generally, eradicate all signs in the built environment that are readable as urban decline.

Broken windows theory reverberated in John's description of why the U-Haul loitering is a "problem" for taskforce members:

> It is a problem because even if there were ten guys standing there, and they were absolutely just looking for work, they were absolutely not littering, they were absolutely not using drugs, or drinking or anything else, the behavior of them standing there, invites other people to come to that area, that it's ok, that this is going to be a hang out place. It's ok for people to come and sleep on the sidewalk, to come intoxicated, to come on drugs. [. . .] It's not so much that I'm against them looking for work. I want everyone to have a job. That's not my problem, but it's what this leads to. It's the next step or the next three steps down the road. If these guys are here all day, maybe they go home at 5 o'clock when U-Haul closes down,

but the other four or five people hang out and invite their friends and it is like a little street party every freaking night. They [the loiterers] don't get that.

Broken windows theory stresses the importance of addressing relatively innocuous crimes, such as loitering, with severity because, as the logic goes, a group of guys standing around a sidewalk looking for work could spiral into more serious criminal behavior and neighborhood deterioration. The theory, as Benjamin Chesluk puts it, gives "an apocalyptic resonance to an open-ended critique of the everyday" such that "every moment of discomfort can be read as a potential broken window" (255). The theory, therefore, lowers the threshold for perceived threats to community well being and justifies preemptive strikes against crimes not yet committed.

Positive loitering, as I argue next, is generally understood by neighborhood participants and CAPS officers as an embodiment of the community will and an exercise of civic duty on behalf of a collective public good (typically defined as public safety and quality of life). As John indicates, positive loitering is the civic engagement of concerned citizens who band together against a common enemy by blanketing "this little corner of Uptown" with visual cues and subtle actions that transmit the "message that we are not going to tolerate this here anymore." It is in this conceptualization that the ambivalence of civic participation becomes clearer, as it is from this rhetorical move (in which positive loitering is seen as civic participation that reflects the will of the demos) that the positive loiterers draw their moral force and legitimacy.

Community Policing and the Ambivalence of Democracy

CAPS's motto is "Together We Can." With approximately 67,000 people attending monthly beat meetings each year, CAPS has certainly contributed much to increasing public involvement (Skogan and Steiner ii). Eric Klinenberg writes that community policing operates on a "principle of social integration and civic renewal," and that "police officers have become the most visible and accessible faces of the state" (76). These sentiments are certainly apparent in the Chicago Police Department's description of the program: "City of Chicago has a new weapon in the fight against crime—and that new weapon is you, the community . . . What makes CAPS innovative is that it brings the police, the community, and other City agencies together to identify and solve neighborhood crime problems" (Chicago). This positing of "the community" as an "innovative" and "new weapon" in crime fighting lends credibility to the program in its claim to work with, through, and on behalf of an active citizenry.

Archon Fung notes that community-policing emerged in response to increasing public concern over crime that was fueled, in part, by the War on Drugs rhetoric of the late-1980s—timing that also corresponds with the introduction of broken windows theory (*Empowered*). Community policing and broken windows both showcase active citizen involvement as the prime method for enacting and justifying crime control, which as Herbert notes, lends "legitimacy because the police would be open to democratic oversight" (448). Fung pushes the democratic trope further by calling CAPS a "model of radical deliberative democracy" and an example of what he calls "street level democracy," which he defines as a "pragmatic, problem-solving alternative . . . that devolves substantial operational authority to the residents of neighborhoods and line-level officials who directly serve them" ("Street Level" 3). Fung also coined the term "participatory devolution," which he articulates as the establishment via CAPS of "hundreds of neighborhood-level structures for problem-solving in the hope that this combination of civic engagement and administrative decentralization—participatory devolution—would be better able to improve neighborhood safety" (*Empowered* 57). Rather than decontextualized, top-down policing, CAPS, according to Fung, is a "deliberative strategy of public action" that "emphasizes local knowledge, cooperation with residents, and embedded ingenuity" (68). Positive loitering, then, emerges as a neoliberal practice that reflects the restructuring of the centralized, bureaucratic police state into community policing that devolves policing work to local citizens—and that is justified rhetorically through democratic topoi such "participatory devolution," "street-level democracy," increased local control, and citizen participation.

Participants earnestly and legitimately understand positive loitering as a productive, citizen-led, community building activity. This sense of collective democratic action is captured in a large-scale positive loitering event to target U-Haul loitering, which was held on Thursday, August 3, 2006, at 7:00 PM in place of the regularly scheduled CAPS meeting. At this event, approximately sixty Uptown residents, six police officers, four babies, six dogs, a journalist, and a four-person Macedonian film crew that happened to be shooting a documentary on U.S. community policing, marched for about five blocks (from the Buena Park Library to the infamous stretch of sidewalk across from U-Haul). When the small mass reached its destination, the five laborers who were working the sidewalk cleared out and disappeared down the street. The group stood around chatting for a few minutes, inadvertently blocking the sidewalk (technically illegal by their own estimation), before the meeting loosely formalized.

An Uptown homeowner, who appeared in his fifties, facilitated the meeting, announcing that the large turnout spoke volumes about what is possible when concerned citizens get involved. Praising the crowd for its "persistent community participation," he said that everyone's "active engagement" would transform Uptown's streets. During a brief brainstorm on how to continue their efforts, one woman suggested the idea of using large flower planters to obstruct the areas where people congregate along Broadway. In reply, the facilitator proclaimed:

> *Now that's innovation. That's the kind of grassroots innovation it takes to clean up these streets. Positive loitering is innovative. Flower pots, too. Anything we can do to make it uncomfortable to hang out in the area is a good thing. [. . .] We are going to create a positive loitering task force to work on this issue [the U-Haul loitering] that is focused on quality of life. The taskforce should not be punitive. It should be kind and geared towards getting people jobs and finding opportunity elsewhere because the way they are living here is not working out for them. We're not against people trying to make a living, but against criminal activity. We need to find positive ways that people can live their lives.*[5]

Broken windows crime theory was explicitly mentioned at this positive loitering event as a respected social theory that inspired their actions. For example, one man provided an example of broken windows in action, saying: "If you see one person smoking a joint, you need to call the police immediately." A woman replied: "Yes, broken windows really works. The people really feel pressure. It shows that we won't tolerate anyone disrespecting the community."

The positive loitering event ended with a round of applause by participants, punctuated with the following praise by one of the organizers: "The fact that you are here means you care. Please get other people involved and let's keep working together towards neighborhood progress. If we work together, things will get so much better. Get your neighbors engaged." The Uptown positive loitering campaign serves as an important example of how "taking it to the street" can occur in direct collaboration with institutional power, such that the "street" becomes a place to galvanize people not in opposition to—but in concordance with—that power. While it is community-driven, positive loitering is also bolstered by the institutional heft of CAPS, which lends ethos, meeting spaces for organizing, and security during public protests. Because of this official link, as well as the tie to market-driven interests of property owners, positive loitering complicates the notion that vernacular democracies are somehow more pure, morally upright, or politically left. This is neither to say that CAPS is nefarious (far form it), nor to suggest that the concerns of positive loiterers are not justified and serious (they are, indeed). It is to say, however, that it is not possible to easily distinguish official/institutional forms of power from vernacular publics. As I have argued throughout this book, the lure of imaging democracy as innately virtuous, or as more authentic, desirable, or pure when practiced "organically" by ordinary people is deeply problematic. In this case, it is not that the positive loiterers are not engaged in democratic practices that have positive social outcomes, it is that the productive capacities of these citizens who are engaged in democratic practices make it harder to see and argue (at least using the rhetorics of democracy) for the connections between the disenfranchised street laborers and the iniquitous distributions of late capitalism. In the end, the evocations and practices of democracy do not remain loyal to any particular ideology or sense of justice, so the useful questions are rarely: Is such and such practice or policy democratic? Or is X or Y in violation of our beloved democratic virtues? One might answer yes to both, and still be faced with human atrocity, depending on one's political orientation in the situation.

For Katie, an Uptown homeowner in her fifties, CAPS and positive loitering actions tapped into a nostalgic and exciting throwback to her participation in the U.S. Civil Rights Movement. Katie's history in Uptown extended back to the 1970s, when she moved to the neighborhood as a social worker. At a CAPS meeting, she voiced her concern about the U-Haul loitering and about people "dumpster diving" in her alley. Although she cared about their welfare, she was deeply torn by the trashy look of the street and by the fact that all of her hard work separating recyclables was ruined each week. She saw a connection between the behaviors and was excited to see her neighbors working together through positive loitering. Katie discussed positive loitering in terms of "community involvement" aimed at reclaiming control of the streets:

> Katie: I am struggling with the homeless . . . well, I don't know if you remember at the CAPS meeting about U-Haul and the positive loitering. I said, well, you know, I feel very guilty about saying this, but here you have dumpster drivers and we have rats in the alley because they are breaking open all of the bags and strewing things all over. By the same token, I know that this is how many of them make their living. [. . .]
> Candice: Were you part of the positive loitering march in Uptown over the summer?
> Katie: I thought this [a positive loitering march] was the perfect opportunity to learn about the neighbors, and I thought it was nice to see a pres-

ence of people. You know, I did mention that I came of age in the 60s, and this was a protest in the same sense. [. . .] It was nice; it was like bringing people together. It shows community involvement. [. . .]
Candice: So, did you see positive loitering as a collective cause? What would that cause be?
Katie: It was about the illegal activities that were going on in the area around. [. . .] That people weren't going to stand for it and let it go on and that people, by having a presence, showed their interests and concern. [. . .]

Katie's comment relies on the trope of civic participation, while simultaneously redrawing clear, moral lines between upright citizens and street denizens. Furthermore, this important concern for the environment, represented in the careful sorting of trash, comes to a head with what might also be her concern for the systemic social injustices—such competing and contradictory pulls in liberal democracy are endemic and ubiquitous facts of citizenship, which is another reason why asking what is or is not democratic is hard to answer outside the concrete contexts of everyday life. And, as I've already said, even then one is faced with intractable endgames and eddies of contradiction. In this case, the good citizens who come out to show their concern are primarily property owners who band together in their desire to get rid of the street market—which is increasingly viewed as interfering with the burgeoning housing market and general urban development, well being, and safety of the neighborhood; and yet, these same good citizens are also often caught in moral dilemmas that pull them this way and that. Although this may not apply unilaterally, positive loiterers I've spoken with express that they care deeply about the contexts and conditions of poverty while also being worried about the safety of their children or the security of their financial property investments (which, given Chicago's explosive condo bubble and then devastating burst, is no joking matter).

Like Katie, John used the "community involvement" trope to describe positive loitering:

I look at positive loitering as community involvement, in that there are so few people that get out and meet their neighbors and talk with their neighbors about things. And honestly, the biggest reason that I have been able to do that is that I have a dog and now I have kids, and those are two avenues for people to have some conversation. And there are a lot of people who saw a lot of things in the community only because they are walking their dog. [. . .] I'm out there walking my dog usually and I just happen across stuff, and then you start talking with other people who have walked their dogs and seen stuff. And it seems that people who walk dogs are the eyes of the neighborhood and getting all those people together to talk about something is why, if we've made any gains, it is in part because of the dog walking.

This detail of the dogs might seem trivial, but I stand behind John in arguing that it is, in fact, notable: "dog walking" has played an important role in positive loitering. In Uptown, the act of dog walking works like urban sociologist Jane Jacob's "eyes on the street" and has become a technique for both policing the streets and for galvanizing "community involvement." Such everyday, passive aggressive tactics, moreover, stand in stark contrast to the hyperpunitive policing strategies that scholars commonly associate with the neoliberal state,[6] as I discuss below.

The Strategies and Logics of Positive Loitering

Herbert and Brown argue that broken windows theory reinforces the "social and spatial distinctions . . . that help legitimate hyperpunitiveness" in urban spaces (756). According to Neil Smith, "hyperpunitive" policing practices in American cities spiked in the 1980s in response to the perceived failure of New Deal policies, the proliferation of expensive social legislation to protect equal opportunity in the 1960s, and the end of the 1980s economic boom (44). Neoliberal processes have been commonly associated with the re-entrenchment and exacerbation of social inequalities, as well as to hyperpunitive policing efforts, in urban cores through spatial practices of exclusion and privatization (Dávila; Duneier; Hackworth; Herbert and Brown; Low).

Punitive measures do occur in Uptown. Residents commonly call 911 at the first sign of misconduct, including for minor offenses like throwing cigarette butts on the sidewalk and standing in the street, which increased police activity in that area. Lester and Melvin reported that, although CAPS police officers are generally "cool" (by which they mean that the officers look the other way when the men are working the sidewalk) and "give us boots and stuff," more severe treatment has occasionally occurred here, according to them:

Marvin: *Some police have come down here and carded us and lined us up against the wall.*

Lester: *They put us against the wall like we are criminals. Search us like criminals and stuff, and they do that shit to us with all these people looking at us, making us look like criminals so that no one wants to work with us.*

Rarely, however, do policing strategies on this sidewalk resemble anything close to what one could rightly call hyperpunitive. The predominant tenor of community policing in this case is not hyperpunitive, but takes the form of nuanced, subtle, and often passive aggressive gestures, such as dog walking, occupying space, and altering the built environment.

Positive loiterers have devised three core strategies, in addition to staging positive loitering events, for addressing the loitering, two of which focus on changing the built environment to make the sidewalk less hospitable. First, the taskforce developed a relationship with the management staff at U-Haul, who agreed to install security cameras that are pointed directly at the sidewalk. They also succeeded in getting U-Haul to erect a fence around its property, and to post signs that instruct customers not to use the men's services. Second, the taskforce encouraged neighbors to consistently walk their dogs down the sidewalk and call 911 at the first sign of law breaking. Third, the taskforce explored—thus far, unsuccessfully—how to narrow the sidewalk either architecturally or with flower planters in order to make it impossible for the men to avoid blocking pedestrians, which would be a crime.

In this discussion, I am making the case that broken windows theory (and, by extension, positive loitering) is as much a theory and practice of spatial rhetorics as one of crime fighting, as both focus on how symbolic, rhetorical forces become enmeshed in the spaces of everyday life. Drawing on the work of Henri Lefebvre, John Ackerman urges rhetoricians to include analysis of spatial and material dimensions of the rhetorical situation, insisting that "rhetorical agency includes the production and maintenance of social space" (85), whereby social space is conceived as a "living laboratory for finding and naming the vitality of everyday life and those structures that oppress it" (88). In arguing that the arrangement and visual appearances, as well as visceral feel, of public spaces communicate something about the health of their neighborhood, Uptown positive loiterers are insisting that materiality is much more than inert matter.

Jane Bennett's argument that objects (materiality, matter, the nonhuman, the built environment) have rhetorical and political freight is also useful here. Objects, for her, should be seen as "actants rather than as objects" (10)—"vibrant matter," as she calls it, has the capacity to "animate, to produce effects dramatic and subtle" (6). Bennett is particularly interested in the active role that objects play in public life and politics—a power she calls "thing-power." Objects in the built environment (whether they resonate as urban decline or indicate the opposite) become tethered to broader rhetorical and affective structures that help define acceptable public behavior, legitimate citizenship, and what constitutes a safe place. Messages transmitted by the environment become targets for positive loiterers to either eradicate or cultivate because they evoke and broadcast perceptions of neighborhood "health."

The positive loiterers, therefore, are not only concerned with eradicating signs of decay in urban spaces, but also in producing new kinds of spaces that better reflect their sense of what good neighborhoods are and what good people should do in them. For example, two positive loiterers, Rob and Mike, described this strategy of changing the built environment to catalyze community involvement in producing more desirable public spaces:

> Rob: There was also talk of putting a green space in there. By putting a green space in there, it would narrow the sidewalk, and if the sidewalk was blocked you could do something. [. . .]
> Mike: Yes, and one of the things they [CAPS and neighborhood participants] thought of was, actually it was suggested by the commander, was installing green space, just a little planter, a couple planters, some type of flowers. Maybe we could do some type of gardening and get people involved in it.
> Rob: The Girl Scouts volunteered to do some work.
> Candice: I wonder what your personal opinions are about these kinds of steps to change the physical environment to deter people from gathering.
> Rob: Well, urban planners would say that the environment is going to have an influence on the amount of crime that exists. Did I think it would work? No, not necessarily. Maybe. I would agree with urban planners that changing the environment does have an influence on the amount of crime in an area. [. . .] This would probably reduce or help influence, but I didn't think that would be the whole solution. [. . .]
> Mike: In terms of physical altering, altering physical areas, I'm a huge proponent of community gardens. There is a pocket garden at Kenmore and Lawrence. It was just totally ignored, it's a little triangle, maybe 20 feet with a muffler in it and beer cans, it was awful. [. . .] There was a lot of drug activity in that corner. [. . .] It gets people talking and interacting. [. . .]
> Rob: So, anyway, that was one invention that we thought would curtail behavior. Creating a community garden. [. . .]
> Candice: Are there any other changes to the environment that were discussed?
> Rob: Cameras. Cameras had a profound effect when cameras were installed.

Here, the logic of altering the built environment is framed not only as a strategy to deter crime but also as a way to inspire community involvement through innocuous activities like public gardening. Although these strategies do insert an argument for proper uses of public spaces that delineate lines between "good" and "bad" citizens, they are not hyperpunitive. In fact, they are productive, community-building practices—as inclusionary as they are exclusionary—that deter the laborers from gathering in public spaces while getting neighbors involved in transforming those same areas into ostensibly beautiful, environmentally conscience spaces.

Positive loitering is a community-building initiative that reverses messages of decay in social spaces both through activities like planting gardens and redesigning the built environment, and through practices in which the bodies of upright citizens become part of the intended signification of neighborhood wellbeing—which is simply to say that the insertion of literal physical bodies into public spaces takes on rhetorical force in and of itself. Such can be seen in the field examples throughout this chapter from the gathering of well-dressed individuals in problem areas to the walking of dogs and infants down the sidewalk. Ralph Cintrón's ethnographic work on embodied rhetorics analyzes the way that particular bodily gestures of Chicago gang members "stitch" together both nondiscursive and discursive qualities of rhetorical performance, arguing that "through its gestures and adornments the body can 'speak' rhetorically, thereby displaying the thought systems that a person identifies with and (implicitly or explicitly) 'argues' for" ("Gates" 6). The stitching together of persuasive messages emitted from the built environment, from bodies in space, and from public rhetorics in circulation about neighborhood health, establish a rhetorical force greater than its parts for what it means to be a good citizen in a good neighborhood.

Positive loiterer Tom eluded to the idea that their own bodily presence in public spaces became part of their strategy, as it involved transmitting a "visual message" that the U-Haul loitering would no longer be tolerated. This Uptown homeowner was fed up with the loitering and sought to take action, arguing that the rhetorical force of their embodied inhabitation of the sidewalk, coupled with changes to the built environment might persuade the street laborers that the community thinks it is a bad idea to hang out:

> *We're sending them the visual message [through positive loitering] that it is not just me [. . .] but it's this group of people, it's the police, it's someone from the Alderman's office occasionally, it's U-Haul, it's Public Storage, it's the car dealership over there, it's the hospital. Everybody is not ok with this and we are all standing here hanging out letting them know how many of us there are. It isn't just one person who moved into a condo and hates black people. It's the whole community. And that's been shocking to them because they assumed it is one or two people who just stared out*

their windows and called the police all day, and I think they were a little surprised by that.

As mentioned previously, various other visual and material rhetorical cues have been deployed by positive loiterers to broadcast that loitering is "not ok": a congregation of neighbors who stand next to the laborers and stare at them until they move; the installation of security cameras; signs posted at U-Haul that discourage patronage; and the documentation (photo and anecdotal) of deviant behavior that is reported to the police. Slowly, the amount of space the men inhabit has been squeezed into a smaller and smaller strip of the public sidewalk—now reduced to about 3' by 15'. If the men step into the street, if they block more than half the sidewalk, if they throw a single piece of trash onto the ground, the police might be called. If someone whistles at a woman, falls asleep, or urinates in public, the police might be called.

This response has led the men to police themselves, in fact, and adopt self-regulatory practices that correct some of the behaviors and bodily habits that the positive loiterers abhor. I am reminded here of Nedra Reynolds's argument that "the process of social construction of space occurs at the level of the body, not just at the level of the city or street or nation" (143). One day, while pointing to the clean street gutters and litter-free sidewalk, Lester reported, "We pick up garbage here. Sweep even. We like to keep it as clean as we can. We keep it neat. Don't block the sidewalk." Melvin added:

> *We are trying to get rid of the bad seeds. I'm an old timer. [. . .] don't want the bad seeds around here no more. All we want to do is come here and work. When U-Haul closes everybody goes home. I go home. He goes home. In the summertime, the bad seeds stick around, and you know what they are fittin' to do. [. . .] We aren't trying to run people away. We aren't trying to make people feel uncomfortable. We have respect for the people who walk down the street. A couple comes past with their dog, we will come to the side and try to give them space. [. . .] We might say, "How are you doing?" or "Have a good day."*

Like the positive loiterers, Lester and Melvin also separate the "good" workers from the "bad," using similar criteria. In an effort to be good citizens, they engage in self-regulatory practices—cleaning up after themselves, remembering to move to the side when someone comes by, and extending polite salutations. As John, the taskforce member, admitted, "They keep things much neater now, and it seems that there are less people there and less trash on the ground." The U-Haul store manager also noted that the laborers who used to come onto their property and harass customers changed their behavior. "We had a lot of complaints," he told me in 2007, "so we asked the men to leave and that is when the hostility started. After awhile they changed. They turned very respectful, polite. They pretty much stay over there now," he said, pointing to the sidewalk across the street.

What emerges in the tensions between the positive loiterers and the men looking for work on the street reveals the problematic way that morality works to smooth over the disconnect between the promise that drives and legitimates neoliberalism (namely, that the market yields the best social outcomes and is the best safeguard of political freedoms) and the inability of the market to deliver the conditions for stable employment and decent living conditions to everyone. Importantly, the point here is not to indict the individual positive loiterers, who are, in fact, engaged in what they understand as necessary, important, and exhausting measures to make their streets safer and more livable, but to consider ways that neoliberal ideologies are activated and entangled in local practices like positive loitering. Central to the positive loitering campaign, furthermore, is the claim that laborers are not engaged in "real" work and are not members of the community. Although the street laborers in Uptown are most certainly participating in a labor market, theirs is deemed an illegitimate and immoral market—dismissed by CAPS and the positive loiterers as a shadow market, a sham, a racket, a hustle, an illegal public nuisance.

The positive loiterers occupy the position of the morally upright and law-abiding, autonomous citizen, and their core arguments for ridding the sidewalk of these men are reasonable in their own right: namely, that these men break the law[7] (many have), block the sidewalk (some do), engage in untaxed, and therefore, unlawful, unsanctioned labor (all do), and detract from the security and beauty of the neighborhood by transmitting messages of urban decline simply through their presence (up for grabs). In contrast, the men who work the sidewalk defend their aims as necessary for survival in a city where employment and housing has remained transitory, if not completely out of reach.

Data on the gaps between wages and housing costs concretely demonstrate the inability of the Chicago housing or labor market to address the material inequity. For example, to afford a two-bedroom apartment at the Chicago-area median of $958 (in 2012), a person would need to work approximately forty hours a week at a wage of $18.42 an hour. Or, to put it another way, someone making the Illinois minimum wage of $8.25 an hour, would need to work eighty-seven hours per week to afford a two-bedroom at the median price (National 62). These calculations, which might seem dire enough, take for granted that a minimum-wage worker has the social capital in place to qualify for an apartment lease and hold over two full-time jobs. Yet, as Harvey argues, within the neoliberal framework, individual success is "interpreted in terms of entrepreneurial virtues or personal failings (such as not investing significantly enough in one's own human capital through education) rather than being attributed to any systemic property (such as the class exclusions attributed to capitalism)" (65–66). "Taking care of oneself" (financially), therefore, becomes a moral imperative through which citizens demonstrate civic responsibility. The comment, "Why don't you get a job!," made at the positive loitering event described at the start of this chapter, crystallizes this moral imperative. In light of this affordable housing data, the sentiment rings even more hollowly for the men who are struggling within the nexus of social services to find stable employment and housing.

Conclusion

A group called Queer to the Left, which played a substantial role in advocating affordable housing in Uptown between 2000–2006, authored a broadside in 2004 called *Gentrification Keywords*. The publication, inspired by Raymond Williams's *Keywords* project, insists that the battle over the meaning of words determines the boundaries of what is possible to say, do, think, and believe. "CAPS" is one of the gentrification keywords, and is defined as follows:

> *Initially a plan in Chicago to place community and public safety concerns in direct dialogue with beat patrol officers. In gentrifying neighborhoods, the process was quickly taken over by new homeowners who have moved into the neighborhood as part of its gentrification. In such an environment, the current CAPS system has become a place where such residents can complain about suspicious people, alleged drug dealing, sex workers, riffraff, and other things that affect their quality of life . . . CAPS is a leading governmental tool of gentrification. (Queer to the Left)*

By increasing interaction between the police and the community, CAPS, and its positive loitering initiatives, offer strategies that are more responsive to citizens' needs, which might result in safer and more aesthetically beautiful streets, but can also, as Queer to the Left suggests, become a way of legitimizing exclusionary practices that pathologize the men working the sidewalk while masking the systemic inequalities that contribute to their economic disenfranchisement.

The positive loitering campaign in Uptown, moreover, consolidates the power of affluent residents and the police through such regulatory practices while making recourse to the rhetoric of democracy—a move that reveals the deep ambivalence within the liberal democratic project. Brown argues that neoliberal discourse is so powerful precisely because it weds a rhetoric of democracy to free market ideology. Neoliberalism, she contends, "wraps itself in the mantle of 'liberty' and 'democracy,'" while rejecting the value of equality inherent in the liberal democratic project ("American" 701). "Equality," Brown insists, is "not a value to be found anywhere in the . . . neoliberal universe"; rather, the "political rationality of neoliberalism is expressly about winners and losers based on entrepreneurial skill" (701). Brown's criticism relies on defining "equality" as economic equality and on the belief that liberal democratic governments should strive toward such equality, institutionalizing corrections to systemic inequality through social welfare programs, and so on. However, in sharp contrast to Brown's formulation of equality, classical liberals who inform neoliberal theory (Friedman, Hayek, Epstein, for example) understand "equality," as Friedman argues, as an equitably distributed "absence of coercion of a man by his fellow man" and from the state (15). Equality, in this sense, is secured by a minimally coercive state that enforces uniform protections of individuals from the coercion of other citizens; that encourages the conditions under which the free market can flourish and individuals can compete in the marketplace; and that establishes the necessary statutes for strong property rights—all of which are seen as a prerequisite for ensuring political freedoms (Friedman, Epstein).

Three interrelated things occur within this neoliberal logic. First, by intertwining market and political freedoms, neoliberal logics lend moral force to arguments that promote free market ideology on the grounds that the free market is foundational to other political freedoms and rights. Thus, the logic goes, increased regulations of markets are undesirable because they can lead to the erosion of individual liberty. Second, social welfare programs are seen as obstacles—if not direct threats—to individual liberties because these programs increase centralized state power (opening a slippery slope toward despotism). Third, welfare recipients are stigmatized not only as drains on the public coffer, but also as irresponsible in their failure to be productive and autonomous contributors to the economic (and, therefore, to the general social) welfare of their communities.

If the neoliberal democratic subject is an active citizen, engaged in and responsible for the transformation of his or her own economic and social position, then, in order to avoid such stigmatization, the disenfranchised subject must be plugged into state-sanctioned, self-directed, industrious activities aimed to achieve economic independence and productivity (Cruikshank). Thus, the retooling of welfare policies increasingly facilitates economic entrepreneurial and self-sufficiency programs that seek to support individuals through this transformative process. Within Uptown, for example, "social entrepreneurial" nonprofits, such as Café Too and The Enterprising Kitchen,[8] are generally accepted by some of the positive loiterers as preferred alternatives to traditional social welfare programs that provide costly services to individuals without bringing about their economic independence. Social entrepreneurial organizations, which operate on market models to generate capital for a social purpose, provide wage-employment and job training to participants who become "active" producers of profitable consumer goods and services (rather than passive recipients dependent on the public dole).

Hazel, a representative from Café Too, met with me in 2010 to discuss their social entrepreneurial business, a nonprofit/restaurant in Uptown that provides job training, employment, and support to homeless individuals, who, in turn, help run the restaurant. In the following exchange, she confirmed the community receptiveness to the focus of social entrepreneurialism on enabling active and economically productive citizens:

> Candice: I know there is a general perception that Uptown is saturated by social service agencies. How does Café Too fit into the broader politics of Uptown? What is the community relationship like?
> Hazel: One, the community sees us providing something that was needed. Another restaurant. There was a hole in the market for brunch spots here. And, for dinner, we have a prix fixe, so we serve a niche in the area. And, two, people come in and say, "oh, those people in the kitchen are trying to better themselves." And a lot of the conflicts that have taken place in this neighborhood over the years have been about the homeless services, and I think there's a small contingency of people who believe that providing homeless services perpetuates homelessness. And, obviously, those of us who work in the field do not believe that. We think we are only mediating homelessness. I think that people in the community see us as a non-profit that is doing something for the community. This is a non-profit that is really trying to ask people to actively do something for themselves, to better themselves. They are not just perpetuating a life on the streets.
> Candice: How do these impressions manifest? Do people come to you and say this?
> Hazel: People have come to us and said, "we think you are one of the good ones."[. . .]. There had been a non-profit organization in our building that had had a lot of conflicts with the neighbors and had not pro-

vided the best example of human services in some people's opinion, and so people were unhappy that another non-profit was coming in when they felt that "oh, we just got rid of one." [. . .] I think because people see us providing something for the community like a restaurant, they see people trying to better themselves. They think, "Oh, that person in the kitchen is getting training so they can get a job," and I think it counters some of the impressions that people have that everyone who is homeless just wants to get a check so they can use. However, a lot of people want to get out of homelessness. It isn't a desire to stay homeless.

Brown argues that neoliberalism not only "normatively constructs and interpellates individuals as entrepreneurial actors in every sphere of life," but "also carries responsibility for the self to new heights" ("Neo-liberalism" ¶ 15) and "constructs prudent subjects through policies that organize such prudence" (¶ 16). The preoccupation with "prudence" seems to ring true in the community support of social entrepreneurialism that Hazel describes above and is certainly a core driver in Uptown's positive loitering initiative—evident in the actions of private citizens who are encouraged by CAPS (and each other) to fix their own "broken windows" and present in the most nuanced activities of the laborers who grow increasingly concerned with how many square inches their bodies occupy and convinced that failing to put a potato chip bag into the trashcan is reprehensible behavior.

Several scholars have attributed the popularity of broken windows, in part, to its compatibility with neoliberalism (Cattelino; Herbert). Herbert and Brown contend, for example, that broken windows helps "legitimate broader neoliberal policies" that regulate urban spaces while obscuring a "consideration of dynamics deeply critical to urban criminality: uneven development; racial segregation; and the social production of fear" (757). The exclusionary effects of local practices bolstered by broken windows logic, they contend, "help entrench racialized social divisions despite their racially neutral language" (771). In fact, it is the "seeming racial neutrality" of broken windows theory that accounts for its widespread popularity because it frames "territorial exclusions as natural and even healthy behaviors of communities," thus, helping to "legitimate spatial boundary construction that may well be motivated by racial antipathy" (771). Herbert and Brown importantly highlight the general public transition from formal and overt racisms toward more informal and insidious forms of racial discrimination indicative of neoliberalism and the so-called U.S. postracial era, in which racism can operate under racially neutral discourse or within rhetorics of empowerment.

Although I think Herbert and Brown's insights help explain some of the undercurrents of Uptown politics, I worry that their focus on racism risks obscuring the systemic economic conditions underscoring the tensions in Uptown—although there is no doubt that racial and class inequity map onto each quite starkly in Chicago. While much could be said about how structures of racial discrimination played a systemic role in producing the circumstances that brought Melvin and Lester to the streets, that greatly limit their opportunities, and that shape how people perceive and engage them, I would be uneasy about a quick dismissal of positive loitering as a racist practice. Such a characterization seems too simple, just as the denigration of the street laborers as morally depraved presences akin to broken windows does. Most positive loiterers who have protested here, along with the beat officers who work on their behalf, have earnest intentions to make Uptown safer in the presence of real crime. In fact, it has been one of my goals here to postpone (or rather, unhinge) the commonplace impulse to name and blame and tell morality tales, whether explicit or implicit, such that we might get at a better sense of the work that democratic rhetoric does in constituting everyday sensibilities, logics, and actions.

That said, I am also concerned that the moral force of positive loitering as a pursuit of citizens working for a better collective life along this strip of sidewalk (and more generally in their neighborhood) works to remove from public view the deeper problems in our society that create the conditions under which people seek underground or alternative employment to begin with. When positive loitering is seen as the will of the people *and* when it is coupled with a broader neoliberal ideology that obscures the market's inability to provide for all and that individualizes poverty as strictly personal failure, it becomes harder to see (and make) public arguments that connect the undesirable social consequences that we experience in our neighborhoods to larger systemic causes of poverty. Throughout my time observing CAPS meetings, I never heard a substantial discussion about the systemic quality of social problems associated with the informal street market, nor what creative solutions might be invented to address them beyond simply keeping the bodies of the unwanted moving or out of sight. While none of this is surprising in a gentrifying neighborhood, I have attempted to identify throughout this chapter *how* neoliberal and democratic rhetoric merges in local civic actions, latch onto affective and emotional structures that circulate in social space, and reinforce (and are reinforced by) the built environment in ways that tacitly enact and justify the restructuring of class (and race) inequities.

In a final turn, I would like to return briefly to the idea that language has the power to shape realities by creating readymade blueprints that influence the range of things that are possible to think, say, do, and believe. Neoliberalism, as a powerful ideology, is one such blueprint that proliferates a vocabulary and set of ideas that work into policy and everyday life in myriad ways. It has not been my goal here to indict individual stakeholders who have complicated relationships to arguments about free markets, community policing strategies, and any number of things, but rather to map the core logics of neoliberalism that work to shape practices, beliefs, and bodily habits and that manifest in everyday rhetorical performances in ways that are both productive and pernicious. That neoliberal practices can be productive, community-building efforts that create public goods; invigorate social relationships and commitments; and lever creative capacities is critically important. The ambivalence of civic participation—and the democratic project itself—is precisely that it offers the primary avenue through which some citizens act to shore up and justify uneven restructuring of the neoliberal state—as well as through which others might critique and seek to change it.

5
Democratic Affects and Public Formations

> Ordinary affects are public feelings that begin and end in broad circulation, but they're also the stuff that seemingly intimate lives are made of. They give circuits and flows the forms of a life. They can be experienced as a pleasure and a shock, as an empty pause or a dragging undertow, as a sensibility that snaps into place or a profound disorientation. They can be funny, perturbing, or traumatic. Rooted not in fixed conditions of possibility but in the actual lines of potential that a something coming together calls to mind and sets in motion, they can be seen as both the pressure points of events or the banalities suffered and the trajectories that forces take if they go unchecked.
>
> Kathleen Stewart, Ordinary Affects

In response to a very direct question like, "What is your position on building more affordable housing in Uptown?," it was not uncommon for an informant to launch into a story about seeing someone defecate in the alley, about their public encounters with smelly things (overturned trashcans, sour alcohol bottles, unwashed bodies), or about some other seemingly unrelated graphic, visceral, fearful, or emotionally jarring bodily encounter. Frankly, I had no idea what to do with these tales at the time or how they related in any way to the study of rhetoric. I scribbled in my notebook: *How do we understand the relationship between these private bodily experiences and this growing collective movement against subsidized housing?* I filed such stories away for quite some time and eventually coded them under "affect." While I realized that, on some level, people were equating affordable housing to the intensification of these negative bodily experiences, I wasn't sure how to account for the raw emotional forces driving this equation, especially since the links between affordable housing development and people's visceral fear, while intuitively clear to me, were semi-conscious, tacit, and rooted in hunch and perception more than in verifiable facts. What I did know is that these kinds of gut experiences were powerful, and that collectively powerful things always seem to have something to do with rhetoric. Such entwinements of affective forces and rhetorical structures are what anthropologist Kathleen Stewart calls "ordinary affects," which she defines as "public feelings," "intensities," and "a tangle of potential connections" (2–4). Their power lies not in symbolic meaning per se, but in the "intensities they build and in what thoughts and feelings they make possible"; ordinary affects are an "animate circuit that conducts force and maps connections, routes, and disjunctures" (3). As social forces, ordinary affects shape, influence, and direct—albeit in a dynamic and often semi-conscious manner.

The "affect" code eventually broadened to include a variety of strong visceral, emotional, and sensual bodily affects that people reported to me and reported most often, given my interview focus, in the context of questions about affordable housing (disgust from smelling urine at a bus stop, deep anxiety when observing a drug interaction, anger at seeing a man passed out in public, horror at seeing a prostitute turning a trick, pinpricks of fear when harassed in the street). Initially, I thought that I might be asking the wrong questions to invite these tales, but eventually concluded that people's strong affective responses to such everyday encounters were enmeshed with their arguments on housing in ways that were in excess of rational political reasoning, yet nevertheless persuasive. But, how do you begin to get at the significance of affect in everyday acts of persuasion, let alone capture the fleeting, not entirely conscious, yet profoundly influential force of the body and its responses? Brian Massumi's insight that the "skin is faster than the word" (25), as well as his distinction between emotions (as situated social responses) and affects (as primal, bodily, animal, pre-cognitive, pre-signifying responses) (*Parables*) should leave us asking whether it even makes sense to think of affective responses as rhetorical. I proceed here with the idea that even if bodily responses are not rhetorical in and of themselves, they become so when similar responses are repeatedly triggered in many individuals over time and when such responses are continually linked to broader ideologies and salient rhetorical formations, for one reason or another.

Before proceeding, let me turn to several brief field examples that illuminate this yoking of everyday sensual encounters to broader public attitudes about affordable housing in circulation:

> One. *Upon asking about the reasons for opposing affordable housing in 2005, an informant answered with a seemingly unrelated story about a time that he took a walk in Uptown, turned a corner and saw two people having sex. His presumption that this was a prostitute and her John is likely to be true.* "I saw this woman pushed up against the fence and they were having sex. Right there, for everyone to see." *His description became more graphic. I asked what this had to do with the proposed new housing. He replied,* "We already have enough problems. That would add to them."

Two. *In 2006, an Uptown homeowner saw a disheveled African American man defecate in her alley. It was getting dark. She believed the man was homeless, and, given the large homeless population in Uptown and myriad social service agencies in place to support it, this is also likely to be true. She explained to me in an interview, visibly shaken by the memory, that she was extremely scared for her safety. It was a "to the core" kind of fear. She recounted this story as part of a long response to a question about her opposition to subsidized affordable housing, though she did not explicitly draw connections between homelessness, the housing, race, and her fears.*

Three. *In 2006, at a community meeting to discuss the proposed affordable housing at Wilson Yard, a woman stood up during the Q & A and passionately denounced the housing idea. With anger and fear audible in her voice, she said that she wants to "go jogging in her neighborhood" without feeling like she is "going to be raped." Others joined by recounting fearful or visceral encounters on the street, among other things, as anecdotal evidence of why affordable housing should not be constructed. Many stories were not directly related to the matter of building 178 units of new subsided housing units for seniors and families making incomes less than the area medium.*

Clearly, there is no direct link between a subsidized housing resident and a homeless man, let alone a rapist or prostitute. Although much could be said about how structures of racism operate in such slippages (and, by the way, how there are real social disorders in Uptown), these lines of inquiry are not the strict focus of this analysis. My concern here is with how these deeply private, emotional, and visceral experiences collectivize and help galvanize consequential publics. As such, I am particularly interested in extending our understanding of topoi to consider, too, the production of emotional commonplaces that forge links between private affects and public tendencies.

In theorizing emotional commonplaces, Sara Ahmed's poignant scholarship on emotion is apt. Ahmed, who refers to the forging of language, bodily sensation, and emotion as a process of "sticking"—examines how rhetorical structures "get stuck together, and how sticking is dependent on past histories of association" (13). The "work of emotion," she argues, "involves the 'sticking' of signs to bodies" (13). Similarly, Jennifer Trainor ethnographically captures the "emotional frames" through which, in her case, "racist discourses become persuasive" (25), and Phaedra Pezzullo emphasizes the relationship between emotion and place, arguing, "The materiality of a place promises the opportunity to shape perceptions, bodies, and lives" through the *"structure of feeling* or one's *affective* experience" (9). Collectively, these scholars foreground a conversation on public persuasion through the concern of how private emotions contribute to the creation of collective valences.

As I have already hinted, documenting how bodily sensations and emotion get "stuck" to language—as well as how they become shared public emotional commonplaces—is not an easy task, in part, because the researcher's own intuitions and bodily knowledge factor into her capacity to perceive such linkages. While intuition contains a powerful knack for comprehending such things, its reliance on subjective, tacit knowledge, and sensation does not set the mind at ease for those seeking objective, verifiable facts. Yet such is the project of this chapter. (And, such a concern, I should add, is not new to the rhetorical tradition in which much has been said about how to help rhetors discover and capitalize on affective and emotional forces as powerful persuasive engines.)

To help ground this rather abstract investigation, I turn to a specific field example of a man who captured on video a "gang riot" that occurred outside his home. The video was posted on a popular local blog called Uptown Update, and eventually circulated to mainstream Chicago and national news outlets, instigating hundreds of comments, dozens of blogs posts, and hundreds of thousands of viewings. Uptown Update served in this case and many others, as a crucial means for Uptowners to document their deeply private and bodily experiences, hitch them to ongoing neighborhood politics, and catalyze a public movement against violence. Because this turn to blogs and cyberpublics might seem quite abrupt, let me explain my reasoning. Critical to this conversation is the capacity for this blog (or any blog) not only to help facilitate the collectivization of individuals' emotions into emotional commonplaces, but also to provide a tangible location for studying such sticking. Uptown Update is one site where people's visceral, bodily experiences have amassed and been recorded, politicized, and made visible through the rhetorical work of individuals who link their everyday observations and sensual experiences to broader ideologies, arguments, and narratives already circulating in Uptown and beyond.

Building on Bruno Latour's network theory, Jeff Rice argues that we might "read the anonymous blogger as enacting a network" and that the "posts and comments that seem to . . . be either scandalous or banal are, in fact, part of a larger discourse of connections and associations" ("Networked" 303). Online media enable participation predicated on the production of connections, on the generation of response (304), and on people, as Rice puts it, "retrieving and assembling a variety of informational experiences" to form "informational relationships" (310). In the crafting of "informational relationships," I also am interested in the affective, embodied qualities of those relationships. The creation of salient public rhetorics also involves the constructing and tethering of emotional frames to powerful rhetorical structures to produce relationships among information, feelings, bodies, language, and people.

This chapter, then, puzzles over how rhetoric is implicated in the processes through which private emotional, sensual, bodily experiences accumulate into—or, at least, contribute to— something we might call collective forces, networks of association, assemblages, rhetorical ecologies, or, more simply, publics. By engaging rhetorical field methods that "plac[e] our bodies within the rhetorical situation we analyze," researchers can become responsive and responsible to such "affective, sensory, and aesthetic dimensions of rhetoric" (Middleton, Senda-Cook, and Endres 393–94). Focusing on the affective qualities of persuasion leads to different kinds of questions about how publics form and how public rhetoric works than are commonly raised in Habermasian public sphere derivatives or other publics theories that foreground rational discursive exchange: How do individuals' everyday sensory experiences or visceral encounters on the street accumulate into collective political forces or contribute to the amassment of publics? How might our conceptualizations of the public better account for these emotive, affective, sensual dimensions of rhetorical force that exist in excess of rational deliberation, or that remain tacit, semi-conscious, and unspoken?

This conversation, therefore, turns to the question of how emotions and bodily sensations become public and, in so becoming, rhetorical. And, once rhetorical, how they become resources for invention and for better understanding the textures of democratic persuasions. With the focus on new media's role in public formation and on how rhetorical structures become tethered to emotional commonplaces in mind, I turn to the field in the following sections to take a closer look at the "gang riot" and its circulation as a video representation. I keep the scare quotes around "gang riot" throughout to honor the controversial use of the term to describe this event. This visual topos, coupled with discourse of an out-of-control "gang riot," added credence and weight to the anti-crime movement; however, there are Uptowners who question the term. As Paul, an anti-poverty and affordable housing activist stated in an interview:

> *The supposed Uptown riot was mostly a bunch of young kids fighting in the street. Ok, yes, nobody wants that, but it was hardly a riot. I had some organizer friends on the South and West sides who laughed at that story because, compared to the violence that takes place there, this was nothing. Cake.*

Whether the events that I will describe were "cake" is beside the point. The street fight is not a novel occurrence in Uptown, nor are daily encounters with myriad other crimes, yet the circulation of this fight as a visual icon catalyzed a public movement that caught the attention of the national media. How and why did this fight become rhetorically salient? While the work of publics and public rhetoric is dynamic and overdetermined, the next two sections examine the critical role that the Uptown Update blog played in providing a genre of civic participation that enabled individuals to document, amass, and translate affective encounters into publicly held emotional commonplaces; stitch these emotional commonplaces to broader neighborhood concerns about and discourses on crime; and organize a public movement against violence.

Public Formation and the Neighborhood Blog

In 2010, I spoke with Greg, a reader of Uptown Update and Chicago blogger, about his thoughts on the power of blogs to produce change in the offline world. He cited the Uptown "gang riot" coverage as exemplary of a blog's capacity to galvanize offline publics and to circulate news beyond contexts of origin:

> *Candice: I am wondering what you think a blog can do?*
> *Greg: It can. . . . well. . . . get the story out as strategically as possible. You know, as widely and strategically as possible. [. . .]*
> *Candice: Do you have an example from Uptown? [. . .]*
> *Greg: Well, the example from Uptown is the man who stood at his window and videotaped a riot and put it up on his Vimeo, and had it carried by Uptown Update. And all of a sudden, it's on the evening news. It's in the newspaper. It's all over media in Chicago.*
> *Candice: So, was it [wider media attention], then, a result from blogging?*
> *Greg: Yeah. It was, it was. . . . the direct result of [. . .] a radicalized citizen picking up a video camera, and saying, "what the hell is going on outside my window"? [. . .] He contacted Uptown Update and Uptown Update mirrored it and suddenly all these other people got to see it and the media follows Uptown Update [. . .] and suddenly it's on the evening news and that came directly from blog-o-sphere.*

As Greg noted, part Uptown Update's power lies in its capacity to "get the story out" as "widely and strategically as possible," which, as you will read, was a remarkable success in this case. But, while I am interested in the capacities of blogs to circulate news stories, it is not the primary aspect of rhetorical power that I am after. Beyond the blog's function as a mechanism of circulation, I am interested in its capacity to facilitate public formation through the sticking of affective structures to ideological and rhetorical structures. In the field example to follow, the "gang riot" video, as a visual topos of a neighborhood gone bad, served as a magnet for what Kenneth Burke calls "Identification," as Uptown residents began discursively linking everyday fearful experiences in the neighborhood to the fight.

"Identification" takes place when people come to recognize kindred spirits in the shared ideas, ideologies, interests, and beliefs of others. Identification, according to Burke, is central to persuasion: "You persuade a man only insofar as you can talk his language by speech, gesture, tonality, order, image, attitude, idea, identifying your ways with his" (*Rhetoric* 55). Because Burke sees division as a fundamental aspect of human sociality, he posits Identification as an attempt to overcome division that might lead to an "acting-together," whereby people who remain separate might yet identify with one another through "common sensations, concepts, images, ideas, attitudes that make them *consubstantial*" (21). Part of what I am suggesting is that the circulation of the "gang riot" video provided a mechanism for bridging division through a process of Identification whereby people could locate their individual fears and seemingly idiosyncratic affective experiences in the context of kindred others and within broader narratives and attitudes about crime, housing, race, aesthetics, and so on. For example, within the Uptown Update comment fields, a contributor who goes by ChicagoCitizen[1] noted the way the "gang riot" video's significance exceeded the capturing of literal events by publicly standing in for the many things people have privately "been witness" to: "I think what galvanized the community about this video was the fact that it caught on camera many of the things. . . . we've all been witness too [sic.]. It wasn't this individual video per se, but the fact that this stuff happens in Uptown."[2] The power of this video lies partly in its capacity to represent, as ChicagoCitizen put it, all the "stuff happen[ing] in Uptown," but it is the genre of the blog comment field that provided the space for people to craft public narratives from their myriad private experiences. The personal anecdotes increasingly became well-worn rhetorical intensities that took on a force independent of the literal events of the "riot." The accumulating weightiness of the links between personal affects and public narratives about crime eventually catalyzed a call for public action.

As far as neighborhood blogs go, Uptown Update is a prominent and popular producer of local news, covering everything from school events to restaurant openings and from community garden initiatives to crime incidents. The blog uses a simple template supported by Blogger that enables chronological postings, hot topics, and event links that run along the right-hand side of the blog, and a moderated comment field box following each posting where people can publish responses anonymously. The blog averages six thousand to eight thousand unique hits per day, according to a cofounder, and more salient postings, such as the "gang riot," might receive twenty thousand hits per day. Like many such blogs, the line between reported hearsay (which is commonly hyperbolic) and journalistic coverage (that aims for "objective" reporting) can become quite blurry and varies story to story. Most entries, however, tend to be rather brief, factual summaries, announcements of events, or descriptions of everyday occurrences. Nearly everyone I spoke with had visited the blog and most had strong opinions that typically fell into the categories, as two informants voiced it, of either "this blog is so useful to me" or "this blog is a shit rag," and, not surprisingly, the attitudes tended to map onto residents' political affiliations and attitudes about public projects and gentrification. A founding member of Uptown Update described the blog as having a "middle of the road political slant." Based on the content of postings, and, in particular, on the conversations in comment fields, the core audience of supportive readers tend to be homeowners, business owners, and long-term renters concerned with safety and crime; those who promote commercial development; and people likely to be exhausted by the radical left-leaning politics of former alderman Shiller who dismissed the "reasonable concerns of regular middle class people," as one homeowner put it.

Uptown Update was founded in 2001 by a renter in his twenties. At the time I interviewed him via e-mail in 2010,[3] he was an Uptown homeowner and worked with three other bloggers, two men in their fifties and another in his thirties. The bloggers choose to remain rigorously anonymous in public.[4] One informant, who enthusiastically supports Uptown Update, classified the blog's power and identity in terms of its anonymity: Uptown Update is "kind of like the Wizard of Oz. They pull the curtain back and it's just. . . . everywhere, nowhere. Some people know who runs the blog, but I don't. But, everybody knows this blog. Everybody reads it." The co-founder shared the following about why he started the blog:

> *I was really disappointed in the amount of coverage our neighborhood received from our Chicago media. I knew there was a lot going on in Uptown and most of the time it seemed like the media turned a blind eye. [. . .] Our mission would be to inform Uptown about what is going on in the neighborhood, share the history of Uptown, and encourage resi-*

dents to make a difference in their community. [. . .] I think Uptown Update is so popular because it fills an information void that exists in the 46th Ward.

Uptown Update, as you will read below, played a central role in providing a space where residents worked to fill this "information void."

On September 17, 2009, my husband called me upstairs. Pointing to his computer, he asked, "Is this *your* Uptown, Candice?" *Huffington Post* was cued up to a story titled, "Uptown Residents Demand Action After Gang Violence Erupts in Streets." I peeked over his shoulder and read the first two sentences: "Uptown residents are furious over escalating neighborhood violence and what they perceive as their alderman's ambivalence to it. Fed up after Ald. Helen Shiller (46th) was not responsive to their concerns about recent shootings and a full-street gang fight, a group of her constituents organized a protest . . . to demand swift action" (Taliaferro). "Yes, Joel," I replied, "That's the one." The actual event that catalyzed this citizen protest took place on August 12, 2009, in the heart of Uptown, on the corner of Leland and Sheridan, at around 9 P.M. At this time and place, a couple dozen African American men brawled, threw bottles and rocks, shouted, cursed loudly, blocked traffic, and taunted one another. Police cars arrived within minutes. The young men scattered. There was no evidence of drawn guns, and, besides the flying projectiles, almost no physical contact among the men.

An Uptown condo owner witnessed this fight from his home. He filmed the fight with his own real-time narrations of the event, titled the video "What a Riot," posted it on Vimeo on August 13, 2009, and forwarded the link and story to Uptown Update. The initial posting on August 13, titled "Street Fighting at Sheridan and Leland," generated over twenty thousand page views in a day and, within two weeks, spawned thirty related Uptown Update posts that yielded 860 comments, totaling over eighty thousand words (e.g., book length).[5] The video quickly gained traction—and was picked up by local and national news. Within days, the story was covered by CBS, ABC, WBEZ (Chicago's NPR), CNN, Fox, and *Huffington Post*, among others.[6]

Once it hit the national media, the video immediately went viral, circulating independent of the circumstances of its origin. The video was uploaded and linked everywhere from YouTube to LiveLeak. The initial event of men fighting in a street one evening generated hundreds more responses within the comment fields of such venues, and inspired all manner of a-contextual linking between the visual topos of the "gang riot" and circulating rhetorics that had nothing to do with Uptown. For example, on August 17, 2009, the New Nation News Reporters Newsroom, a white nationalist message board,

17. Screen shot of initial "gang riot." Uptown Update post.

linked to Fox News's coverage with the title "Gangs of Gorillas Stage Riot in Chicago," eliciting racist comments like: "Niggers are such criminal primates, they should not even be allowed to live among our race at all!!!" Or, a year after the "riot," on June 24, 2010, a YouTube posting titled, "An Almost lol Chicago gang fight caught on tape," received nearly 160,000 views, and inspired comments like: "Deleted scene from Planet of the Apes?" "Is this change Obama?" The video, in its various channels of circulation, had been viewed over 400,000 times as of 2012.

While there is no direct connection between these latter egregious racist comments and the people in Uptown who witnessed and responded to the actual events of the video, one bears witness to the power of the visual topos to connect a network of ideas, people, and sentiments. The video representation of the street fight initiated a chain of consequential linking that stitched together general associations of urban street fights, ideological stuff, situated everyday events, and individuals' strong emotions (fear, anger), eventually emerging in rhetorical situations far removed from the place of origination. Studying the social in terms of network means, as Latour has argued, tracing the "very peculiar movement of re-association and reassembling" (*Reassembling* 7). Jeffrey Grabill has helpfully called the "study of the rhetorical" the "study of particular kinds of associations that are actively created and re-created. The rhetorical is and creates particular kinds of connections" (195). The visual topos of the "gang riot" became a political actor as people put the topos to work both at the local level (where Uptown residents can be seen linking other crimes, fears, and concerns to it, and using it as leverage to collectively fight crime) as well as in national contexts far removed from Uptown (where people used the topos to forward racist ideologies, political diatribes against President Obama, and anti-police sentiments). "Actors," for Latour, are not only humans, but also any "thing," human or nonhuman, with agentic capacity within the network (chairs, the Internet, genres, institutions, bodies, spaces). And, while Latour is referring to material agencies, I would add rhetorical and affective structures to the list of "things" that contain "agentive capacity." Grabill theorizes the public in terms of a network, interpreting Latour's "thing" or "assemblage" as the "issue—the matter of concern—that brings people together and also the assembly itself" (199).

An attunement to how "things" assemble into a public movement against crime, in our case, exponentially expands the purview of what counts of a "matter of concern." But, how do we draw a boundary around what matters when what matters includes everything from shit in the alley to housing policy in the 1960s and from a crashing real estate market to the genre of blog comment fields? When rhetorical intensities have agentive forces that include the overdetermined and dynamic enmeshments of ideology, affect, public discourse, spaces, contested histories, and so on, how do you decide what to include in your study? As Fleckenstein et al. write of ecological/networked methodology, "What is constant is not a *kind* of context" that might constitute the whole of the assemblage, but "the *act* of circumscribing a boundary and the permeability of that boundary" (399). In seeking to comprehend both the rhetorical forces in circulation within a social space and the processes/things that enable this circulation, one can never capture the totality of every "thing" that matters. Here, we reach the methodological paradox of ecological and networked perspectives that seek to abandon container models of the rhetorical situation yet must ultimately redraw boundaries. But, even given this paradox, adopting such a perspective still shifts the focus of one's rhetorical study from symbolic content to capturing the circulation, accretion, dynamism, affects, and consequences of rhetoric.

Within five days of the street fight, several Uptown Update blog entries rallied for a "peaceful protest" against violence, targeted to Alderman Shiller, whom they saw as negligent in her response to crime. The bulk of the organizing efforts occurred within Uptown Update's comment fields. A high-profile press conference held at Truman College about Chicago's bid for the 2016 Olympics, hosted by Shiller, provided the opportunity for ample media coverage. Writing under various monikers within the comment fields, people organized the protest. Here is just a sample of general calls for a protest:

I think a group of 300–400 people marching would get the media's attention. I suggest Tuesday.

I no longer feel safe and hate having to leave my apartment for fear of what is on the streets. i dont [sic.] know what we should and can do, but something is better than listening to this every night. ideas?? anyone?

Tomorrow night. 6PM . . . Polite. Civil. No chants or songs, just signs and people. Public safety is more important than any legacy project. [. . .] The media will be there. Tell your friends and neighbors to be there.[7]

Let's converse with her [Alderman Shiller] in a civil and open minded manner. Should she decay into the political speak, politely ask her to go back on point. [. . .] If you are with the group, you are part of the group and your actions reflect upon all of us. Short version: behave yourselves. [. . .] Be civil. Be respectful. [. . .] We already own the moral high ground. Don't give it up by being a d**k.[8]

On August 17, 2009, at 6:00PM, over one hundred protesters arrived at the press conference with signs that read: "Every Uptown Resident Deserves To Live In A Safe Neighborhood." "We Will Not Let Violent Crime Take Over Our Community." "Whose Child is Next Helen?" "No More Shooting, No More Death on Uptown's Streets." "We Care About the Safety of ALL Uptowners." After the formal presentation, several protestors and members of the media asked the alderman to discuss her lack of public responsiveness to the "gang riot" and other recent crimes in the neighborhood. This discourse dissolved into rabble-rousing questions, which prompted Shiller to exit the event abruptly through the backdoor to avoid the large crowd waiting out front. The protestors chased after her for several blocks, shaking their signs with local media camera crews in tow, and yelling things like: "Talk to the People, Helen." "I am not voting for you again. You are awful." "We are trying to do our part, why aren't you?" "Don't run away like a coward!" The angry chanting eventually devolved into a group cadence, complete with handclapping and fists shaking at the heavens: "Run, Helen, Run! Run, Helen, Run! Run, Helen, Run! Run, Helen, Run! Run, Helen, Run! Run, Helen, Run!"[9]

While the protest was modest in size, the story was picked up by local and national media, most commonly framed as concerned citizens banded together to "demand action" from an apathetic government official against gang violence and crime. After the protest, hundreds of responses were written in Uptown Update's comment fields, many of them calling for more citizen participation. "UptownVoice" called for another protest to keep the momentum going:

> *Right [at] this moment, with the local and (growing) national spotlight on our local community, as well as the absolute disregard for it from our "Alderman" Shiller, we have the energy and the momentum to force the change WE WANT and WE NEED. Why should we accept a publicly-elected official who uses our hard-earned tax dollars for wasteful projects? Who ignores our concerns? Who turns a blind eye to the eye-sores in our neighborhood? And who refuses to stop our violence? We should not. Let's petition. Let's [. . .] protest. Let's use our voice for a better Uptown. One that reflects the diversity, the beauty, and the energy at its core.*[10]

"UptownHero" issued another call for action:

> *NOW WHAT? [. . .] we have had an unusual confluence of events that worked to our advantage in highlighting both our frustration with crime and the lack of support from Shiller. In the past week, we had the posting of the video which finally allowed us to show proof that we were not a bunch of Yuppie complainers followed shortly by the Olympic meeting. [. . .] there are no more scheduled events for which we can rally [. . .] We got our press, we did our marches, etc. and now we have no particular 'rallying' point. [. . .] so I ask the Uptown Community. . . . what are you going to do personally to make sure that all of the gains we made the past week are not lost, that they do not fade away?*[11]

Beyond this function as a space for rally calls, the comment field served as a place for people to make visible their everyday street encounters and to transform their personal anecdotes into public narratives about the state of crime. For example, in the aftermath of the release of the "gang riot" video, two Uptown Update participants attributed the success of their protest to the blog as a site that helps previously isolated individuals share information:

> GreenCitizen: *I am sure there are lots of blogs out there. But I believe the reason UU [Uptown Update] is so popular is that before it existed, there was a black hole in the 46th where no information could escape the ward office. Now with so many people meeting in one place to share info and piece things together, we all are much better informed.*[12]

> AnotherUptownMan: *"Thanks to Uptown Update for bringing Uptown's most valuable assets, it's [sic.] residents, a way to share information and connect! The unfortunate incident of the gang activity at Leland and Sheridan probably would have never made the news if a resident did not film it, and if Uptown Update weren't there to feature it!"*[13]

Uptown Update played a key role of informing, "piec[ing] things together," and helping people to feel empowered in numbers. The blog offers a site where people—"Uptown's most valuable assets"—can capture disturbing everyday happenings and circulate the story to a wide, captive audience. For example, "Mr. Uptown" encourages this practice of citizen reporting:

> *What if local residents just start documenting the things they see around Uptown [. . .]? Do you have a cell phone? Does it have a camera? You can snap a photo of this and send it to another cell phone that can upload it to Google and start building a digital map. See some drug use. Take a photo and sms it. Include the location. Plot it on a Google Map.*[14]

From this example, we see that Uptown Update helped make visible and amass the experiences of individuals who previously felt isolated and fearful, and through this amassment, people can be seen "identifying" with one another. This sense of publicly depends, in part, on the collective crafting of "informational relationships," as Jeff Rice puts it, and, as I am arguing, the tethering of those relationships to emotional commonplaces. My opening examples of such linking showed how fearful, visceral, emotionally powerful encounters in the street become hinged to broader narratives playing out in the neighborhood about affordable housing.

Within Uptown Update's comment fields, Uptown residents can be observed linking the "gang riot" to the proposed Wilson Yard affordable housing development in the following four examples:

Example One. Just wait until Wilson Yard is full of gangbangers. . . . if you think it is bad now . . .

Example Two. Wonder why it happened in that location? Take a look at the number of low income, very low income, and extremely low income housing projects there are in a one block radius. Do you think a single one of those involved in the riot went home to unsubsidized housing?

Example Three: Schiller [sic] can't point her finger at the police when she alone is responsible for ensuring an extremely high concentration of gang activity via massive low-income relocation to the ward. And the Wilson Yard debacle will only exacerbate the situation to levels that should give all of us great pause. I can only hope that this may be the start of what makes the city reconsider who will live in Schiller's [sic.] Wilson Yard fortress.

Example Four. Watch the news [coverage] tonight [of the fight] [. . .] Hopefully, they will tie this story into Wilson Yard.[15]

That it might seem natural for people to link their fear of urban anarchy to their opposition of affordable housing is testament to the power of technology to transform the visceral fear of rampant gang violence into a kind of metaphoric force that stands in for all criminal or derelict behavior in Uptown—a force made available to people sitting at home who are also able to easily express and aggregate that fear into a public will.

Paul, the affordable housing activist mentioned above, responded to such comments that link general fear from street encounters, the "gang riot," and affordable housing:

For me, so much of what that blog is doing is based in amplifying fears that people have. Fear of black people. Fear of poor people. Fear of violence. Fear of drug culture. Some of those fears are legitimate. There are drug transactions and there is real violence, but a bunch of people taking photos and videos from behind their closed curtains is not having a positive impact on what is happening. It is not addressing what is happening on the streets in a real way. Not that any person can do that. But the way the stories are portrayed and the so called discussions that emerge in the comments people make are mostly fear based and lopsided [. . .] So,

> the people they see on the streets [. . .] or the housing that attract more of "those" people [. . .] become the easy and unified target of all that fear and frustration that keeps them from living out their vision of what the neighborhood could be. [. . .].

While Paul called out the way that affordable housing could "become the easy and unified target" of fear or an obstacle to people's "vision of what the neighborhood could be," some blog commenters responding to the video and its aftermath on the Uptown Update called for the end to such linkages. In particular, they felt that drawing those connections would discredit their arguments about crime and perpetuate the "rich versus poor" stereotypes that are often dismissively attached to their cause. As "NotParadise" phrased it: "mentioning [sic.] punks and affordable housing in the same narrative is alderman Shiller pointing to an 'unintended' correlation in a defensive manner."[16] Within the comment fields, "UptownExerciser" posts a letter draft to Shiller about her "tardy" public response to the "gang riot." In it, the writer denounced the linking of affordable housing to crime for similar reasons:

> You [Shiller] state that the media coverage and protest was the strategy of your opposition to attack you by saying that affordable housing equates to crime. First of all, [. . .] I am not your opposition and I am not trying to polarize the community. I am a concerned resident of your ward who would like to see an improvement in safety in his neighborhood. [. . .] Secondly, I honestly do not believe all affordable housing equates to crime. I believe that [low income] housing can benefit everyone in the community with proper planning and cost-effective funding from the multiple government sources (local, state and federal).[17]

While my fieldwork and countless examples in public discourse can attest to the fact that many opponents did link affordable housing and crime, many do not. Regardless, affordable housing proponents have, as UptownExerciser's letter accuses, used this strategy of pitting the rich against the poor to cast their opposition into a morally abject position. The "gang riot" video proved to be such a powerful rally point for some protestors of crime because it helped disrupt the "rich vs. poor" narrative that is often imbricated onto Uptown politics, offering a new avenue for rhetorical invention that generated universal arguments situated in public safety that are hard for anyone to dismiss. The image of men on the verge of erupting into serious violence on a street where children play is universally alarming. When one's complaints about safety are not voiced as an opposition to affordable housing and its occupants but to violent crimes that "no thinking person" wants, as "Insanity" argues below, the argument has more legs:

> *I think the most insulting thing, year after year, is the 46th Ward Office's stance, is that it is Rich versus Poor. That hollow argument is slowly crashing down. Finally. The issue is gang activity, and a neighborhood that [. . .] lacks any attractive or inspiring hope for new business development. [. . .] No thinking person who lives in Uptown, doesn't appreciate the diversity up here. No thinking person who lives here, wants crime. And NO thinking person up here, wants to be placed in a bogus fish bowl of the "Rich versus the downtrodden." Because as we've seen in the last 2 weeks. . . . that argument doesn't hold any water.*[18]

Not only do the comment fields provide a space where people connect and transform their private encounters into matters of public concern, but they also become a site at which people can craft arguments against crime within and against the discourses (e.g., "rich versus poor") that tend to constrict arguments over contested public space in Uptown.

Greg, the blogger mentioned earlier, described his perception of the persuasive strategies used by the Uptown Update bloggers regarding the "gang riot" video and subsequent public organizing against crime. His explanation cut to the core of how persuasion works (within the blog genre) through affective registers:

> *Greg: They [the Uptown Update bloggers] were really astute. You know they were really strategic. [. . .] They were very Machiavellian about it. [. . .] They know very well. . . . that, if you want to bring somebody on board you've got to meet them in terms of their values and their feelings, so everything that they write is so emotionally charged. So, it's like, a slot machine. Like pulling the lever of some sort of civic, you know, sidewalk issue in Uptown that, that makes the people in Uptown upset or afraid and boom. [. . .] It's effective. It's not necessarily fair. It's more like Alinsky's rules. But it works.*
> *Candice: How do you think it works?*
> *Greg: Nobody, nobody's going to agree with you. Or they might agree with you but nobody is going to get behind you if they just, if you're just in mental agreement. [. . .] That's fine, but I'm not going to go fight a war for you. But if you somehow linked to like, homeland and country and apple pie and if threatened then yeah maybe I would. And they do that linkage.*

Candice: You mean linking to these dreams or fantasies or whatever that people have or desires?
Greg: About what a neighborhood should be. About what Uptown should be. And what it isn't. You know they, they paint that, that contrast you know and it's not just a contrast of facts and figures: it's an emotional one, too.

While, as Greg suggested, the linking of emotional frames (whether situated in collective fears or dreams of "apple pie") can be done explicitly, such connections are often quite implicit, even if patterned and even when specious.

The brief field example of circulating rhetoric shared above offers a glimpse into what Jenny Edbauer Rice calls the ecological and viral nature of how rhetoric works in the world. Responding to Sara Ahmed's work, Rice articulates Ahmed's aim as one that "theorizes how language affectively articulates a social imaginary within which political discourse is lodged" ("The New" 205). We become "so strongly invested in (or glued to) certain structures of belief that they seem like part of our own identity. To borrow Kenneth Burke's well-worn term, we are 'identified' with structures of ideology through an affective investment" (205). In the section that follows, I take a close look at the how the comment field genre facilitated the processes of affective investment in Uptown politics.

Genres of Civic Participation and Democratic Affects

Blog comment fields are commonly perceived as virtual spaces where rational debate dissolves into hyperbolic, pernicious, and ineffectual rhetorics that remain far afield from romanticized visions of democracy-in-action. While we might begrudge the tendency toward the breakdown of social decorum in these spaces or the circulation of racist/sexist/classist/etc. discourses, the comment field is a genre of civic participation that provides a space where individuals can do the rhetorical work of linking everyday occurrences, private encounters, and affective experiences to broader narratives already in circulation. We might say that all genres are genres of participation in the sense that genres emerge through social exigencies as tools that help us interact, work, and shape the world, but I am using this specific term "genres of civic participation" to refer to genres that explicitly help us carry out civic action and engage in democratic debate.

Genre predecessors to the blog comment fields include the letter to the editor and comment drop boxes. Other contemporary examples of genres of participation include different forms of social media, such as Facebook and online community forums/message boards. Even if they fail to facilitate opinion formation through interaction, debate and dialogue, information sharing, the crafting of public rhetorics, and public formation, these genres of civic participation are designed to do so. Such genres are defined more than anything by their capacity to help people do democracy (or at any rate to engage others civilly through discursive exchanges), their potential for politicizing people, and their possibility for organizing collective action. While not all comment fields share these features, Uptown Update's are exemplary of what I mean by genre of civic participation in that they have helped individuals form public opinion, carry out civic action, engage in democratic debate, and do collective public work. But, in saying this, I stress that I do not see democratic practice as something transcendently virtuous or intrinsically emancipatory—though I do believe that online media offer tools that can be used to participate in democracies and forward "democratic" aims. As I have argued throughout this book, democracy does not come equipped with a clear moral compass; people with radically different political agendas can adhere their varied social projects to the language and practices of democracy.

The Uptown Update blog (and its comment fields, in particular) provides an example of democracy-in-action, according to the co-founder of the blog, because the blog offers a space where people can voice and challenge opinions: "I think that people sharing their political opinions facilitates democracy. We often have commenters engage in long discussions about policies or events in Uptown. It is good to see both sides, you don't have to agree, but you can accept that there are differing views." The comment fields in Uptown Update were the site where several protests, including the one described above, were organized in a short amount of time, largely by people who did not know each other, yet shared concerns about crime. Uptown Update's comment function is a simple open textbox that allows users to publish comments anonymously. The comment field provided a place where individuals' fears were transformed from a series of unconnected, private stories into weighty public sentiments that inspired offline protests that drew local and national media attention. Speaking of social media more generally, Robert Glenn Howard argues that participatory media offers "inexpensive and seemingly endless avenues for everyday people to participate in public discourse" (256). The accessibility to the means of participation (at least to those with Internet connections) makes such media tantalizingly democratic.

The comment field feature of a blog certainly offers an abundantly accessible and cheap tool for participating in a public discussion and for circulating one's argument that "half the time," as blogger Greg put it, is "shit." Yet, as he discusses below, the comment fields are also "fertile ground" with the power to "generate community":

> Candice: So, I wanted to ask you what value you see in comment fields?
> Greg: Half the time they're shit.
> Candice: There's something to them, no?
> Greg: I think it's a fertile ground. [. . .] I think their value is that sometimes the debate that can arise under a blog post in the comment thread can be. . . . it can really give you a sense of what the debate is that is going on, what public opinion is, what the opinions of specific people are. [. . .] It's giving people a sense that they're not alone. You know, that they're not alone. That they're not the only people thinking certain things. It can help generate community around issues.
> Candice: How so?
> Greg: Because people are connecting. It's a discussion. It's not just one-off comments. I'm commenting on this blog post. It starts with that and then it becomes people discussing the things that they've said above and above and above and now you've got a conversation going, launched by whatever the topic of the blog post was.

Within Greg's comments, we see a refrain that was common in my interviews that the blog helps people feel less alone, and builds dialogue around important shared issues.

For all of the scholars who seek the democratic potentiality of participatory media, there are a litany of those who would be quick to point out shortcomings, including a lack of readers, a dearth of consequences in the "real world," diminished capacity for drawing attention to one's message in the wash of voices, and access issues. Jodi Dean, moreover, warns us that the increased participation of new media genres does not equate to better democracy. Dean argues that everyone is a participant via content creation, but no one is a reader and nothing amounts to anything that "might actually affect change": "Interacting with others online feels good. It feels like action, like one is doing something, like one is making a difference. One might argue on a blog for hours on end, failing to convince another person of a single point, and *still* feel efficacious and involved. But this feeling is unconnected from any larger collective practice that might actually affect change" (Dean 40). While I certainly concede that Dean's point is salient in many instances, in Uptown, I'm focused precisely on the moments when online participation, in fact, does affect change. But contrary to Dean's point that "one might argue on a blog for hours on end" without changing anyone's mind, I would like to add that there is another way to think about how a blog (and its comment fields) affect change. As I have said throughout this chapter, the accumulating weight of these comments can have impact without changing minds through processes of Identification. The value, as a point of public formation, lies somewhere other than in "convinc[ing] another person of a single point." The comment fields figure citizenship as participation (which would include writing and posting comments, linking and sharing information, and reading), rather than through explicit persuasion of others through rational debate.

While not all blogs "affect change," my case study demonstrates the way that blog comment fields can transform private affects into public emotions. The capacity of the genre to serve as a repository of scattered, embodied, and affective experiences is key. Once they are "voiced" in public, these private observations and sensations take on a collective force through the linking of somatic experience to broader narratives about crime, urban development, and so on. People who previously felt alone in their private fearful encounters suddenly begin feeling like they are part of something greater than themselves. They recognize themselves in the stories of others. There are others who are afraid and who want to do something about it. Suddenly, strangers are talking to each other in the comment fields, realizing there is a growing group of like-minded individuals. They begin assigning blame for the things producing their fears, and identifying common enemies and obstacles. They devise plans of action. Dean's fear that we are only producers of content and not readers is challenged by these people who begin to organize to affect change in the world within the genre she discounts as ineffectual.

In the following, informants explain that while "minds" are not necessarily changed through participation with Uptown Update, private fears are aggregated into public sentiments that gather force. In 2010, a longtime Uptown homeowner, Michelle, discussed her experiences with neighborhood politics and the role of Uptown Update in her activism. She extended this role to include the blog's critical capacity to not only "share information," but also help her and others galvanize a public. While Michelle said that she didn't "know if it [Uptown Update] changes core beliefs," she thought it "definitely changes surface beliefs." The example she provided had to do with the increasing sense of fear that she had after reading about crime on the blog, which made her change the way she walked through the neighborhood. As she put it: "I am now literally afraid to walk North of Montrose and I never used to be afraid to walk anywhere. [. . .] And I am sure that all of that was happening before Uptown Update and I would walk up there but I didn't know what was happening." In other words, the blog served as an aggregate of fear that, in fact, did change behavior. Her reading of Uptown Update prompted her to join an effort to reduce criminal activity, oppose affordable housing construction at Wilson Yard, and make Uptown, as she put it, a "happier, more beautiful, and safer place to live for everyone."

Michelle had the following to say about the Internet's role in organizing on behalf of public safety and against Wilson Yard's affordable housing, among other projects:

> *The Internet has brought that element [small town hall] back of personal connections and investment in politics. I think it is just fabulous. I think it's just a boon for democracy because that is how we not only understand one another, but we share information and I have learned so much from people sharing their information. You begin to understand why people are concerned because they tell their personal stories. People see things happening on the street or around the neighborhood and all these personal stories add up to more than one person's story. [. . .] It used to feel like I was alone, experiencing these terrible things in the neighborhood. The website [Uptown Update] makes me feel like I am part of something bigger. I see other people seeing what I see, thinking what I think. The blog gave us a place to organize and it felt like we were getting something accomplished.*

As indicated by Michelle, Uptown Update plays a key role in creating a public through the sharing of information and personal stories that eventually "add up to more than one person's story." Where Michelle, who has lived in Uptown over two decades, "used to feel like [she] was alone, experiencing these terrible things in the neighborhood," the blog's capacity to transform one's private encounters into public issues of concern (over time and through the slow accumulation of like-minded people who share similar experiences) helped her understand her individual experiences as "part of something bigger." The blog comments play an important role in creating connections among disparate experiences and, from those connections, a sense of publicity. Individuals in Uptown observe something on the street and post it. Others see their own experiences and fears reflected in those they read and momentum is gained without changing opinions. What is accomplished is the production of exigency.

Below, Edward, an affordable housing advocate, shared a similar observation of how Uptown Update has the effect of aggregating people's individual experiences, fears, and opinions into weighty public forces without necessarily changing their minds:

> Candice: Some people in Uptown have called the Uptown Update an example of civic participation, citizen action, and even democracy. What do you think?
> Edward: Eh. It is. . . . well. . . . yeah, it's dialog, I guess. But, I don't think anybody's opinion changes or anything. I think people take from it what they already pre-thought in their head.
> Candice: You don't think people's minds are changed?
> Edward: No. No, no, no. I think they come in with a view and they take out from those things whatever their view is. And they will read somebody's comments and say yes, that's exactly what I'm thinking or feeling, so, therefore, I'm now right because somebody else thinks that or feels that. So changing minds is not the important thing.
> Candice: What is the important thing, then?
> Edward: So, people have their observations and thoughts by themselves and then they come to Uptown Update and read articles or comments where other people say similar things and it kind of legitimizes their feeling that this whole neighborhood is overrun by gangs or whatever the fear is. So, as I was saying, the fears might be warranted or not, but they become something bigger because of the blog. So, nothing changes the minds but I guess something does change because people share the fears and those fears gain momentum and shape.

Edward's description of how the blog aggregates people's fears into "something bigger" that can "gain momentum and shape" speaks to my point about how "structures of feelings," as Edbauer Rice puts it, that circulate in a social space can latch onto not only raw visceral experiences, but also to other rhetorics, in this case, about housing.

Personal affects are pulled into pre-existing narratives or social tendencies that incline us toward translating individual responses into dynamic but structured emotional commonplaces that stitch affect, public emotions, and broader rhetorical structures. Drawing on Steven Shaviro's work on networks, Edbauer Rice argues, "To say that we are connected is another way of saying that we are never outside the networked interconnection of forces, energies, rhetorics, moods, and experiences. In other words, our practical consciousness is never outside the prior and ongoing structures of feelings that shape the social field" ("Unframing" 10). Kathleen Stewart talks about these affective structures as not exactly working through semantic meanings, but through "pick[ing] up density and texture as they move through bodies, dreams, dramas, and social worldings of all kinds," such that their "significance lies in the intensities they build and in what thoughts and feelings they make possible" (3). Edward's comment helps us understand how the nuanced, personal, emotional responses of individuals cohere into publics that increasingly see their concerns as social, political, collective, and actionable.

Conclusion

As a way of wrapping up, I want to return to my original point of departure, which had to do with how to account for the affective, sensual, emotional aspects of my fieldwork as rhetorical objects of study. Even as such things are difficult to capture—as they are experienced extra-linguistically—it is even harder to factor in how affective structures become embedded in the economies of rhetorical force. What was clear is that somatic stories came up in fieldwork all the time as persuasive forces that were linked to the topics at hand. With the simple example below, you see how the perception of one's neighborhood is experienced, in part, as bodily sensations. And, while we may dismiss these sensations as irrelevant in the workings of everyday democracy, I want to suggest that as primitive, intimate forces of persuasion, we are wise not to deny their power in politics. In 2007, I asked Jake about his impression of Uptown:

> Candice: Tell me about your perceptions of Uptown. What kind of a place is this? How would you describe it to others?
> Jake: Well, it can be very funky.
> Candice: What do you mean by this?
> Jake: Well, I don't know if you knew this, but the Wilson stop [one of Uptown's stops on Chicago's public train system] was just voted the smelliest in the city.
> Candice: Smelliest? I didn't know about that, but yeah. . . . it's pretty bad. It does almost always smell like a toilet bowl. That's true.
> Jake: Yes, it is so gross here sometimes. It could be a great neighborhood, though. I mean, we have the lake and diverse people and cool restaurants. Interesting history. Blah blah blah. But sometimes it is just so disgusting.

As with the affective stories that opened this chapter, I had completely dismissed the relevance of this treatise on the smelly eL station at the time of the interview. In trying to understand people's arguments about affordable housing and neighborhood politics, I would have initially disregarded this passage as an unrelated, idiosyncratic exchange. But, let us consider that it might be telling that this individual chose to begin with this detail. It was smell (and other bodily affects) that began this chapter, after all, along with the concern about how such things become rhetorical when they become enmeshed with broader public sentiment.

Smell, in particular, in addition to its links to memory, is one of those deeply intimate bodily sensations that really impress upon a person, gets under their skin. When you smell something, you are literally ingesting particles of the thing you smell, taking that thing into your own body. There is no way to avoid having a sensual, embodied relationship to a smell. It momentarily becomes part of you. The point here is not to be gross, but to think about the power of such an experience when it becomes something more than just a guy experiencing a rancid smell some afternoon while waiting for the train. In fact, what I have been trying to get at is the way that smell, and other bodily experiences, become public, and, in becoming public, become part of the valences that make up rhetorical force. Smells (or name that bodily sensation) are directly tied to our everyday sense of wellbeing, and as smells (or other fearful, sensual, bodily things) become public affective structures that are attributed to causes and constructed as obstacles to the good life, a growing sense of publicness emerges around not only shared interests but also shared bodily/affective/emotional experiences.

Beyond my interest in the general crafting of emotional commonplaces that link personal affect and public rhetorics, I have been compelled by the genre of the blog comment field for its potential to aggregate (and capture) affective valences and link them to broader rhetorics. As Uptown residents themselves have stated, the power of this aggregation does not lie in changing people's minds but in intensifying the sense of an emerging public to which they belong and to which they imagine might have force in the offline world. Where effective arguments in public contexts (such as in town hall meetings) typically require citizens to formally bracket their private interests or translate them in term of public issues, such as public safety, the comment field inverses this "requirement" as a public space where private, visceral, emotional, and embodied anecdotes are an accepted and expected commonplace. The accumulation of similar stories becomes public sentiment over time as individuals translate them into universal justice claims. Working with Oskar Negt and Alexander Kluge's public sphere theories, Jamie Daniel argues that the formal requirement of disinterestedness in the public sphere works to the advantage of the powerful who are better positioned to translate their private interests into universal public ones than are those who are systemically disenfranchised (in Daniel's case, Chicago public housing residents), whose claims in the public sphere are often presented in the form of personal anecdotes, which are easier to dismiss as matters of private concern.

In this case study, the comment field is one place where affluent citizens can be seen expressing their private, embodied experiences and then doing the rhetorical work of translating them into public matters. In Uptown, the affluent homeowners who might oppose affordable housing and support commercial development gain more traction by rooting their justice clams in terms of universal public appeals (such as public safety), than in private claims (such as the protection of property investments or desires for aesthetic upgrades). As several residents stated earlier, such subjective arguments merely lock citizens concerned about public safety into a rhetoric of "rich vs. poor," which casts them into a morally suspect role, rather than into morally righteous citizens concerned with the general welfare of all. By studying the ways that affective structures become tethered to the ideological and the rhetorical, we might not only better understand, study, and make visible these processes, but also discover agency in finding ways to unhinge and reconfigure these linkages.

Conclusion

From the Thicket

> So it is that the study of ordinary democracy is at war with itself. On the one hand, the intention is to identify and celebrate the distinctive character of democracy as it is actually practiced to sustain and improve local communities. On the other hand, by focusing on the raw particularity of what ordinary citizens actually say in a local setting, the inquiry shreds the illusions that sustain democracy as a political ideal. One studies ordinary democracy out of a love of democracy, and one finds little that is loveable. The choice seems to be between delusion and cynicism.
>
> Robert Hariman, "Amateur Hour"

If I began my study of democracy with a desire to capture how democracy works in everyday life and might work better, I left with a more pragmatic understanding that the ideals that drive democratic rhetoric and practice unravel in the messiness of ordinary life, yet remain poignant resources in the day-to-day wrangles of people collectively working to "sustain and improve local communities," as Robert Hariman suggests above. The move toward a situated pragmatism seems the only response to this choice "between delusion and cynicism"—a pragmatism that refuses defeat from the impossibility of realizing the idealized ends of political projects, yet remains inspired by them. During my fieldwork, I heard much talk about democracy and observed the practices of democracy materialize before my eyes. This book has attempted to provide a map of and methods for studying the places of invention within democracy.

Throughout this book, I have spoken at length about publics (what they are, what they do, how we theorize and study them, the conditions under which they form and operate) both within the abstractions of democratic theory and within the ethnographic analysis of publics-in-action. Uptown politics, I have found, provided an exemplary field site for thinking about democracy and the passions that erupt at the heart of its key metaphor—the so-called rational public sphere. Of the many competing publics in Uptown that I have encountered, however, "Fight Club," a caricaturized vision of Chantal Mouffe's space of agonism, offers perhaps the best metaphor to describe what can transpire from the stalemate at democracy's core.

On the evening of September 1, 2005, over one hundred curious Uptown residents, community organizers, activists, and industrial designers paid five dollars to participate in an event called Fight Club, hosted and created by designer Paul Hatch.[1] Fight Club is conceived as a raw and gritty debate between two verbal adversaries on controversial issues, such as sex and violence, human cloning, and the legalization of marijuana. *New York Times* writer Bradford McKee described the event as a "rhetorical mosh pit." Fight Club has only two rules: "First Rule of Fight Club: There can only be one winner. Second Rule of Fight Club: There are no debate rules" ("Fight Club"). Uptowners came to see a "fight" about gentrification between Randall Lehner of the Uptown Neighborhood Council and Rian Wanstreet of the Organization of the NorthEast. Though over-simplified, these organizations represented the commercial and urban development interests associated with Uptown's middle-class home and business owners and the interest of halting gentrification on behalf of the neighborhood's poor, respectively. Fight Club's website describes the event as follows: "What is Fight Club? . . . The two Fighters take extreme for and against stances to debate the merits and pitfalls of the chosen debate topic. The surrounding audience or 'crowd' openly add their spice to the debate from all sides" ("Fight Club").

As people filed up a flight of stairs to the second floor of a rehabbed warehouse on the West Side of Chicago, they entered a large industrial loft space with high ceilings, exposed air ducts, and hardwood floors. In the center of the room, there was a large circle outlined in white chalk on the floor: this was the fighting ring. Lehner and Wanstreet debated from within the ring, while the onlookers heckled, questioned, and listened to a deliberation over salient matters of public concern that was intended to persuade them. Hatch had to break up the fight several times because the debate kept devolving into a loud, volatile, and incomprehensible shouting match, complete with shaking fists, groans, boos, and shrieking women. This Fight Club on gentrification was an eruption of passion. Hatch admitted: this one "got a little out of control."

According to those I interviewed who attended the event, the cacophony of opinions in the room rendered all arguments incoherent. While Wanstreet was declared the "winning fighter," participants viewed the decision as meaningless because everyone was just rehashing the same old affordable housing arguments—mostly about the Wilson Yard development. No one was listening. Informants I spoke with called it a "zoo," a "debacle," and something akin to "Mad Max Thunderdome." One of the core purposes of Fight Club, Hatch explained, is to provide the "common man" with access to multiple perspectives about important public issues. Hatch describes the goals of Fight Club as democratic:

> Paul Hatch: It [the gentrification debate] was definitely an ethical debate. But, it isn't pushing ethics that this is about. [. . .] [T]he point is to stress the opening up of questions instead of giving an answer. The goal is not at the end of Fight Club that we all come to an agreement that gentrification is good or bad. [. . .] We are looking at two sides of the same coin. Fight Club usually comes to an end before there is consensus with the audience. It had more to do with the atmosphere and gut feelings about who fought the most and the best. [. . .] The actual idea of Fight Club is to bring these heady, rational debates—that tend to be over intellectualized—down to the common man, down to regular people, to street level.
> Candice: To what end?
> Paul: To what end? So that regular people also have access to awareness and these segments of ongoing scandals, ethical questions and change. [. . .] I think Fight Club has a format that offers a democratization, a street level, version of something. [. . .]
> Candice: So, what makes this democratic for you?
> Paul: People have the chance as audience members to participate and engage. It is spontaneous. The audience does get irate sometimes. [. . .] These are the visceral reactions that make up Fight Club. It is important. Whether they are shouting Bullshit, or whether they shout "no, that's not true, just this morning. . . . I . . . ." In a democracy, the voice of the small person is just as important as the person in the spotlight, and [. . .] in this community because you have an organization on the microphone saying this is what we want for Uptown, and then, there is a barrage of people's opinion saying "that is absolute crap, and that's not what I want. What I want is this, this, or this." There is a leveling out, and it is not the people with the microphone that have the last say [. . .]. The forum is fitting for this type of change, and it gives more folks the chance to say what they think. What people say is not always correct. People say things like, "You know it is just my opinion, but . . ." You know people are giving personal, anecdotal evidence to backup their opinions.

Hatch described a version of the public that includes passions and bodies in space, as well as reasoned arguments and rhetorical flair. It is a public that includes gut feelings and personal anecdotes. It is a public geared toward the "opening up of questions instead of giving an answer" and that is not fixated on reaching consensus. This is a public driven just as much (if not more) by "what I want" as by what is best for all. If debating about what is in the interest of the public good is a goal in such a model, there is no consensus about the constitution of that good. As one participant aptly said, the "truck had driven far away from consensus" on whether gentrification was desirable or not in Uptown.

Fight Club is an extreme and melodramatic performance of democratic publics-in-action, perhaps, but in the end, it might be a more accurate description of how things can actually work out when competing publics come to head. At this event, public debate became a dramatization of debate, serving more as entertainment and spectacle than as productive argument making or collective problem solving across difference. Here, argument became rarefied into either/or binaries (gentrification: pro or con, you decide), and the radically complex and nuanced histories, ideologies, and stakes that underscore urban development in Uptown and the stances Uptown citizens hold were flattened out. The shouting match that ensued had everyone laughing, angry, or withdrawn by the end—and, in the end, it was debate, if not democracy itself, that was the thing heckled and dismissed as ineffectual and bankrupt.

It seems to me that this is, in part, what Habermas meant when he argued that there is an "anarchistic core" at the heart of the liberal democratic public sphere—revealing of ideological stalemates perpetually on the verge of erupting into violence (or becoming mere spectacle). The Fight Club might both enact and test the limits of Karen Tracy's "reasonable hostility," a communication norm that "recognizes competing values" and that creates public space for "strongly worded argument" and "[p]assionate, angry talk," both of which can "be a sign that ordinary democracy is working" (203). At any rate, Fight Club is instructive in its demonstration that spaces for citizens to debate and evidence of democratic participation do not necessarily yield social goods that we might associate with "democracy." As Jacques Rancière has argued, and which Habermas's comment implies, "There is only one good democracy, the one that represses the catastrophe of democratic civilization" (4). Or, to soften the blow, we might say, the good democratic government is the one that directs our actions toward democratic designs, as Barbara Cruickshank argues. Yet, as I have argued throughout, "democracy" cannot, finally, determine the shape of those designs: those can only be fleetingly determined, as Kenneth Burke says, in the rhetorical wrangle of the human barnyard.

The quest for perfected publics or forms of democracy might not be the best way to pursue democratic designs. Many have said the same, only to direct us away from the abstract, idealized conceptions of democracy that float above "real life" toward the promises of a grounded, situated, contextualized, everyday model of democracy as a way of mitigating the paradoxes of liberal democracy. While I am intellectually indebted and tethered to such studies of everyday publics, my fieldwork reveals that the paradoxes of democracy are exhibited in the most grounded everyday publics—publics that are radically diverse, educated, morally driven, and engaged in projects passionately taken to be in interest of the public good. In looking for the promises of democracy in miniature form, then, I mostly found miniature versions of problems that play out on larger scales.

The pursuit of a moral high ground, the search for perfected forms of democracy, and the presumption that democracy—if only practiced better or more purely—would yield more virtuous social flowers, distracts us not only from this as an impossibility, but also, more importantly, from understanding the power of democratic rhetoric and ideals within the very contextual circumstances of our everyday lives. And, as I've said, learning how to discover, examine, and use democracy to garner rhetorical force—to locate the places of invention within democracy, in other words—can only be done from within particular spaces and times. The goal, then, is not to perfect democracy as a teleological end point, but to think about how the power it does afford is, or could be, deployed here but not there, now but not then, by us but not them, and so on. This orientation toward a pragmatic immanent democratic public practice does not sit comfortably, as I have also said, because all manner of projects can be supported in the name of democracy and through the deployment of its rhetorical forces. This latter line of thought, however, merely evokes the double-edged nature of the public work of rhetoric that has been theorized since the Classical era. Rhetoric is powerful stuff that can generate force for those we think moral and those we think not and, in most cases, we will never be able to draw a clear line that separates the two. As ancient rhetoricians attested, the best way to arm a citizenry against the pernicious use of rhetoric is to train people in the art of rhetoric, which, too, is a sentiment that lurks behind my impulse to look at and map rhetoric forces at work in the world.

One of the primary rhetorical moves in democratic rhetoric (beyond evoking democratic commonplaces like equality, liberty, justice, and so on) is the linking of one's position to an assumed moral high ground and/or vision of social justice, and, inversely, denigrating opposing positions as immoral or as obstacles to social justice. This general rhetorical impulse, in turn, tends to be motored by the commonplace of "the marginal" (we are the unheard, voiceless, wronged, systemically disenfranchised) or through "rights discourse" (our rights have *either* been impinged, revoked, and/or ignored *or* we should have the right to additional consideration, resources, and/or power). Such alignment with the morally righteous or marginal (whether tacitly or not, earnestly or not, warranted or not) is, of course, a powerful rhetorical tactic in democracies. The problem, as my informants and I have demonstrated throughout this book, is that such tactics are not reserved for particular political positions, but can and are deployed across material conditions and the ideological spectrum. If the moral core of democracy is flexible, and its language and practices capable of supporting incommensurable projects, does this ambivalence point to the bankruptcy of democracy? So long as democracy helps generate rhetorical force and capacities to work together for collective public goods, I'm not willing to answer yes to that question—though the prospect of democracy's innate goodness seems doubtful. The virtue, where discovered, is not to be found in transcendent ideals, but in the purely immanent labors and manifestations of democracy.

And thus, the inclination toward reading rhetoric-in-action differently is calling for an engagement with a form of reading that postpones critical judgment (at least for awhile) in order to look at the relationship between the many arguments circulating within social and material terrains *and* the terrains that shape and are shaped by those arguments—to look, in other words, at the fullest sense of the places of persuasion. This call for reading rhetoric deeply in places, as I have argued, is well suited for rhetorical ethnographic methods. Tracing the places of invention within democracy facilitates a mapping of arguments and strategies within the contexts of their use. When is it useful to speak of democracy in support of our goals? How can we think outside of the language and narratives of democracy? But because democratic rhetorics and tactics can be so easily turned on their head—even in earnest but ideologically incompatible projects—the question is from where might people discover rhetorical force (within democracies) that does not rely on democracy, or at any rate that does not necessitate (1) the creation of moral scapegoats as the primary strategy; (2) the insistence of moral superiority and noncomplicity in systemic injustice; (3) the tendency to rely on abstract, ambiguous ideas that float above the complexities of everyday life, excluding the material and affect dimensions of persuasion; or (4) the capitulation of hope for collective public action in the face of—fill in the blank here—neoliberalism, global capitalism, widespread economic and environmental collapse, political corruption, the pervasive corporatization of culture, and so forth.

In short, from where might ideological underpinnings emerge that can inform and inspire clear and persuasive oppositional political positions that attend to the ambivalence and radically immanent nature of democracy? What all of this suggests is that the question of how to get beyond the democratic paradoxes or how to perfect democracy can supplant the question of how to discover the available means of persuasion in *this* democracy here and now in the micro-level of everyday publics. In the end, I am doubtful that appealing to democracy—even if one aligns with its ideals—is always the best tactic for pursuing whatever it is we are perceiving as democratic aims (social equality, liberty, fairness, equal representation, justice, more livable lives with less pain and suffering for the most, etc.).

This desire to locate political agency in small actions that make a difference —rather than in wholesale revolution—is, of course, not a novel political response. Such a turn in contemporary politics, among other things, might signal an exhaustion with the modernist dialectical movement through history— inclined always toward a presumed transcendent telos wherein oppressive regimes are overthrown by progressive social revolution that create new forms of oppression that, in turn, inspire new cycles of revolution, drawing us closer to our teleological desires. If there is one thing that the field taught me about democracy, it is that this mythos of an historical progression toward an idealized telos is simply not how politics work—while there are historical moments that can erupt into wide-scale social change that is more just or beneficial for more of the population, I do not imagine such change as developmental progression toward a telos, but more as a stable-for-now social state that might just as easily backslide as improve in the future, and, moreover, as a state that is always contested and that always benefits people unevenly across the social landscape. Besides ordinary people must live out their lives within the ordinary places they inhabit as they wait for large-scale social revolution to occur or not.

Or perhaps, more of us are simply feeling that this turn to small, ordinary, situated political agencies—our little jab jabs enacted in kairotic openings (salient opportunities) for change that emerge in particular spaces and times—is the best available response to an increasingly vast, complex, and interconnected political and economic system of global capitalism within which we are networked, nested, entangled, emplaced, and complicit in ways we can know and ways we cannot, in ways we can control and ways we cannot. In either case, what I am saying is very simple in the end: even if there is need to contemplate long-term goals (telos) as doing so helps guide our practices and even if it remains critical to examine how systems and structures shape our everyday lives, the most promising political agency is perhaps to be found in the ordinary, idiosyncratic rhythms and exigencies of particular places and times. In some sense, this book has documented how "small" engagements within everyday publics create significant change—sometimes more tangible, like the outcome of affordable housing at Wilson Yard, and sometime indirect and felt, like the increasing capacities for action among Uptown's citizens who, through their engagement, learn dispositions and skills, build networks and tools, and galvanize arguments and evidence that enhance the places of invention within which they dwell, act, write, and speak, and from which they draw upon as resources for getting small things done in the immanence, the thicket, the textures, the places of everyday life.

In this sense, this ethnographic project might be summed up as an argument and blueprint for how ordinary people can act within larger structural and economic forces to create change and make a difference in the world. Such small actions could easily be laughed at or dismissed, perhaps, in the face of models of social revolution that call for wholesale and far-reaching change, but to me the small actions I witnessed in the field are profound, even heroic, responses to the impossibly complex and ungraspable, incomprehensible complexities inherent in the places we dwell. In company with these ideas, Thomas Rickert theorizes a thoroughly emplaced human agency as "both occasioned and conditioned by surrounding lands, communities, and forces" (15). Beyond and entangled with human agency, Rickert's and my concerns are with the material conditions; affective valences; ways of relating, thinking, speaking built into an environment; tools and processes; natural resources, constraints, and forces; and many other qualities, large and small, systemic and locally idiosyncratic, that constitute the world. Agency here points to something that is modest, infinitesimal, fleeting, but also grounded, concrete, tangible, felt, embodied, and tailored to the environs of the everyday. Here is an agency that is not earth shattering, perhaps, but no less profound. Both mundane and cosmic.

I am probably sounding either too romantic or mystical here, so let me pull on another thread of my argument, which stresses that all the small actions I witnessed in Uptown, and that we may witness and participate in within our various lives apart from this space, are not to be valorized as morally upright or somehow more just *because* of their proximity to ordinary life. The problems of adjudicating the content of democracy, justice, morality, and action on behalf of the public—and the impossibility of doing so without eliminating perspectives and voices from the table—travels all the way down to the smallest of public actions. Let me wrap up this section by drawing on three field examples of small actions, which all, perhaps fittingly, have to do with, as Voltaire's Candide would have it, "tending one's own garden." The metaphor of "tending your garden" has to do with imagining small private actions as also productive activities that respond to the local conditions in which we dwell.

> *Uptown Garden One:* Positive loiterer John wrote of addressing the U-Haul loitering on Broadway Street as something akin to "tending a garden." In addition to day laborers hanging out there, the sidewalk inhabitants have included drug dealers, prostitutes, harassers, and drunks. After years of working on the loitering with his neighbors and the police, John reported that things "had gotten better," but he told me that as soon as neighbors relax, the men start setting up camp, lining the sidewalk with chairs and coolers filled with alcohol. This strip, he said, is "like tending a garden [. . .]. Keep it nice and neat. But if you get distracted with something else, [. . .] the weeds come very quickly. There's no break. You have to continue to weed it to make it look good. . . . So the minute you stop putting pressure on them they're coming back." He expressed that it is exhausting, time consuming, and, at times, disheartening to keep up the activism on the streets because people have lives and kids and jobs. Social action is a commitment to showing up everyday you can to work on important collective problems together. Social change is a "long-term process" that "you have to stick with."

> *Uptown Garden Two:* Annabelle is a local and national affordable housing activist, and a long-term Uptown affordable housing resident. In reflecting on her experience organizing in the 1990s, she told me about traveling to D.C. to testify as a tenant representative at HUD hearings. She said she was often "the only black person in a room of white people," but that she "felt [. . .] on the side of right." Recounting her work with fellow tenants and Uptown's Organization of the NorthEast, she talked not only about her pride in their efforts at preserving affordable housing, but also about how hard that work was. Beaming, she said, "You know, amazing work can happen when people get together and make it happen," but "It's hard." Her activism with others saved some of the Uptown buildings, but in the process, she shared that "we just about burnt ourselves out. I got tired after the struggle and left it, felt safe, I was tired of it all. Just went back to living my life." In 2010, her HUD building was again in jeopardy and after time off, she was "right back in the fight." The process of fighting for social justice and for one's rights is "like a garden that needs tending. You've gotta keep tilling the earth. Works never done but you get tired. It takes a lot of work and education. Building relationship and trust."

Uptown Garden Three: In the summer of 2010, I worked at the Ginkgo Organic Gardens, nestled between two brownstones on Kenmore Street in Uptown. Ginkgo is a community garden founded in 1994 as a "response to local hunger." Seeing both a "surplus produce in urban gardens that ended up on the compost pile" and that area non-profits were "unable to afford fresh produce for the homeless and low-income people they serve," Ginkgo aims to "solve both problems" by providing nearly 1,500 pounds of produce each year to Uptown organizations (Ginkgo). On my first day, I found a regular gardener and said, "Hi, I'm here to garden!" He said, "Great, let me show you a few things that need to be done." So, every Saturday for eight weeks or so, I helped with things like turnip picking, beet washing, weeding, manure spreading, and flower picking. Each week, the produce was inventoried, bundled, and loaded onto two flatbed trollies attached to bikes. Each week volunteers bicycle-delivered the produce to a farmers market of sorts that is part of Heartland Alliance's Vital Bridges Program, which provides food to homeless and low-income individuals living with HIV/AIDS. For the farmers I chatted with, food politics was as important as creating a means of distributing organic food to the poor. The farmers were meticulous about producing organic food, as well as using heirloom seeds to sustain a pocket of biodiversity in response to mass farming practices. At least one farmer I interviewed saw their work at creating an alternative market and distribution circuit as a counter-response to the systemic inequalities and means of distribution of capitalism. This person felt that farmers markets are great in the sense that they help out the local farmers, but that the markets themselves are expensive and, generally, not for poor people.

But, what of these gardens? What dent do these small practices make? Perhaps, not much of one, if we demand large-scale systemic change as the only change that matters, but all of these collective public activities create a space for ongoing deeply situated and productive responses to the world. We might have much to say about the differing politics and commitments that underscore what it means to tend each garden, the way that each garden privileges one set of rights and public goods over others, or how some salient matters are glossed over in order to carry on with the tilling that seems most pressing to each gardener. These are small measures—what Hardt and Negri call the politics of immanence—or what I have referred to as actions that result from a deep attunement to the places of invention. These gardens, and the world's infinite others, the weight of a million small measures, are profoundly substantial, but no more pure, morally clear, or free of radical contest. Assessing and engaging in such small, collective public actions (and training others with the capacities to do so) within the very contexts of those actions seems one of the simplest but most important fruits that my field delivers to us.

Closing Thoughts

When I first set out to do this research, there was something exciting to me about the prospect of observing and participating in "democracy-in-action." I think I was blinded by something that wasn't there to begin with, looking for obstacles that thwarted democracy and hoping to get a better sense of how to do democracy better. But, the limits of democracy presented everywhere as the limits of deliberation; the limits of defining (let alone fighting for) ideals like equality, justice, and so forth; the fleeting nature of collaboration; the exhaustion of democratic terms and slipperiness of democratic rhetoric; and the sheer impossibility of acting from a space of "virginal innocence," as Ananya Roy puts it. The turn toward pragmatism for rhetoricians, given our preoccupation with the shaping force of symbols, typically means engaging in what Richard Rorty has called "redescription," which involves the invention of new vocabularies that help us reshape entrenched practices, discursively close the gap between ideals and material practices, and facilitate the "ability to think of people wildly different from ourselves as included in the range of 'us'" (192). Pierre Bourdieu similarly argues that to "change the world, one has to change the ways of world-making" (23). Rhetoric constitutes one of the "ways of world-making."

The stakes of thinking about the constitutive nature of rhetoric and language, as these theorists allude, centers on the following idea: the power to remake our everyday lives resides, in part, in our capacities to see how rhetoric structures our lives and, in seeing, to craft anew our rhetorics. Such power and such labors, as I have argued, rely on visibility—of seeing and keeping the sightlines open in our collective social imagination for rhetorical invention and timely action that takes into consideration the paradoxes of democracy and the recalcitrance of materiality in shaping persuasion. Ultimately, for me to conclude that "democracy is ambivalent" is radically unremarkable. So, let me suggest that the importance of this ambivalence might play out most significantly for the political left. Here Brian, a longtime Uptown housing activist who self-identifies as a "lefty," says the following about the rhetorical exhaustion and identity crisis of the left:

> Candice: You mentioned that the left has lost some of their energy. What do you think has happened to the political left in Uptown? It does seems

like these perspectives [which are not leftist ones] seen in Uptown Update, Fix Wilson Yard and so on have been more unified in their message and more effective in their activism recently.
Brian: Well, I don't know about that entirely. I think that the left is working on so many different issues and everyone is spread out. But some of the problem is that we are saying some things that are similar to the right, or whatever you want to call them, like we are being left out or that this is unjust or that those in power are turning a deaf ear or whatever. It feels like we can't get a clear message together because we are spread out so much and the strategy of saying those kinds of things that used to unify us, like we don't have a voice or we are fighting for the people or whatever, just doesn't cut it anymore because they say it, too, even though they mean something different.

Brian's discussion of the lack of unifying vision and the capaciousness of a democratic rhetoric that is no longer closely tethered to leftist politics demonstrates the one-two punch that leftists face. These comments are profound in that they point to the question of what rhetorical strategies are available to the "left," given my argument that democracy is ambivalent to its very core and given a complex conception of power and its complicity in all political projects.

As I have suggested throughout, the use of democratic rhetoric as a morally righteous sword of the left proved to be ineffectual in Uptown, not just because people with opposing projects were engaged in the same arguments and strategies, but also because the arguments justifying "rights to" affordable housing for the poor, for example, were typically made by vilifying, simplifying, and denying how the complexities of capitalism shaped the experiences of middle-class residents who were underwater in mortgages or business owners who were on the brink, and how these lived realities were influencing the positions of their opponents.

Brian certainly leaves us with the important question of what a leftist politics—that emerges from these ideas of complicity and the radical ambivalence of democracy—might look like. If we can say, as Brian seems to, that the left presents as rhetorically bankrupt when drawing on democratic appeals to moral high grounds, because these appeals can be used by radically incommensurable political projects, then part of what is called for are new arguments that retain the broad aims of the political left, which we might boil down to a response to the systemic structural inequities of capitalism through the redistribution of goods. Such arguments might best be discovered within logics that lie in excess of democracy. It is, finally, to say that to answer the question of where we might find the powers of democratic persuasion might be to say: *not* in the standard logics, rhetorics, or practices of democracy. At least, not solely in.

Let me also suggest that abandoning the quest for a perfected democracy is not the same as abandoning the project of democracy. While the idealized, public sphere—rooted in the metaphor of deliberation as the primary site and mechanism of democracy—cannot capture all of the nuanced dimensions of everyday democracies, it retains a heuristical quality of keeping in our collective memories the language and practices through which we can oppose that which we perceive as pernicious and unjust and work toward that which we value and find socially just. It is to highlight, then, the simple idea that while more democracy is not the solution to democracy, the project does provide a rhetorical toolkit and a set of practices that help maintain in the public imagination very important questions about equality, human rights, and just, collective life. I see democratic rhetoric, finally, in raw pragmatic terms—as a discursive stuff capable of inspiring action and of providing strategies for making sense of and shaping our lives that limit and constrain, generate and make possible, our various experiences.

Epilogue

Exiting the Parlor

> Imagine that you enter a parlor. . . . When you arrive, others have long preceded you, and they are engaged in a heated discussion. . . . You listen for a while. . . . then you put in your oar. Someone answers; you answer him; another comes to your defense; another aligns himself against you. . . . However, the discussion is interminable. The hour grows late, you must depart. And you do depart, with the discussion still vigorously in progress
>
> Kenneth Burke, *The Philosophy*

Entering and exiting a fieldsite reminds me of Kenneth Burke's famous parlor metaphor for public debate and humanity's "unending conversation." Indeed, the textures, histories, politics, and dynamics of the field long preceded my time in Uptown (and the time of everyone I met), and all such matters will continue rolling along long after I make my exit and after my field informants make theirs. But, before I exit, let me bring you up to date. Not long after Wilson Yard's ribbon cutting ceremony in 2010, Helen Shiller publicly announced that she was retiring after serving twenty-four years as Uptown's alderman (1987–2011). Near the end of Shiller's term, Carol Marin of *Chicago Tonight* interviewed her:

> Marin: Are you a mellow Marxist now?. . . . Is Helen Shiller of today different than the one who got elected in '87?
>
> Shiller: Helen Shiller in 1987 said, we should be able to make sure that everyone has a place in this city [. . .]. And when we do development, especially when we do development that comes from money and resources that is there explicitly on the backs of people who have nothing—in other words, because they have nothing we get extra money here to do something—that when we do that we should make sure that the people who are here today will be here when that's complete to be able to benefit from it. [. . .] We have to have a city where it's not just inclusive of our diversity but we're serious [. . .] about making sure that we all have a place here and we benefit in the improvements

that are being made. [. . .] That's the same Helen Shiller that was here before. ("Alderman Shiller")

Of course, in high-Uptown style, not everyone shared or valued this perception of Shiller's legacy as a city-official who used her power to promote balanced development. In the Uptown Update blog comment fields, Shiller's announcement inspired vitriolic statements like "ding dong the witch is dead," "Can we release doves?," and "I think my condo just appreciated $50,000 in one day" ("Ald. Shiller"). There were also more measured critiques of Shiller: "Supplying a voice to the voiceless is laudible [sic]. Doing so at the expense of voices you may not agree with is deplorable. What we've always needed was someone who could and would listen to everyone." This critique that Shiller did not always listen to the voices of her more affluent constituents is probably fair. From 1987 on, she made explicit moves to preserve affordable housing, grant or stymie building permits, and support ordinances in a manner that forwarded her vision of "balanced development" that ran counter to the hopes of some of her constituents.

James Cappleman—a licensed clinical social worker who has worked with homeless, HIV/AIDS, and impoverished communities—became Shiller's successor in 2011. Prior to his aldermanic win, Cappleman was a public figure and community organizer in Uptown. Cappleman is a complicated figure, generally supported by the diverse contingency featured in this book that prioritized urban development, public safety, and aesthetic upgrades over—as their opponents might put it—countering systemic inequality through affordable housing construction and resource expansion for the poor. Cappleman's website corroborates this sense of his "primary focus" as "promoting economic development to create more shopping, dining, entertainment, and employment opportunities" and with addressing "public safety." Yet, he has also worked closely with local social service agencies to deliver better, more efficient services to the poor, which he articulates as an aim of "improving the delivery of services by advocating the use of outcome metrics to measure the performance of various city departments and social services to ensure greater efficiency and use of their limited resources" ("Meet James").[1]

However, the matter of how Cappleman has enacted his support of Uptown's most disenfranchised has become a point of major public contention—one that reenergized Uptown's political left and earned him a reputation of being waged in a "war" against the poor. Let me share two representative actions that speak to this contention—first, in early 2013, Cappleman moved to close down a Salvation Army mobile unit that stopped regularly in Uptown to hand out food to the homeless. Nancy Powers of the Salvation Army reportedly said that Cappleman "decided he felt the unit was pulling homeless into the area, and he does not want us to feed them" ("Ald. Cappleman"). Cappleman and Powers eventually negotiated a plan to continue the services, but not before he alienated a lot of stakeholders in his ward. Second, around the same time, Cappleman was working on a city ordinance that "would prohibit cubicle-style sleeping-room hotels in residential communities" (Bowean), and target Uptown's most notorious Single Room Occupancies (SROs), such as the "cage-style" Wilson Men's Hotel.

These two public actions catalyzed a series of oppositional protests, along with two left-leaning community groups, Uptown Uprising and Social Workers Against Cappleman. Uptown Uprising began in March 2013 as a "community coalition" dedicated to "maintain[ing] Uptown's affordability, diversity and character" and to "informing the Uptown community about the various attacks our alderman and his developer donors have been waging against the poor and working-class of our neighborhood" (Uptown Uprising). Social Workers Against Cappleman galvanized in August 2013 as a group of social workers fed up with Cappleman's consistent use of the refrain "I am a clinical social worker" to justify his actions against the poor; the group claimed, "Alderman James Cappleman is intent on destroying the beloved Uptown community, and he is inappropriately using his past as a Social Worker as a means to his end" (Social).

Cappleman's perceived attack on the Salvation Army food truck was the last straw that gave "birth" to Uptown Uprising. The group launched a social media campaign and staged a protest on March 6, 2013, in which over two hundred activists gathered outside of Cappleman's office chanting things like "Food and housing is a right, not just for the rich and white" (Sosin). Journalists Emmanuel and Woodward noted that some activists "accused Cappleman of being 'at war' with poor people," which an alderman's representative called a radically unfair characterization. Along with these protestors, who dressed as condiments and food carts, were animal rights activists who showed up as human-sized pigeons to voice their dissent about a completely different matter involving the capture and removal of pigeons from Uptown's core public spaces. The alderman, who was also working on an ordinance to increase fines for pigeon feeding, felt that the pigeons—and more precisely their copious poop smears that blanketed busy public sidewalks and left gooey streaks along the storefronts that flanked Wilson at Broadway— reduced the capacity to catalyze economic development. The animal rights folks were particularly incensed that he allowed an Indiana farmer to capture the pigeons without knowing his intentions to use them at a pigeon shoot (Emmanuel). As many have said, only in Uptown.

Cappleman's appointment into office and the strong re-emergence of Uptown's left, represented an ideological swing in who held official power and who occupied the position of the marginal. Arguments now circulating about civic participation, justice, and democracy are similar to those I witnessed during my time in the field—but those who can most effectively make use of the various arguments shifted after Cappleman took office. This fact, in the end, demonstrates, once more, the moral, political, and ideological flexibility of the democratic project and its rhetorics. Another book could be written picking up from here, but I'll leave that storytelling to others. Simply, the rhetorics of democracy have aligned with new ideological content in the new political context—and the beat goes on.

Uptown Uprising activist Stavraoula Harissis, who reportedly "started the Facebook page that spawned" the first protest in March, told reporters that characterizing Cappleman as being at "war with the poor" is a "really sensational way to put it"; continuing, she added, "I don't see it as this person is at war with the poor. I see it as this system that we're living in is at war with people" (Emmanuel and Woodward). Harissis's statement might be the most productive public comment made on the matter, and one that is lost in the vilification of Cappleman and his actions. While measured stances can deflate the oomph of a protest, let me pull out some of the nuance of Harissis's insight regarding the systemic quality of the problem of poverty, and do so by returning to the case of whether it is better or not to keep SROs like the Wilson Men's Hotel open. This question is a salient one playing out in Chicago as I type this in 2015.

On July 30, 2014, the City of Chicago passed a six-month moratorium on issuing "permits for conversion or demolition of existing single-room occupancy buildings and resident hotels" to give the city time to create legislation aimed at preserving the housing. The ordinance stresses that the "loss of these effectively irreplaceable forms of affordable housing could force low income households into homelessness, subjecting many more persons and families to inhumane living conditions and increased crime," which would "add to the already practically overwhelming burden on public and nonprofit agencies that provide [. . .] support to this population" (City of Chicago). While Cappleman reportedly stated days before the vote that he would oppose the ordinance out of principle, he supported it in the end. Cappleman explained his reasoning for wanting to shut down SROs like the Wilson Men's Hotel as part of a desire to "provide humane housing options" (Byrne) and to "send a message that we as a city can't allow our neighbors to live in cages" (Brown, "Where").

Let me offer an account of a day in the life of the Wilson Men's Hotel to give some weight to Cappleman's driving argument that human beings deserve better living conditions. The Wilson (which has operated as substandard housing since the 1920s) is pretty dismal. Here's a description published in 1992 (so add over *twenty* years of wear and tear to get us to 2015):

> A cubicle room is generally seven by five feet [. . .] There is a steel bed frame [. . .]. To maximize ventilation, cubicles have wire mesh ceilings [. . .] A low-wattage bulb suspended from the chicken wire is the only light source. And there is a four-inch gap between floor and wall for further ventilation. [. . .] 4 AM is the same as 4 PM. One hears constant cursing, groaning, farting, belching. There are guttural guffaws and childlike exclamations of "Well I'll be damned," or "Fuck you." There are also the incessant sounds of wheezing vacuum cleaners, sloshing water buckets, rolling bottles, singing radios and TVs. [. . .] One way to get a handle on it is to stay put in your room [. . .] as stories, arguments, and explanations fly overhead between 'Nam' vets, out-of-work truckers, [. . .] day laborers, and mentally and emotionally damaged people, some placid and resigned, others ready to snap at the mention of a wrong word. (Watson)

Cappleman quite earnestly, in my opinion, desires better living conditions for the people who dwell in such places. Unlike his most extreme critics, I don't accept that he is simply paying empty lip service or telling a "cock-and-bull story" (Brown, "Where"). Yet, as housing advocates argue, derelict as they may be, it would be worse to eliminate this housing before viable alternatives are in place to accommodate everyone, as the units stand in as the last resort before homelessness. SROs can run as little as $300, providing a last stop housing option for people who would otherwise end up on the streets or cycling in and out of already overflowing shelters. Such is the situation Chicago faces: place the poor in inhumane living conditions or eliminate inhumane housing, potentially landing people in worst situations. To do the latter without being able to afford replacement housing is to choose the worse option, homeless advocates would argue. So, while all may agree that SROs like Wilson are poor housing options, Cappleman's critics are skeptical about what happens once the housing is demolished.

Uptown, with one of the few concentrations of affordable housing and SROs on Chicago's largely gentrified North Side, is an epicenter for discourse that captures the broader tensions reflected within Chicago's housing problems. While there is no space left to sort through those arguments here with any nuance, within the public discourse, I discovered many of the same basic housing topoi that I discussed in Chapter One—which, on the one hand, draw links between poverty and housing, stating that the concentration of shoddy housing either causes or perpetuates poverty, or, on the other hand, states that we live in a (capitalist) society that by necessity creates permanent abject material inequity that we must contend with such that maintaining affordable housing becomes a justice imperative. Both broad perspectives can reach an agreement that the poor should be living in better housing, but beyond that abstract assent all else seems up for wrangle.

In the end, the people of Uptown know how to get things accomplished in the company of dissenting others. So many block clubs, organizations, initiatives, web presences, and strong contending voices have emerged over the decades. Affordable housing gets built and destroyed, streets get cleaned up, new parks are built, commercial development happens, and protests occur across the political spectrum in an "unending conversation" about the public good. For all that Uptown's citizens have to teach us about the limits, frustrations, and stalemates of democracy, they have just as much to share with us about how to get collective work done that results in concrete changes. And so, let me close this book by expressing my thanks to the people of Uptown, and my hope that their collective conversations, actions, and wrangles over how to live and act among radically different others may continue. Exiting. . . .

Notes

Introduction

1. The popularity of the public sphere burgeoned in the US after Habermas's *Structural Transformation* was first translated into English in 1989.
2. Habermas locates the historical precedence and material foundation of the public sphere in the seventeenth- and eighteenth-century print explosion (and attendant salon and coffee house culture) that facilitated the formation of rational, moral subjectivities capable of engaging in deliberative democracy.
3. McGee also considered consciousness itself as a material outcome of rhetoric, as well as the consciousness of consciousness and the modes of production of various forms of consciousness (18–30).
4. Foucault has a parallel interest in the interface between rhetoric and materiality. Rhetorical structures are "always given through some material medium" (*Archaeology* 112), and their materiality is "constitutive of the statement itself" because "a statement must have a substance, a support, a place, and a date" (113).
5. To clarify, highlighting the experiences, voices, and stories of marginalized peoples and cultures is incredibly valuable and not mutually exclusive from the aims of rhetorical ethnographies. I am asking what value ethnographies might have when documenting how power (or capitalism) operates perniciously or when capturing marginal experience is not the central aim. What other inquiries might we have instead of (or in addition to) these (which have, of late, dominated the ethnographic gaze)?
6. Affordable housing advocates successfully pushed for mandatory setaside ordinances that require a portion of TIF funds be used for affordable housing.
7. The use of quotations indicates a direct transcription. Where I edited quotations, I indicate this with ellipses in square brackets: [. . .]. All names are pseudonyms, with a few noted exceptions for very public figures who gave me permission to use their real names in public matters. In two cases,

a single person has two "field" names to further protect his or her identity. With permission, interviews were digitally recorded in public settings like cafes. Interviewees were selected based on their participation in Uptown politics, civic actions, businesses, community organizations, and blogs. Interviews lasted between forty-five minutes and 140 minutes.

Chapter 1

1. The definition of affordable housing is slippery. I use the terms affordable and low-cost housing interchangeably throughout the book to refer to a variety of housing types that fall into the Department of Housing and Urban Development's definition of affordable housing (no more than 30% of a household's income is used for rent/mortgage and utility payments) as it applies to their categories for low-income (households earning 51–80% of the area median), very low-income (31–50% of the area median), and extremely low-income (0–31% of the area median).

2. I entered the field to study the Tax Increment Financing Policy.

3. Affordable housing has sat at the crux of these political wrangles since the 1950s, serving as the material foundation that enables low-income residents to remain in the neighborhood, according to some, and, given its relative concentration, as an obstacle to economic revitalization, to others. Uptown's varied housing stock—which now includes substandard apartments, subsidized affordable buildings, single-family homes, brownstone flats, mansions, SROs, homeless shelters, and more—has facilitated the neighborhood's radical diversity and fueled public conflict since the postwar years.

4. For a breakdown of inventional heuristics in Classical rhetoric, see Corbett and Connors 1999, Lanham 1991, and Crowley and Hawhee 2009.

5. Muckelbauer leans on Aristotle's sense of topoi in the *Physics* as "pure surfaces that enable the very action of locating," arguing that topoi exist in "reciprocal and generative fusion of body and place" (137).

6. The doctrine of kairos insists that the timing of arguments is central to persuasion. But, as Rickert argues, kairos has an often ignored spatial and material aspect; namely, the exigencies and textures of place will, more than anything, give rise to the opening up of the opportunities and affordances of kairos.

7. While I am not suggesting that "inhabitation" must involve literally placing one's body in a place, I am suggesting that there are things one cannot capture about rhetoric-in-action by not being there, such as affective valences, bodily knowledge, kairos, performance, and so on. This necessity of presence is, perhaps, the most significant justification for rhetorical field methods.

8. Some space and place theorists separate these terms, along the lines of the bare materiality of the built and natural environment and the ideological frames we invest in those environments, respectively. Because the interplay of these concepts is important to my thinking, and because I want more mileage out of the terms commonplace and places of invention, I use space and place interchangeably here, though I employ the term *place* most

prevalently as a way of evoking the enmeshment of the literal materiality of environments with ideological investments, political textures, everyday practices, and rhetorical structures. The fusion of such things constitutes the places of invention.

9. See Paul Siegel's dissertation work *Uptown, Chicago: The Origins and Emergence of a Movement Against Displacement* for more on this subject.

10. These questions and the topoi that follow emerge through my fieldwork and rhetorical analysis of archival materials, public discourse, and interview transcripts on Uptown history, Chicago housing, and Uptown's contemporary debates.

11. Commercial trains were established by 1919 that connected passengers from Milwaukee to Chicago via the Wilson stop in Uptown.

12. Landmarks, such as the decaying Uptown Theater, continue to stand as ghostly reminders of this "Golden Era" that sharply contrast with the visible signs of poverty. Such material haunts are summoned in public discourse as the peak from which the neighborhood has fallen and to which it might return.

13. The report was named after Jack Meltzer, who completed the work. UCC's *Meltzer Plan* highlights the general substandard quality of the converted housing units (*First Draft* 16).

14. Models Cities was initiated on November 3, 1966, under the U.S. Demonstration Cities and Metropolitan Development Act in response to the failed postwar urban renewal efforts of the 1940s and 1950s. Model Cities attempted to balance the competing interests of the government with the very diverse citizens who lived in so-called urban slums. In Chicago, the program was subject to the strong-arm hold of Mayor Daley, who reined in citizen participation by appointing board members who supported the party line, which generally amounted to the use of federal money to support development plans aimed at revamping the business core and demolishing dilapidated housing.

15. Although JOIN spearheaded the anti-urban renewal movement in the 1960s, the group was defunct during the Truman College controversy. In the wake of JOIN's efforts, Chuck Geary of the Voice of the People formed the Poor People's Coalition in 1968 to oppose the Uptown Model Cities program.

16. While I've focused on Truman College, Uptown's battle over housing throughout this period is prolific. For example, Slim Coleman and the Heart of Uptown Coalition worked together on several housing initiatives; in 1975, they sued to halt construction of the upscale Pensacola Place, eventually obligating the developer to reserve 20% of the new units as Section 8 units (Fisher).

17. The Wilson Yard debates (1998–2010) galvanized groups on both sides of the housing divide. Groups like Queer to the Left, Jesus People, COURAJ, and Organization of the NorthEast worked as advocates for affordable housing; groups like Uptown Chicago Commission, Uptown Neighborhood Council, and Fix Wilson Yard opposed it.

18. Shiller came into power during an era, according to Neil Smith, when

American cities experienced a general backlash against failed liberal policies of the New Deal, the liberalism of the 1960s, and the end of the 1980s economic boom that manifested in the form of "deregulation, privatization and emerging cuts in welfare and social service budgets" (44). Smith associates such scalar changes with what he calls the revanchist city to highlight an increasing desensitization to the concerns of the poor.

19. In Uptown, what "progress" entails is debatable. Uptown resident Glenn Charlton responded to McCarron by saying, "'Progress' is in the eye of the beholder . . . From the eyes of this beholder, Helen Shiller is progress. She is a shining beacon in the cold and calculating darkness of this decade" (2).

20. In her first year, Shiller was arrested for trespassing while participating in "Tent City," an action to draw attention to homelessness, and to prod the CHA to rehabilitate two scattered-site buildings at 4526 N. Magnolia and 4657 N. Malden (Casuso and Heard 3). Protestors showed up at a vacant lot that was designated for CHA scattered-site housing, and proceeded to illegally pitch tents, fabricate shelters from scrap wood, and start campfires in metal barrels (Randle 3).

21. Not only does this statistic signify a gradual increase of homeowners, but it also highlights the fact that renters make up the majority of Uptown's population. The extent to which homeowners should be regarded in urban planning projects, given this renter majority, becomes a major point of contention, especially in instances where substantial portions of property taxes are funneled into development projects to which a contingency of homeowners are opposed [see Chapter Two].

22. ONE gained national prominence in the 1980s and 1990s for its affordable housing campaigns. Like the UCC, ONE is an umbrella organization that represents a cross section of Uptown stakeholders, including individuals, block clubs, religious institutions, businesses, and other community groups.

23. This history is documented in *Saving our Homes*, which was collaboratively written by ONE and Loyola researchers Philip Nyden and Joanne Adams.

24. Rather than owning individual units, members collectively own the building through the purchase of stock in the cooperative corporation, which is, in theory, controlled through democratic decision-making processes that include all members (*Affordable Housing Cooperatives* 6).

25. SROs are rooms for rent that typically have shared baths and kitchenettes. Uptown has a variety of SROs that range from flophouses to well-maintained buildings managed by reputable nonprofits. Project-based public housing is funded by the Department of Housing and Urban Development; the subsidy is attached to units in a building. Low-income subsidized rentals here refer to affordable rental units subsidized by state or federal funds. Limited equity co-ops are forms of affordable, nonspeculative, resident-controlled homeownership, in which members of the co-op own shares in the corporation.

26. Developing Accountability to the People (DGAP) is dedicated to tak-

ing "action on social-justice issues" and to creating and preserving a "participatory and democratic society through collaborations among organizations and individuals" ("DGAP"). Formed in 2006, DGAP evaluates Chicago's performance in key areas, such as housing and education.

27. In the Housing Choice Voucher program, subsidies travel with the tenant. Vouchers can generally be used to pay for any market-rate apartment with a willing landlord.

Chapter 2

1. In 1998, the Wilson Yard Redevelopment Taskforce conducted a survey in six languages to gather community input. There were 1,762 respondents. Survey results were presented at two community meetings in October 1998. In June 1998 and June 2000, the public was invited to participate in charrette planning sessions to discuss survey results, brainstorm, and voice dissent. The current proposal is based on the survey results and the input gathered at these charrettes.

2. "Extremely low income" households make up to 30% of the Chicago Area Median Income (AMI) ($0–22,600 for a family of four in 2006); "very low income" households make 30–50% of the AMI ($22,600–37,700); and "low income" households make 50–80% of the AMI ($37,700–59,600). These are HUD categories ("Median Income").

3. In Uptown, the question of who counts as a legitimate stakeholder is paramount. The genealogy suggests that a stakeholder is one who *literally* holds the stakes of a property. It is a term tied to land, ownership, and property. Stakeholders have vested interest in what happens to a particular place because they own part of it. Not everyone in a particular place is necessarily a stakeholder, in this sense. But, what qualities allow one to be a stakeholder in Uptown? Do property owners have more stake than renters? Do long-time residents have more stake than new ones? Are the homeless staked? Do people in subsidized housing have a stake? When I refer to stakeholders I use the broadest definition: Uptown's renters, homeowners, business owners, workers, politicians, activists, homeless individuals, and so on.

4. I asked several UNC members why they chose to don orange t-shirts. Here's the story I heard: out of a desire to appear as a unified group, someone suggested a "protest uniform." The safety orange color was offered as a standout, others agreed, and the rest is history.

5. Hauser and Fleming's work is critical to my own, but I am not sure either rids the public sphere of Habermas's idealistic core. (Note: I am not sure I do either, and, frankly, I am ambivalent about critiques that fixate on Habermas's idealism as a reason to dismiss his work.) What exactly is at stake in eradicating idealism from the public sphere? Would it entail denouncing the possibility of reaching agreement through deliberation? Where does such denouncement leave us? Ultimately, if one aim of the public sphere is to derive the content of a public good that might guide collective action—there remains the need to *do our best*. Yes—of course—power inequity, access problems, incommensurable politics, etc. will thwart us; formal and in-

formal exclusions to the public always exist. We reach a stalemate. But then what? Suddenly, the public sphere takes on a pragmatic, heuristical value in generating the things we should keep in mind when trying to engage each other in public debate. This heuristical quality, as both Fleming and Hauser contend, helps inform emergent processes in concrete situations and times and sharpens our capacities to collectively imagine, define, and work toward some shared goal, however tentative and problematic.

6. See Montag on the material constraints of the public sphere, the limits of communicative action, and the violent underbelly of democracy.

7. The sale of single-family homes dropped 15% between 2005 and 2006 (Umberger).

8. These agencies include Chicago's Department of Housing, the Illinois Development Agency, the Chicago Housing Authority, U.S. Department of Housing and Urban Development, and the Housing Choice Voucher program.

9. Other critiques of the process include that there were no trained facilitators at the charrettes; that the decks were stacked for affordable housing; and that the survey was unscientific and biased.

10. Wilson Yard is partially funded through Tax Increment Financing (TIF), which captures incremental property tax growth over twenty-three years, redirecting it toward projects within a given geographic area. While TIF law requires public hearings for all TIF proposals and a formal municipal approval process, "state law does not require the City to respond to those comments or act on public input regarding TIF districts." See Neighborhood Capital Budget Group, "The TIF Process." Shiller, therefore, was not legally required to initiate the extensive community-based process that she did to determine what to build at Wilson Yard.

11. The perception that the housing at Wilson Yard will become "Cabrini—Green" is racially charged. Cabrini—Green, one of the most infamous Chicago public housing high rises, was demolished under the CHA's Plan for Transformation. For a detailed history, see Fleming's *City of Rhetoric*.

12. This fear is compounded by the Chicago's Plan for Transformation, a ten-year, $1.5 billion overhaul of public housing that called for the demolition of approximately 22,000 of CHA's 39,000 units, the construction of 8,000, and the rehabilitation of 17,000. The plan called for the massive relocation of tens of thousands of public housing residents into mixed-income low-rises and into the private rental market with Housing Choice Vouchers. The worry that the Wilson Yard would be solely populated by voucher holders, thus functioning informally as public housing, is commonly expressed.

13. In response to a decline of federal money available for local redevelopment after 1970, the Tax Increment Allocation Redevelopment Act was adopted in 1977 by the Illinois legislature to grant municipalities a tool that could be used to prompt urban development (*Review of TIF* 4). The TIF policy was developed to empower local municipalities with the autonomy to make major decisions, such as allocation of funds and choice of development, once an area has been designated a TIF zone (*TIF Handbook* 18). Any incremental taxes that are generated as a result of increased property value within the designated area is paid to the municipality and placed into a special tax

fund, which is used to purchase bonds to pay for redevelopment projects in the area (2).

14. Fix Wilson Yard "evolved as a grassroots effort by dedicated volunteers in the Uptown community" to stop the project through legal injunction. The organizers wrote in August 2008, "Despite years of trying to work with the public officials to develop a responsible use of taxpayer dollars, they were not willing to listen. This summer, without announcement, they began pre-construction preparation, leaving us no choice but to start the legal battle" ("What is").

Chapter 3

1. While the message board comments are public, I added an extra layer of protection by using pseudonyms in place of the original screen names (which were already generic and anonymous).

2. While the Buena Park Message Board was still receiving posts in 2012, the traffic had tapered off around 2009, when the Uptown Update blog began taking over the social function of community dialogue.

3. The Uplift Mural is in Alderman Helen Shiller's ward (46th), and the "Roots of Argyle" is in Alderman Mary Ann Smith's Ward (48th). The 48th Ward dips into the upper third of the neighborhood.

4. The reference to the glamorous historical past is evoked by the repeated image of the Essanay Movie Door. The studio is now home to St. Augustine College, where the door is still in use.

5. Because of the public nature of the "Roots of Argyle" mural, I have not used a pseudonym, with Mr. Elder's permission, for quotations in which he discusses his experiences with the mural.

6. An official of Alderman Mary Ann Smith's office supplied these minutes as public documents.

7. I am not implying that such sidestepping is intentional. I think the conflation of equal representation of racial diversity and social justice often occurs hegemonically in the US.

8. *Our America* is a collection of narratives about living in Chicago public housing told by two boys, LeAlan Jones and Lloyd Newman, who lived in the Ida B. Wells development. Reporter David Isay trained kids to conduct interviews within the community. LeAlan and Lloyd were these kids.

9. The trouble with Mouffe is that, although she valorizes agonism as a means of keeping democratic contestation alive, she doesn't necessarily help those on the ground who require immediate, decisive action. Representing instances where people have acted through and in response to democratic paradoxes seems a valuable move in the interest of maintaining argumentative sightlines.

10. Carmen Marine building is not utopic. In 2006, the *Chicago Tribune*, for example, covered the sketchy dealings of board members who allegedly broke fair housing law by bumping friends and families up to the top of long waiting lists and screening out African American and Latino applicants (Olivo). In providing a model of collective homeownership for people who

would not otherwise be able to afford property, affordable co-ops like Carmen Marine are an inventive responses to the intractable problem of material inequity in a capitalist democracy where private homeownership is valorized as a cornerstone of society and a marker of success.

Chapter 4

1. A word on the timing of the positive loitering marches. The events are sometimes staged during regularly scheduled CAPS beat meetings, often at 7:00 P.M. Laborers typically arrive when U-Haul opens at 7:00 A.M. and vacate when the store closes between 7 and 8:00 P.M. During summer months, when the weather is nice and the daylight long, some men remain on the sidewalk after closing, hanging out in a manner that seems to have little to do with finding work.

2. Each of Chicago's twenty-five policing districts contains several geographically bound "beats" staffed by officers who get to know residents and local concerns during long-term rotation periods. During this study, Uptown was largely situated in the 23rd district, and fell into the jurisdiction of seven beats: 2024, 2033, 2311, 2312, 2313, 2322, 2323.

3. Chicago's anti-loitering laws have a contentious history. In 1992, Chicago passed an anti-loitering law that increased the police's authority to disperse public congregations. Loitering was defined as the gathering of persons in a "place with no apparent purpose," and led to the arrest of 42,000 between 1992 and 1995. In 1999, the U.S. Supreme Court deemed the law unconstitutionally vague (Strosnider 102). The city revised this law in 2000, redefining loitering as "gang loitering" that applies to persons "remaining in any one place under circumstances that would warrant a reasonable person to believe that the purpose or effect of that behavior is to enable a criminal street gang to establish control over identifiable areas, to intimidate others from entering those areas, or to conceal illegal activities" (City Clerk, 2002).

4. The second chart, "Lowest Crime Statistics Ranking," counters the commonplace argument that Uptown is crime ridden. In fact, Uptown's two districts (20 and 23) have consistently been ranked among the lowest citywide for both violent and property crimes. I selected this date range (2005–2009) because it was the timespan of my fieldwork on positive loitering. The third chart, "Comparison of Reported Crimes in Uptown and Surrounding Lakefront Neighborhoods," is a snapshot of a single year, providing a comparison of the areas. The Web tool ClearMap only allows for a search over the last twelve months, so I included a search closest to the date range of the fieldwork.

5. The quotations from this event were not audio recorded but were captured via extensive field jottings taken at the event and written up immediately after the event.

6. Scholars characterize neoliberalism as an economic and political ideology that posits individual liberty as a foundational social tenet best safeguarded by a noninterventionist state. In additional to punitive policing measures, core characteristics of neoliberalism include the retrenchment of the

Keynesian welfare state, the devolution of state services, and the increasing reliance on informal labor practices and regulatory mechanisms (Harvey).

7. As a result of citizen pressure on U-Haul, the organization agreed to press charges for trespassing. At least thirteen cases were heard in 2007 for U-Haul trespassing. The citizen-led CAPS Court Advocacy Subcommittee, which is spearheaded by individuals also involved in positive loitering, pressured Uptown citizens to show up for the hearings as "silent witnesses." The subcommittee trains citizens to become court advocates, which entails supporting victims and reporters of crime and putting passive aggressive pressure on judges to extend harsher sentencing.

8. The Enterprising Kitchen was an Uptown social entrepreneurial effort founded in 1999 to provide workplace skills to women working toward self-sufficiency. The organization involved participants in all aspects of the production of natural soaps and spa products. Uptown's Café Too opened in 2005 and provides culinary and restaurant skill training to homeless and impoverished individuals.

Chapter 5

1. While Uptown Update is a public blog, I have added an extra layer of protection by using pseudonyms in place of the original screen names (which were already generic and anonymous).

2. "If This Had Been Released Two Weeks Ago." *Uptown Update.* 27 August 2009. Comment Fields.

3. I requested a face-to-face or phone interview, but the informant preferred to respond via e-mail. I submitted a round of questions and asked a couple of follow-up questions.

4. The blog's authors have retained anonymity even in the face of a controversial subpoena that would have forced them to reveal their identity. See Chapter Two.

5. Not every article was about the August 13 gang video, but all were related to crime or the alderman's tardy response to safety concerns. All thirty articles on Uptown Update are included because conversations in the comment fields linked back to the incident at Leland and Sheridan. The count does not include the hundreds of comments to articles on local and national media, such as CBS, *Huffington Post*, etc.

6. CBS Leads with the story (Aug. 14), "Uptown Residents Say Neighborhood is Under Attack"; Fox News picks up the story (Aug.14), "Uptown Rioting Caught on Tape"; WBEZ interviews the man who shot the video (Aug. 18); *Huffington Post* covers the story (Aug. 17) "Uptown Residents Demand Action After Gang Violence Erupts in Streets"; and CNN uses the video footage to introduce a story on "Chicago's Deadly Streets" (Aug. 24).

7. The first two comments are from "Time to March?" *Uptown Update.* 15 August 2009. Comment Fields. The final is from "And the Inevitable Result." *Uptown Update.* 16 August 2009. Comment Fields.

8. "Signs for Monday's 'Peaceful Protest.'" *Uptown Update.* 16 August 2009. Comment Fields.

9. "Shiller Olympics." 16 August 2009. Comment Fields.
10. "Share Your Aldermanic Encounters." *Uptown Update.* 19 August 2009. Comment Fields.
11. "Uptown Update: Just a Little Press Conference at the CAPS Beat 2312." *Uptown Update.* 18 August 2009. Comment Fields.
12. "CBS Leads Newscast with Story about Uptown Violence." *Uptown Update.* 14 August 2009. Comment Fields.
13. "Time to March?" *Uptown Update,* 15 August 2009. Comment Fields.
14. "If This Had Been Released Two Weeks Ago. . . ." *Uptown Update.* 27 August 2009. Comment Fields.
15. "Street Fighting at Leland & Sheridan." *Uptown Update.* 13 August 2009. Comment Fields.
16. "If This Had Been Released Two Weeks Ago. . . ." *Uptown Update.* 27 August 2009. Comment Fields.
17. "Gang Fight Caught on Video at Sheridan and Leland." *Uptown Update.* 29 August 2009. Comment Fields.
18. "CBS2: Uptown Residents Want Answers From Ald. Shiller." *Uptown Update.* 18 August 2009. Comment Fields.

Conclusion

1. I did not use a pseudonym for Hatch, with his permission, because of the public nature of the event.

Epilogue

1. While measuring outcomes is important for program improvement, such metrics are double-edged. I cannot speak to Cappleman's use, but the focus on "outcome metrics" is a commonly named hallmark of the neoliberalization of social services.

Works Cited

Ackerman, John. "The Space for Rhetoric in Everyday Life." *Towards a Rhetoric of Everyday Life: New Directions in Research on Writing, Text, and Discourse*. Eds. Martin Nystrand and John Duffy. Madison: U of Wisconsin P, 2003. 84–117.
Affordable Chicago: The Next Five Year Housing Plan, 2004–2008. Chicago: Chicago Rehab Network, June 2003.
Affordable Housing Conditions and Outlook in Chicago: An Early Warning for Intervention. Nathalle P. Voorhees Center for Neighborhood and Community Improvement. Chicago: University of Illinois at Chicago, March 2006.
Affordable Housing Cooperatives: Conditions and Prospects in Chicago. Nathalie P. Voorhees Center for Neighborhood and Community Improvement and the Chicago Mutual Housing Network: University of Illinois at Chicago, June 2004.
Ahmed, Sara. *The Cultural Politics of Emotion*. New York: Routledge, 2004.
"Ald. Shiller Will Not Run for Re-Election." *Uptown Update. Uptown Update*, 2 Aug. 2010. 15 Aug. 2011. <http://www.uptownupdate.com/2010/08/ald-shiller-will-not-run-for-re.html>.
"Alderman Shiller Stepping Aside." *Chicago Tonight*. WTTW. 2 Aug. 2010.
"Area Median Income: 2014." *City of Chicago*. 16 May 2014. <http://www.cityofchicago.org/city/en/depts/dcd/supp_info/area_median_incomeamichart.html>.
Aristotle. *On Rhetoric: A Theory of Civic Discourse*. 2nd ed. Trans. George A. Kennedy. New York: Oxford UP, 2007.
Bawarshi, Anis. *Genre and the Invention of the Writer: Reconsidering the Place of Invention in Composition*. Logan: Utah State UP, 2003.
Beauregard, Robert A. *Voices of Decline: The Postwar Fate of U.S. Cities*. New York: Routledge, 2003.
Bennett, Jane. *Vibrant Matter: A Political Ecology of Things*. Durham: Duke UP, 2010.
Bennett, Larry. *Neighborhood Politics: Chicago & Sheffield*. New York: Garland Publishing, 1997.
Biesecker, Barbara, and John Lucaites. "Introduction." *Rhetoric, Materiality, and Politics*." Eds. Barbara Biesecker and John Lucaites. New York: Peter Lang, 2009. 1–16.
Blair, Carole. "Contemporary U.S. Memorial Sites as Exemplars of Rhetoric's Materiality." *Rhetorical Bodies*. Eds. Jack Selzer and Sharon Crowley. Madison: U of Wisconsin P, 1999. 3–15.

Blair, Carole, Greg Dickinson, and Brian L. Ott. "Introduction: Rhetoric/Memory/Place." *Places of Public Memory: Rhetoric of Museums and Memorials*. Tuscaloosa: U of Alabama P, 2010. 1–54.
Bleeden, David, Caroline Gottschalk-Druschke, and Ralph Cintrón. "Minutemen and the Subject of Democracy." *Marcha!: Latino Chicago and the Immigrant Rights Movement*. Eds. Amalia Pallares and Nilda Flores-González. Urbana: U of Illinois P, 2010. 179–97.
Bourdieu, Pierre. "Social Space and Symbolic Power." *Sociological Theory* 7.1 (1989): 14–25.
Bowean, Lolly. "At Uptown Cubicle Hotel, a Fight to Stay Open." *Chicago Tribune*. 31 Mar. 2013. 28 Jul. 2014. <http://articles.chicagotribune.com/2013-03-31/news/ct-met-mens-hotel-20130331_1_cubicle-hotel-affordable-housing-uptown>.
Bratt, Rachel G., Michael E. Stone, and Chester Hartman, eds. Introduction. *A Right to Housing: Foundation for a New Social Agenda*. Philadelphia: Temple UP, 2006. 1–19.
Braun, Bruce, and Sarah J. Whatmore. "The Stuff of Politics: Introduction." *Political Matter: Technoscience, Democracy, and Public Life*. Eds. Bruce Braun and Sarah J. Whatmore. Minneapolis: U of Minnesota P, 2010. ix–xl.
Brouwer, Daniel C., and Robert Asen. "Public Modalities, or the Metaphors We Theorize By." *Public Modalities: Rhetoric, Culture, Media, and the Shape of Public Life*. Eds. Daniel C. Brouwer and Robert Asen. Tuscaloosa: U of Alabama P, 2010. 1–32.
Brown, Mark. "Ald. Cappleman Orders Salvation Army to Stop Feeding the Poor in his North Side Ward." *Chicago Sun-Times*. 1 Mar. 2013. 28 Jul. 2014. <http://www.suntimes.com/news/brown/18574177-452/brown-ald-cappleman-orders-salvation-army-to-stop-feeding-the-poor-in-his-north-side.html#.VEVifMZPQds>.
———. "'Where is He Going to Put These People?'" *Chicago Sun-Times*. 27 Feb. 2013. 28 Jul. 2014. <http://www.suntimes.com/news/18522480-452/where-is-he-going-to-put-these-people.html#.VEViy8ZPQds>.
Brown, Wendy. "American Nightmare: Neoliberalism, Neoconservatism, and De-democratization." *Political Theory* 34.6 (2006): 690–714.
———. "Neo-liberalism and the End of Liberal Democracy." *Theory and Event* 7.1 (2003). Project Muse. 10 Jan. 2007.
Buck, Thomas. "Board OK's Renewal Aid for Uptown: 3.5 Million Fixed for Project." *Chicago Tribune*. 9 Apr. 1965: 3. ProQuest Historical Newspapers. U of Illinois at Chicago, U Lib. 5 May 2006 <http://proquest.umi.com>.
Burke, Kenneth. *A Grammar of Motives*. Berkeley: U of California P, 1969.
———. *Language as Symbolic Action: Essays on Life, Literature, and Method*. Berkeley: U of California P, 1966.
———. *The Philosophy of Literary Form: Studies in Symbolic Action*. 3rd ed. 1941. Berkeley: U of California P, 1973.
———. *A Rhetoric of Motives*. Berkeley: U of California P, 1969.
Byrne, John. "In Uptown, Freshman Alderman Angers Advocates for the Needy." *Chicago Tribune*. 9 Mar. 2013. 31 Jul 2014. <http://articles.chicagotribune.com/2013-03-09/news/ct-met-cappleman-uptown-homeless-20130309_1_uptown-neighborhood-james-cappleman-homeless-people>.
Calhoun, Craig. "Introduction: Habermas and the Public Sphere." *Habermas and the Public Sphere*. Ed. Craig Calhoun. Cambridge: MIT Press, 1992. 1–48.

Carrithers, Michael B. "Why Anthropologists Should Study Rhetoric." *Journal of the Royal Anthropological Institute* 11.3 (2005): 577–83.
Casuso, Jorge, and Jacquelyn Heard. "Homeless Group Hopes to Prod CHA with Tent City Vigil on Uptown Lot." *Chicago Tribune* 11 Oct. 1988: 3.
Cattelino, Jessica R. "The Difference That Citizenship Makes: Civilian Crime Prevention on the Lower East Side." *PoLAR* 27.1 (2004): 114–37.
Charlton, Glenn R. "Shiller Praise." *Chicago Tribune* 11 Sept. 1988: 2.
Chesluk, Benjamin. "'Visible Signs of a City Out of Control': Community Policing in New York City." *Cultural Anthropology* 19.2 (2004): 250–75.
"Chicago Community Area Data." Rob Paral and Associates. n.d. 15 Feb. 2013. <http://www.robparal.com/ChicagoCommunityAreaData.html>.
Chicago Police Department. "What is CAPS?" 15 Mar. 2007. <http://egov.cityofchicago.org/city/webportal/portalContentItemAction.do?contentOID=10912&contenTypeName=COC_EDITORIAL&topChannelName=HomePage>.
Cintrón, Ralph. *Angel's Town: Chero Ways, Gang Life, and Rhetorics of the Everyday.* Boston: Beacon Press, 1997.
———. "Democracy and Its Limitations." Eds. John Ackerman and David Coogan. *The Public Work of Rhetoric: Citizen-Scholars and Civic Engagement.* Columbia: U of South Carolina P, 2010. 98–116.
———. "'Gates Locked' and the Violence of Fixation." *Towards a Rhetoric of Everyday Life: New Directions in Research on Writing, Text, and Discourse.* Eds. Martin Nystrand and John Duff. Madison: U of Wisconsin P, 2003. 5–37.
City Clerk of Chicago. "8–4–015 Gang Loitering: Chicago Municipal Code" 2002. 2 Sept. 2007. <http://www.chicityclerk.com/legislation/codes/ chapter8_4.html#015>.
City of Chicago. "Moratorium on Issuance of Permits for Conversion or Demolition of Existing Single-Room Occupancy Buildings and Residential Hotels." Ordinance 02014–5685. 25 Jul. 2014.
Clair, Robin P. "Reflexivity and Rhetorical Ethnography: From Family Farm to Orphanage and Back Again." *Cultural Studies, Critical Methodologies* 11.2 (2011): 117–28.
Clifford, James. "Introduction: Partial Truths." *Writing Culture: The Poetics and Politics of Ethnography.* Eds. James Clifford and George E. Marcus. Berkeley: U of California P, 1986. 1–26.
Condit, Celeste M. *The Meanings of the Gene: Public Debates about Human Heredity.* Madison: U of Wisconsin P, 1999.
Conquergood, Dwight. "Ethnography, Rhetoric, and Performance." *Quarterly Journal of Speech* 78 (1992): 80–123.
———. "Rethinking Ethnography: Towards a Critical Cultural Politics." *Communication Monographs* 58 (1991): 179–94.
Consigny, Scott. "Rhetoric and Its Situations." *Rhetoric & Philosophy* 7.3 (1974): 175–86.
Corbett, Edward P. J, and Robert J. Connors. *Classical Rhetoric for the Modern Student.* 4th ed. Oxford: Oxford UP, 1999.
Creswell, John W. *Qualitative Inquiry & Research Design: Choosing Among Five Approaches.* 2nd ed. Thousand Oaks, CA: Sage Publications, 2007.
Crowley, Sharon. *Towards a Civil Discourse: Rhetoric and Fundamentalism.* Pittsburgh, PA: U of Pittsburgh P, 2006.
Crowley, Sharon, and Debra Hawhee. *Ancient Rhetorics for Contemporary Students.* New York: Longman, 2009.

Cruikshank, Barbara. *The Will to Empower: Democratic Citizens and Other Subjects.* Ithaca, NY: Cornell UP, 1999.
Daniel, Jamie. "Ritual of Disqualification: Competing Publics and Public Housing in Contemporary Chicago." *Masses, Classes, and the Public Sphere.* Eds. Mike Hill and Warren Hill. New York: Verso, 2000. 62–82.
Dávila, Angela. *Barrio Dreams: Puerto Ricans, Latinos, and the Neoliberal City.* Los Angeles: U of California P, 2004.
Davis, Diane. *Inessential Solidarity: Rhetoric and Foreigner Relations.* Pittsburgh, PA: U of Pittsburgh, 2010.
Dean, Jodi. *Blog Theory: Feedback and Capture in the Circuits of Drive.* Malden, MA: Polity Press, 2010.
Deutsche, Rosalyn. "Art and Public Space: Questions of Democracy." *Social Text* 33 (1992): 34–53.
"DGAP's Mission." *Developing Government Accountability to the People.* 15 May 2008. <http://www.dgapchicago.org>.
Dingo, Rebecca. *Networking Arguments: Rhetoric, Transnational Feminism, and Public Policy Writing.* Pittsburgh, PA: U of Pittsburgh P, 2012.
Druschke, Caroline Gottschalk. "Watershed as Common-place: Communicating for Conservation at the Watershed Scale." *Environmental Communication: A Journal of Nature and Culture* 7 (2013): 80–96.
Duneier, Mitchell. *Sidewalk.* New York: Farrar, Straus and Giroux, 1999.
"DUR Study Gives College Site Facts." *Chicago Tribune.* 2 Mar. 1969: N10. ProQuest Historical Newspapers. U of Illinois at Chicago, U Lib. 10 Nov. 2007 <http://proquest.umi.com>.
Electronic Frontier Foundation. "Chicago Development Critics Fight for Anonymity." 21 Aug. 2009. 10 Jun. 2014. <https://www.eff.org/press/archives/2009/08/21>.
Eliasoph, Nina. *Avoiding Politics: How Americans Produce Apathy in Everyday Life.* Cambridge: Cambridge UP, 1998.
Emmanuel, Adeshina. "Pigeon Poop Hurts Economy, Safety in Uptown, Officials Say." *DNAinfor Chicago.* 30 Jan. 2013. 31 July 2014. <http://www.dnainfo.com/chicago/20130130/uptown/pigeon-poop-blame-for-poor-economy-crime-uptown-officials-say>.
Emmanuel, Adeshina, and Benjamin Woodword. "Rally Ouside Cappleman's Office Protests 'War on the Poor'." *DNAinfor Chicago.* 7 Mar. 2013. 31 July 2014. <http://www.dnainfo.com/chicago/20130306/uptown/residents-rally-outside-capplemans-office-protest-war-on-poor>.
Endres, Danielle, Leah Sprain, and Tarla R. Peterson. "The Imperative of Praxis-Based Environmental Communication Research: Suggestions from the Step It Up 2007 National Research Project." *Environmental Communication: a Journal of Nature and Culture* 2.2 (2008): 237–45.
Epstein, Richard. *Skepticism and Freedom: A Modern Case for Classical Liberalism.* Chicago: U of Chicago P, 2003.
Finnegan, Cara A., and Jiyeon Kang. "'Sighting' the Public: Iconoclasm and Public Sphere Theory." *Quarterly Journal of Speech* 90.4 (2004): 377–402.
First Draft of the Uptown Planning Proposal. Chicago: Jack Metzler and Associates, 1962.

Fish, Stanley. "Boutique Multiculturalism, or Why Liberals are Incapable of Thinking About Hate Speech." *Critical Inquiry* 23.2 (1997): 378–395.
Fisher, Alison. "The Battle for Uptown." *Area Chicago*, n.d. 15 Aug. 2014. <http://areachicago.org/the-battle-for-uptown/>.
Fix Wilson Yard, "What is Wilson Yard?," Fix Wilson Yard. n.d. 18 Aug. 2008. <http://www.fixwilsonyard.org/index.html#Update>.
Fleckenstein, Kristie S., Clay Spinuzzi, Rebecca J. Ricky, and Carole C. Papper. "The Importance of Harmony: An Ecological Metaphor for Writing Research." *CCC* 60.2 (2008): 388–419.
Fleming, David. *City of Rhetoric: Revitalizing the Public Sphere in Metropolitan America.* Albany: SUNY Press, 2008.
Foucault, Michel. *The Archaeology of Knowledge.* New York: Routledge, 2002.
———. "The Subject and Power." In *Power.* Ed. James D. Faubion. New York: The New Press, 2000. 326–48.
Fraser, Nancy. "Rethinking the Public Sphere: A Contribution to the Critique of Actually Existing Democracy." *Social Text* 25/26 (1990): 56–80.
Fraser, Nancy, and Axel Honneth. *Redistribution or Recognition? A Political-Philosophical Exchange.* New York: Verso, 2003.
Fremon, David. "Chicago's Uptown: Struggling or Thriving on Diversity?" *Illinois Issues* 25. 1990. 20 Jul. 2008. <http://www.lib.niu.edu/1990/ii901125.html>.
Friedman, Milton. *Capitalism and Freedom.* 40th ed. Chicago: U of Chicago P, 2006.
Fung, Archon. *Empowered Participation: Reinventing Urban Democracy.* Princeton, NJ: Princeton UP, 2004.
———. "Street Level Democracy: Pragmatic Popular Sovereignty in Chicago Schools and Policing." American Political Science Association Annual Meeting. Atlanta, September 1999.
Garnett, Nicole S. "Private Norms and Public Spaces." *William & Mary Bill of Rights Journal* 18.1 (2009): Ginko Organic Gardens. 15 August 2013. <http://www.ginkgogardens.org>.
Gitlin, Nanci, and Todd Hollander. *Uptown: Poor Whites in Chicago.* New York: Harper Collins, 1970.
Grabill, Jeffrey T. "On Being Useful: Rhetoric and the Work of Engagement." *The Public Work of Rhetoric: Citizen-Scholars and Civic Engagement.* Eds. John M. Ackerman and David J. Coogan. Columbia, SC: U of South Carolina P, 2010. 193–208.
"Greater Chicago Housing and Community Development." Chicago Metropolitan Agency for Planning. n.d. 20 Jul. 2008. <http://www.chicagoareahousing.org/List_CCA.asp>.
Greene, Richard. "Rhetorical Materialism: The Rhetorical Subject and General Intellect." *Rhetoric, Materiality, and Politics.* Eds. Barbara A. Biesecker and John Louis Lucaites. New York: Peter Lang, 2009. 43–65.
Guy, Roger. "We Shall Not Be Moved: Hand Williams Village and the Legacy of Advocacy Planning. *Humanity & Society* 37.3 (2013): 159–75.
Haas, Peter, Philip Nyden, Thomas Walsh, Nathan Benefield, and Christopher Giangreco. *The Uptown Housing and Land Use Study.* Chicago: The Center for Urban Research and Learning, December 2002.
Habermas, Jürgen. *The Structural Transformation of the Public Sphere: An Inquiry into*

a Category of Bourgeois Society. Trans. Thomas Burger with Frederick Lawrence. Cambridge: MIT Press, 1989.

Hackworth, Jason. *The Neoliberal City: Governance, Ideology, and Development in American Urbanism*. Ithaca, NY: Cornell UP, 2007.

Hafferkamp, Jack. "Who Owns the Neighborhoods?" *Chicago*. Nov. 1979: 194–99.

Hamilton, David. "The Politics of Affordable Housing." *Affordable Housing in the Chicago Region: Perspectives and Strategies*. Eds. Phil Nyden, James Lewis, Kale Williams, and Nathan Benefield. Housing Affordability Research Consortium, Chicago 2003.

Hardt, Michael, and Antonio Negri. *Multitude: War and Democracy in the Age of Empire*. New York: Penguin Books, 2005.

Hariman, Robert. "Amateur Hour: Knowing What to Love in Ordinary Democracy." *The Prettier Doll: Rhetoric, Discourse, and Ordinary Democracy*. Eds. Karen Tracy, James P. McDaniel, and Bruce Gronbeck. Tuscaloosa: U of Alabama P, 2007. 218–49.

Hariman, Robert, and John Lucaites. *No Caption Needed: Iconic Photographs, Public Culture, and Liberal Democracy*. Chicago: U of Chicago P, 2007.

Harvey, David. *A Brief History of Neoliberalism*. Oxford: Oxford UP, 2005.

Hauser, Gerard A. "Attending the Vernacular. A Plea for an Ethnographical Rhetoric." *Rhetorical Emergence of Culture*. Eds. Christian Meyer and Felix Girke. Oxford, NY: Berghahn Books, 2011. 157–72.

———. *Vernacular Voices: The Rhetoric of Publics and Public Spheres*. Columbia: U of South Carolina P, 1999.

Hawhee, Debra. *Moving Bodies: Kenneth Burke at the Edges of Language*. Columbia, SC: U of South Carolina P, 2009.

Herndl, Carl, Goodwin, Jean, Honeycutt, Lee, Wilson, Greg, Graham, Scott, and Niedergeses, David. "Talking Sustainability: Identification and Division in an Iowa Community." *Journal of Sustainable Agriculture* 35.3 (2011): 436–61.

Herbert, Steve. "Policing the Contemporary City: Fixing Broken Windows or Shoring Up Neoliberalism?" *Theoretical Criminology* 5.4 (2001): 445–66.

Herbert, Steve, and Elizabeth Brown. "Conceptions of Space and Crime in the Punitive Neoliberal City." *Antipode* 38.4 (2006): 755–77.

Hess, Aaron. "Critical-Rhetorical Ethnography: Rethinking the Place and Process of Rhetoric." *Communication Studies* 62.2 (2011): 127–52.

Hirsch, Arnold. "Urban Renewal." *Electronic Encyclopedia of Chicago*. Chicago Historical Society. n.d. 1 Jan. 2008. <http://www.encyclopedia.chicagohistory.org/pages/1295.html>.

Howard, Robert Glenn. "The Vernacular Mode: Locating the Non-institutional in the Practice of Citizenship." *Public Modalities: Rhetoric, Culture, Media, and the Shape of Public Life*. Eds. Daniel C. Brouwer and Robert Asen. Tuscaloosa: U of Alabama P, 2010.

Illinois State Board of Education 2012 School Report Card. 10 Jan. 2013. <http://www.isbe.net/assessment/report_card.htm>.

Jacobs, Jane. *The Death and Life of Great American Cities*. NY: Random House, 1961.

Joravsky, Ben. "Helen's Voters: Democracy at Work in the 46th Ward." *Chicago Reader*. 20 Mar. 2007: 8.

———. "The Right Fight." *Chicago Reader* 11 Dec. 2008. 23 May 2014. <http://www.chicagoreader.com/chicago/the-right-fight/Content?oid=1103941>.
Kass, John. "Class Struggle Divides Uptown: Middle-Class Development at Odds with Housing for the Poor." *Chicago Tribune*. December 27:2 (1987).
Kelling, George L., and James Q. Wilson. "Broken Windows." *Atlantic Monthly* Mar. 1982. 3 Apr. 2007. <http://www.theatlantic.com/magazine/archive/1982/03/broken-windows/304465/>.
Klinenberg, Eric. "Bowling Alone, Policing Together." *Social Justice* 28.3 (2001): 75–80.
Knight, Cher Krause. *Public Art: Theory, Practice, and Populism*. Malden, MA: Blackwell Publishing, 2008.
Krueckeberg, Donald A. "The Grapes of Rent: A History of Renting in a Country of Owners." *Housing Policy Debate* 10.1 (1999): 9–30.
Lanham, Richard A. *Handlist of Rhetorical Terms*. 2nd ed. Berkeley: U of California P, 1991.
Latour, Bruno. *Reassembling the Social: An Introduction to Actor-Network Theory*. Oxford: Oxford UP, 2005.
Lee, Pamela. "Public Art and the Spaces of Democracy." *Assemblage* 35 (1998): 80–86.
Lefebvre, Henri. *The Production of Space*. Trans. Donald Nicholson-Smith. Cambridge, MA: Blackwell Publishing, 1991.
LeFevre, Karen B. *Invention as a Social Act*. Carbondale: Southern Illinois UP, 1987.
LeMesurier, Jennifer. "Somatic Metaphors: Embodied Recognition of Rhetorical Opportunities." *Rhetoric Review* 33.4 (2014): 362–80.
Lewis, Jim, Phil Nyden, and Kate Williams, eds. *Affordable Housing in the Chicago Region: Perspectives and Strategies*. Chicago: Housing Affordability Research Consortium, 2003.
Lindquist, Julie. *A Place to Stand: Politics and Persuasion in a Working-Class Bar*. Oxford: Oxford UP, 2002.
Low, Setha. *Behind the Gates: Life, Security, and the Pursuit of Happiness in Fortress America*. New York: Routledge, 2003.
———. *On the Plaza: The Politics of Public Space and Culture*. Austin: U of Texas P, 2000.
Lyden, Jacki and Chet Jakus. *Landmarks and Legends of Uptown*. Chicago: 1980.
Lydersen, Kari. "Living Room or Work Space?" *Chicago Reader* 20 Nov. 1998.
Lyons, Arthur, and James Hardy. "The Crisis in Housing: Thinking the Unthinkable." *Affordable Housing in the Chicago Region: Perspectives and Strategies*. Eds. Phil Nyden, James Lewis, Kale Williams, and Nathan Benefield. Chicago: Housing Affordability Research Consortium, 2003.
Mailloux, Steven. "Sophistry and Rhetorical Pragmatism." Introduction. *Rhetoric, Sophistry, Pragmatism*. Cambridge: Cambridge UP, 1995. 1–31.
Maly, Michael T. *Beyond Segregation: Multiracial and Multiethnic Neighborhoods in the United States*. Philadelphia: Temple UP, 2005.
Maly, Michael T., and Michael Leachman. "Rogers Park, Edgewater, Uptown, and Chicago Lawn, Chicago." *Cityscape: A Journal of Policy Development and Research* 4.2 (1998): 131–60.
Massumi, Brian. *Parables for the Virtual: Movement, Affect, Sensation*. Durham: Duke UP, 2002.

McCarron, John. "Shiller Guards Against Uptown Progress." *Chicago Tribune* 1 Sep. 1988: 1.
McGee, Michael. "A Materialist's Conception of Rhetoric." *Rhetoric, Materiality, and Politics*. Eds. Barbara A. Biesecker and John Louis Lucaites. New York: Peter Lang, 2009. 17–42.
mcclellan, erin daina. "Place, Space, and Language: Vernacular Performances in and about a 'Successful' Urban Public Square." *Liminalities: A Journal of Performance Studies* 4.1 (2008). 5 Aug. 2014. <http://liminalities.net/4-1/>.
"Median Income and Income Limits for Section 8 Program." U.S. Department of Housing and Urban Development. 5 Apr 2006. 9 Sep. 2006. <http://www.huduser.org/datasets/il/il07/index.html>.
Meyer, Christian, and Felix Girke, eds. *The Rhetorical Emergence of Culture*. New York: Berghahn Books, 2011.
Middleton, Michael K., Samantha Senda-Cook, and Danielle Endres. "Articulating Rhetorical Field Methods: Challenges and Tensions." *Western Journal of Communication* 75.4 (2011): 386–406:
Miller, Carolyn. "The Aristotelian Topos: Hunting for Novelty." *Rereading Aristotle's Rhetoric*. Eds. Alan Gross and Arthur Walzer. Carbondale: Southern Illinois UP, 2000. 130–46.
Montag, Warren. "The Pressure of the Street: Habermas's Fear of the Masses." *Masses, Classes, and the Public Sphere*. Eds. Mike Hill and Warren Montag. New York: Verso, 2000. 132–45.
Mouffe, Chantal. "Art and Democracy: Art as an Agnostic Intervention in Public Space." *Open* 14 (2008): 6–15.
———. *The Democratic Paradox*. New York: Verso, 2000.
Muckelbauer, John. *The Future of Invention: Rhetoric, Postmodernism, and the Problem of Change*. Albany: State U of New York P, 2008.
National Low Income Housing Coalition. *Out of Reach 2012: America's Forgotten Housing Crisis*. 2012. 15 July 2012. <http://nlihc.org/sites/default/files/oor/2012-OOR.pdf>.
Neighborhood Capital Budget Group, "The TIF Process: Understanding the Process Step-by-Step." *Neighborhood Capital Budget Group*. 2005. 8 August 2006. <http://www.ncbg.org/tifs/tif_process.htm>.
Nyden, Phil, James Lewis, and Kale Williams. *Affordable Housing in the Chicago Region: Perspectives and Strategies*. Eds. Phil Nyden, James Lewis, Kale Williams, and Nathan Benefield. Chicago: Housing Affordability Research Consortium, 2003.
Nyden, Philip et al. "Saving Our Homes: The Lessons of Community Struggles to Preserve Affordable Housing in Chicago's Uptown." Chicago: The Center for Urban Research and Learning and the Organization of the NorthEast, 1996.
Paley, Julia. "Towards an Anthropology of Democracy." *Annual Review of Anthropology* 31 (2002): 469–96.
Palmer, Laurie. "Artists Against Artist Housing." *Trashing the Neoliberal City: Autonomous Cultural Practices in Chicago from 2000–2005*. Copenhagen, Denmark: Learning Site, 2007. 9.
Pezzullo, Phaedra. *Toxic Tourism: Rhetoric of Pollution, Travel, and Environmental Justice*. Tuscaloosa: U of Alabama P, 2007.
Pipes, Richard. *Property and Freedom*. New York: Vintage Books, 1999.

Podmolik, Mary Ellen. "44% of Cook County Homes with a Mortgage are Underwater." *Chicago Tribune* 24 May 2012. 10 Jun. 2014. <http://articles.chicagotribune.com/2012-05-24/business/chi-44-of-cook-county-homes-with-a-mortgage-are-underwater-20120523_1_negative-equity-underwater-homeowners-zillow-chief-economist>.
Queer to the Left. *Gentrification Keywords*. Chicago: Crossroads, 2004.
Quintilian. *Institutes of Oratory*. Trans. H. E. Butler. Cambridge: Loeb Classical Library, 1936.
Rai, Candice. "Power, Publics, and the Rhetorical Uses of Democracy." *The Public Work of Rhetoric: Citizen-Scholars and Civic Engagement*. Eds. John M. Ackerman and David J. Coogan. Columbia: U of South Carolina P, 2010. 39–55.
Rancière, Jacque. *Hatred of Democracy*. Trans. Steve Corcoran. New York: Verso, 2006.
Randle, Wilma. "CHA Chief, Ald. Shiller Propose Private Help in Fixing CHA Flats." *Chicago Tribune* 18 Oct. 1988: 3.
Rawls, John. *A Theory of Justice*. Cambridge: Harvard UP, 1999.
Read, Sarah, and Jason Swarts. "Visualizing and Tracing: Research Methodologies for the Study of Networked, Sociotechnical Activity, Otherwise Known as Knowledge Work." *Technical Communication Quarterly* 24.1 (2015): 14–44.
Reynolds, Nedra. *Geographies of Writing: Inhabiting Places and Encountering Difference*. Carbondale: Southern Illinois UP, 2004.
Review of Tax Increment Financing in The City of Chicago. Department of Planning & Development, July 1998.
Rice, Jeff. *Digital Detroit: Rhetoric and Space in the Age of Network*. Carbondale: Southern Illinois UP, 2012.
———. "Networked Exchanges, Identity, Writing." *Journal of Business and Technical Communication* 23.1 (2009): 294–317.
Rice, Jenny Edbauer. *Distant Publics: Development Rhetoric and the Subject of Crisis*. Pittsburgh: U of Pittsburgh P, 2012.
———. "The New 'New': Making a Case for Critical Affect Studies." *Quarterly Journal of Speech* 94.2 (2008): 200–12.
———. "Unframing Models of Public Distribution: From Rhetorical Situations to Rhetorical Ecologies." *Rhetoric Society Quarterly* 35.4 (2005): 5–24.
Rickert, Thomas. *Ambient Rhetoric: The Attunements of Rhetorical Being*. Pittsburgh: U of Pittsburgh P, 2013.
Roeder, David. "Shiller on Tightrope Over Development Plan in Uptown." *Chicago Sun-Times* 12 Apr. 2006.
———. "Taming Chicago's $1.7 billion TIF monster." *Chicago Sun-Times* 28 Sep. 2013. 12 Jun. 2014 <http://www.suntimes.com/22832518-761/taming-chicagos-17-billion-tif-monster.html#.VEVrAsZPQds>.
———. "Uptown Plan Alive Despite Theater Loss, Developer Says." *Chicago Sun-Times* 4 Apr. 2006: 47, 52.
———. "Wilson Yard: 'Wonderful' or 'Debacle'?" *Chicago Sun-Times* 19 Apr. 2006: 63.
Rorty, Richard. *Contingency, Irony, and Solidarity*. Cambridge: Cambridge UP, 1989.
Roy, Ananya. "Praxis in the Time of Empire." *Planning Theory* 5.1 (2006): 7–29.
Saldaña, Johnny. *The Coding Manual for Qualitative Research*. Thousand Oaks, CA: SAGE Publications, 2009.

Selzer, Jack. "Habeas Corpus: An Introduction." *Rhetorical Bodies*. Eds. Jack Selzer and Sharon Crowley. Madison: U of Wisconsin P, 1999. 3–15.

Severinsen, Kay. "First Step to Safe Neighborhoods - Be a Good Neighbor: 'Positive Loitering' and Community Watch Groups Making Areas Safer." *Search Chicago Homes*. 19 Aug. 2010. 20 Aug. 2010. <http://searchchicago.suntimes.com/homes/2613608,safe-neighborhoods19.article>.

Sharp, Joanne, Venda Pollack, and Ronan Paddison. "Just Art for a Just City: Public Art and Social Inclusion in Urban Regeneration." *Urban Studies* 42.5/6 (2005): 1001–23.

Siegel, Paul B. *Uptown, Chicago: The Origins and Emergence of a Movement Against Displacement, 1947–1972*. Diss. University of Illinois at Chicago, 2002.

Skogan, Wesley G. and Steiner, Lynn. *Community Policing in Chicago, Year Ten: An Evaluation of Chicago's Alternative Policing Strategy*. Chicago: Chicago Community Policing Evaluation Consortium, 2004.

Skogan, Wesley G., and Hartnett, Susan. *Community Policing, Chicago Style*. New York: Oxford UP, 1997.

Smith, Janet L. "The Space of Local Control in the Devolution of US Public Housing Policy." *Geografiska Annaler* 82.4 (2000): 221–33.

Smith, Neil. *The New Urban Frontier: Gentrification and the Revanchist City*. New York: Routledge, 1996.

Social Workers Against Cappleman. "About." Facebook.com. 8 Aug. 2013. 1 Aug. 2014. <https://www.facebook.com/socialworkersagainstcappleman>.

Sosin, Kate. "Hundreds Protest Cappleman Over Salvation Army Fallout." *Windy City Times* 6 Mar. 2013. 20 Jan. 2014. <http://www.windycitymediagroup.com/lgbt/Hundreds-protest-Cappleman-over-Salvation-Army-fallout/41846.html>.

Spinuzzi, Clay. *Tracing Genres Through Organizations: A Sociocultural Approach*. Cambridge: MIT Press, 2003.

Stewart, Kathleen. *Ordinary Affects*. Durham, NC: Duke UP, 2007.

Strosnider, Kim. "Anti-Gang Ordinances After City of Chicago v. Morales: The Intersection of Race, Vagueness Doctrine, and Equal Protection in the Criminal Law." *American Criminal Law Review* 39.1 (2002): 101–46.

Sweet, Lynn. "Shiller & poor vs. yuppies in Uptown." *Chicago Sun-Times* 15 Nov. 1987: 5. Access World News. U of Illinois at Chicago, U Lib. 1 Jun. 2006 <http://infoweb.newsbank.com>.

Taliaferro, Tim. "Uptown Residents Demand Action After Gang Violence Erupts in Streets." *Huffington Post* 17 Sep. 2009. 12 May 2010. <http://www.huffingtonpost.com/2009/08/17/uptown-residents-demand-a_n_261175.html>.

Tax Increment Financing in Illinois: A Legislative Issue—September 1995. Tax Payers' Federation of Illinois, 1995.

Tax Increment Financing Handbook. Illinois Department of Commerce and Community Affairs, 1999.

Thornton, Jerry. "'Tent City' Residents Vow to Stay." *Chicago Tribune* 14 Oct. 1988: 4.

Tracy, Karen. *Challenges of Ordinary Democracy: A Case Study in Deliberation and Dissent*. University Park: The Pennsylvania State UP, 2010.

Trainor, Jennifer S. *Rethinking Racism: Emotion, Persuasion, and Literacy Education in an All-White High School*. Carbondale: Southern Illinois UP, 2008.

Umberger, Mary. "Chicago Feels Housing Chill." *Chicago Tribune*. 26 Jul. 2006. *Access World News*. 10 Aug. 2006.

"Uptown Gains in Drive to Rout Rooming Houses." *Chicago Daily Tribune* 18 Oct. 1931: D2.

"Uptown Model Cities Plan Receives Praise, Criticism." *Chicago Tribune* 17 Apr. 1969: N1. ProQuest Historical Newspapers. U of Illinois at Chicago, U Lib. 10 Nov. 2007 <http://proquest.umi.com>.

"Uptown Neighborhood Council—Who We Are." *Uptown Neighborhood Council*. Mar. 2006. 15 Aug. 2006. <http://www.uncchicago.org/about_us/index.html>.

"Uptown Resident." *Chicagoist*. 8 Feb. 2007. Weblog Comment. 2 Mar. 2007 <http://www.chicagoist.com>.

Uptown Uprising. "About." *Facebook.com*. 6 Mar. 2013. 30 Jul. 2014. <https://www.facebook.com/UptownUprising/info?ref=page_internal>.

Wacquant, Loïc. "Scrutinizing the Street: Poverty, Morality, and the Pitfalls of Urban Ethnography." *American Journal of Sociology*. 107.6 (2002): 1468–1432.

Watson, Carl. "Men in Cages: Reflections on Skid Row Society." *Chicago Reader*. 5 Nov. 1992. 15 Jul. 2014. <http://www.chicagoreader.com/chicago/men-in-cages/Content?oid=880810>.

"What is Wilson Yard?" *Fix Wilson Yard Website*. Aug. 2008. 18 Aug. 2008. <http://www.fixwilsonyard.org/index.html#Update>.

Whelan, Dominique. *Problem Solving Case Studies*. Chicago: Chicago Community Policing Evaluation Consortium, 1995.

Young, Iris Marion. *Justice and the Politics of Difference*. Princeton, NJ: Princeton UP, 1990.

Zukin, Sharon. *Landscapes of Power: From Detroit to Disney World*. Los Angeles: U of California P, 1991.

Index

Ackerman, John, 15, 40, 161
aesthetics, 3, 9, 14, 19, 24, 32, 35, 42–43, 56, 60, 64, 115, 124–125, 128, 153–154, 166, 176, 197, 212
affect, 6–8, 10–12, 14–16, 19, 24, 28, 30, 34, 37, 65, 114, 144–146, 154, 161, 170, 172–197, 203, 205, 218
affordable housing. *See* housing
agency, 8, 10, 12–14, 16, 18–19, 79, 161, 182, 197, 204–205
agonism, 16, 33, 72, 115, 130, 136, 199, 223
Ahmed, Sara, 174–175, 189
Aristotle, 7, 16, 35–36, 218
Asen, Robert, 11, 25, 78–79, 116–117

Bawarshi, Anis, 37
Bennett, Jane, 12, 37, 161
Bennett, Larry, 9, 49–52
Biesecker, Barbara, 14
Blair, Carole, 8, 14, 114–115
blog comment field, 5, 100, 175, 178–197, 212, 223
blogs, 5, 9, 26–27, 30, 76, 100, 108, 123, 175–197, 212, 218, 223, 225
bodies, 3, 6–8, 14, 17–19, 27–28, 37–41, 65, 117, 139, 144, 154, 163–164, 169–176, 182, 192, 194–197, 200, 218. *See also* rhetoric: and embodiment
broken windows theory, 147, 151–157, 160–161, 169
Brouwer, Daniel, 11, 25, 78–79, 116–117
Brown, Elizabeth, 153, 155, 160, 169

Brown, Wendy, 167, 169
Buena Park Neighbors, 58, 108, 123–124
built environment, 2, 6, 18, 41, 133, 144, 153–154, 161–163, 170, 205, 218. *See also* social space
Burke, Kenneth, 22, 37, 66, 178, 189, 201, 211
business owner, 22, 25–26, 53, 74, 90, 94, 135, 179, 199, 209

capitalism, 22–25, 29, 44, 51, 61, 103–106, 109, 116, 127, 166, 203–204, 207, 209–210, 217
censorship, 31, 121–128
Chicago, 45, 47, 58, 79, 133, 155–156, 165–166; Tax Increment Financing, 22; Uptown neighborhood, 2, 45–65, 79–83
Chicago Alternative Policing Strategy (CAPS), 101, 121, 144–146, 149, 151–152, 155–158, 165–166, 169–170, 224–225
Cicero, 13
Cintrón, Ralph, 15, 20, 37, 98, 163
circulation, 6–8, 11, 13–21, 25, 28–29, 32, 34, 37–43, 59, 79, 82, 114–118, 124, 137, 139, 141, 144, 163, 173, 175–194, 203, 214
citizen, 2–3, 6, 9, 13, 21, 29, 30, 31–33, 42, 44, 61, 66, 75–76, 78, 82, 89, 92–94, 97–99, 101, 107–112, 117, 119, 124, 140, 143–146, 149, 152–153, 155–159, 163–171, 177, 180, 184–185, 194, 196–198, 201–202, 216, 219, 225
citizenship, 6, 32–33, 97, 99, 102, 113, 117, 147, 154, 159, 161, 192, 219

civic participation, 3, 9, 26, 71, 110, 146–149, 155–156, 159, 171, 177, 184, 189–195, 214
classism, 11, 22–23, 59, 60–61, 80, 90–91, 100, 133–134, 189
Coalition of Uptown Residents for Affordability and Justice (COURAJ), 57, 74, 90, 92, 102, 106
commonplaces, 8, 10, 15–17, 29, 34–37, 39–42, 46, 51, 53–54, 58–59, 61, 64, 72, 77, 94, 113, 118, 139, 174–177, 185, 194, 196, 202–203. *See also* topoi
community gardens, 68, 101, 162–163, 168–169, 178, 205–207
community policing, 30, 143–171
condo owner. *See* homeowner
Condit, Celeste, 33
Conquergood, Dwight, 15, 17
consensus, 3, 5, 9–11, 72, 75–76, 78, 88–92, 95, 115–116, 118, 121–123, 126–127, 130, 135, 200–201
Consigny, Scott, 36
Corbett, Edward, 36
crime, 30, 64, 74, 81, 96, 145–146, 149–157, 161–162, 170, 176–179, 182–185, 187–188, 190, 192, 214, 224–225
Crowley, Sharon, 13, 25–26, 35–37, 137, 139, 218
Cruikshank, Barbara, 14, 75, 78, 168, 201

Daniel, Jamie, 196
Davis, Diane, 7
Dean, Jodi, 191–192
democracy, 1–2, 5, 9–15, 26, 116, 136, 198–210; and ambivalence, 9, 23, 25–26, 30–31, 64, 66–109, 124, 130, 141–171, 190, 199–210, 214–216; and censorship, 121–128; and class politics, 133–134, 138; and consensus, 72, 75, 89–92, 115–116, 120–128, 130, 135; and equality, 11, 29, 32–33, 42–45, 52, 57–59, 66, 72, 76, 82, 88–89, 102–105, 110–113, 131, 134, 137–139, 147, 167, 202, 204, 208; everyday, 8, 12, 24–25, 29–30, 45, 64–65, 109, 113–114, 136, 142–143, 145–146, 195, 210; and housing, 23, 29, 31–35, 41–65, 66–109; and invention, 7, 28–30, 67, 110–118, 123, 136–142, 198, 202–203; liberal, 10, 66, 72, 76, 98, 105, 113, 115, 117–118, 122, 128, 130, 134, 159, 167, 202; and the market, 52, 59, 63–64, 93–98, 157, 165–171, 207; and morality, 29, 63, 66, 76, 78, 82, 87, 94, 98, 104, 106, 109, 121–122, 125, 157–159, 165–167, 190, 197, 202–203, 209, 214, 217; paradoxes, 9, 72–109, 136–140, 141–142; and property, 97–105; and publics, 9–14, 23–24, 66–109, 115, 127, 133, 198–210; and public art, 110–142; online, 124–127, 175–197; ordinary, 12, 75, 198, 201; and taxes, 33, 83, 97–105; and violence, 9, 13, 23, 67, 76–77, 88, 112, 127–140, 201, 222; and virtue, 9, 14, 30, 75, 157–158, 190, 203; visual icons, 111, 115–119
democratic, 21, 26, 28, 30–31, 66–109, 113–117, 121–123, 127–128, 130, 133, 136, 138–139, 143–144, 167, 170, 189–195, 200–204, 214, 220–221; contests, 115–116, 127, 130, 138–144, 189, 200–204, 221, 223; process; 83–88, 90, 93, 127, 130–133; rhetoric, 2–3, 7–14, 14, 23, 25, 28–30, 41–42, 44, 63, 66–109, 113–114, 117, 122, 144–147, 156, 158, 167–171, 198, 202, 214; rights, 31–33, 51, 53, 63–65, 82, 88, 93–94, 105, 167, 170, 176, 201–204, 208–210, 214; subjectivity, 12–14, 75–78, 167–168; topoi, 8, 10, 23, 29, 31–35, 37, 41–42, 44, 58–65, 66–109, 113, 117–119, 121–122, 140, 156
Deutsche, Rosalyn, 110, 115–116, 136
development. *See* urban development
Dickinson, Greg, 114–115
Dingo, Rebecca, 79
displacement, 22, 32–33, 42–43, 45, 47, 49–54, 57, 64, 98, 114, 128
diversity, 2, 9–10, 29–30, 35, 47–49, 52–53, 56, 62–63, 77, 80–81, 105, 110–142, 146, 184, 188, 211, 218; and democracies, 29–30, 77, 110–142, 223
doxa, 6, 124, 136–140
Druschke, Caroline, 16, 98

ecological, 7, 11–12, 15, 18–19, 28, 78–79, 114, 139, 176, 182–183, 189. *See also* rhetorical ecologies
Edbauer, Jenny. *See* Rice, Jenny Edbauer

embodiment. *See* bodies; rhetoric: and embodiment
emotion, 6, 8, 12, 23–24, 27–28, 30, 81, 144, 170, 172–177, 182, 186, 188–189, 192, 194–196
Endres, Danielle, 15–17, 176
equality, 29, 32–33, 35, 42–45, 57–59, 63, 66, 72, 74, 76, 82, 88–89, 93, 102–105, 110–113, 131, 134, 136–139, 147, 160, 166–167, 202, 204, 207, 208, 210, 212
ethnography, 8, 15–21, 24–28, 33, 41. *See also* rhetorical fieldwork
exclusion, 11, 21, 72, 77, 88, 105, 110, 113, 115, 120, 122, 128, 130, 132–133, 136, 140, 147, 160, 163, 166, 169, 222

Federalist Papers, 9–10
field methodologies. *See* ethnography; rhetorical fieldwork
fieldsite, 13, 18, 20–21, 24, 32–33, 41, 64, 211
fieldwork, 13, 15, 19, 22, 26–28, 30, 33, 43, 81, 93, 104, 146, 149, 152, 187, 195, 198, 202, 224
Finnegan, Cara, 116–117, 140–141
Fix Wilson Yard, 58, 107–109, 209, 219, 223
Fleming, David, 11, 13, 15, 76–77, 221–222
Foucault, Michel, 33, 78, 217
Fraser, Nancy, 11, 76, 134
freedom, 29, 31–33, 42, 59, 66, 97, 113, 122, 126, 165, 167

Geary, Chuck, 50, 219
genre, 6, 8, 14, 16–17, 20–21, 37–38, 41, 117, 177–178, 182, 189–196
gentrification, 2–3, 22–23, 25–26, 29, 32–33, 43, 47, 52–54, 56, 64, 68, 70–71, 74, 79, 90, 92–98, 104–105, 114, 128, 132, 141, 145, 148, 166, 170, 179, 199–201, 215
Grabill, Jeff, 12, 15, 182
Greene, Richard, 14

Habermas, Jürgen, 10–11, 28, 76–77, 125, 176, 201, 217, 221
Hariman, Robert, 116–117, 198
Harvey, David, 166, 225
Hauser, Gerard, 11–13, 15, 76–77, 221–222
Hawhee, Debra, 35–37, 218

Herbert, Steve, 153, 155–156, 160, 169
Herndl, Carl, 16
Hess, Aaron, 15–16
homelessness, 2, 34, 42, 49, 64, 93, 95, 100, 110, 131, 145, 158–159, 168–169, 174, 207, 212–215, 218, 220–221, 225
homeowner, 25–26, 30, 33–34, 42, 52–57, 60–61, 71, 74, 80–81, 83–84, 89, 92, 94, 109, 120–123, 135, 142, 146, 152, 157–158, 163, 166, 174, 179, 192, 197, 220–224; as topos in democracy, 97–105
housing, 2, 5, 8–9, 22–23, 26–27, 31–65, 67–109, 120–123, 141–142, 144, 165, 214–223; affordable, 8, 22–23, 26–27, 29, 31–35, 41–65, 67–109, 120–122, 128, 147, 165–166, 172–174, 178, 182, 185–187, 193–197, 205–206, 209, 212, 214–217, 220; definition of, 218; and democracy, 23, 29, 31–35, 41–65, 67–109; and the free market, 29, 33, 42–49, 52–54, 56, 64, 79–82, 89, 93–98, 114, 127, 132, 157, 159, 165–166, 182; and neoliberalism, 58–63; public, 2, 34–35, 51, 57–61, 79, 91, 95–96, 100, 120, 142, 222; as a right, 31–32, 53, 63–64, 82, 88, 93–94, 105, 209, 212–213; and segregation, 47, 52, 133; topoi, 32–35, 42–46, 53–54, 58–65, 172–174, 185–186, 215–216

Identification, 178, 185, 189, 192. *See also* Burke, Kenneth
immanence, 6, 11–12, 14, 24–25, 29, 38–39, 203–204, 207
immigration, 2, 35, 45, 47–49, 110, 128, 131–132
inequality. *See* equality
invention. *See* rhetorical invention

Jobs Or Income Now (JOIN), 50–51, 219

kairos, 12, 15–17, 19, 38, 77, 114, 139, 204, 218
kairotic. *See* kairos
Kang, Jiyeon, 116–117, 140–141
Kuumba Lynx, 118–119, 127

land speculation, 22–23, 34–35, 42–47, 53–54; and racism, 47
Latour, Bruno, 12, 39, 116, 175, 182

Lee, Pamela, 115, 136
Lefebvre, Henri, 28, 40, 161
LeMesurier, Jennifer, 15
Lindquist, Julie, 15, 36–37
Lucaites, John, 14, 117–118

market logic, 3, 29, 42–45, 49, 52–59, 79–82, 93–98, 119, 132, 146–148, 157, 165–171, 207
Massumi, Brian, 173
materiality, 5–19, 24–25, 27–28, 30, 32–42, 46, 51, 63–67, 77–79, 83, 89–90, 104, 106–107, 113–114, 117–118, 136–140, 144–146, 154, 161, 164–165, 174–175, 182, 203, 205, 208, 216–219, 222
mcclellan, erin, 15
McComiskey, Bruce, 139
McGee, Michael, 14, 217
Michaels, Walter Benn, 133–134
middle-class, 23, 42, 44, 50, 52, 59–61, 81, 104–105, 109, 179, 199, 209
Middleton, Michael, 15, 17, 176
Miller, Carolyn, 39–41, 139
morality, 33, 43, 45, 60, 63, 66, 82, 84, 94, 97–98, 101, 104, 106, 116, 121, 126, 139, 154–155, 157–159, 165–167, 183, 187, 207, 217; ambivalence, 23–26, 29, 63, 66, 76, 78, 87, 104, 106, 109, 121–122, 126, 130, 146, 170, 190, 197, 202–203, 205, 209, 214
Mouffe, Chantal, 72–73, 88–89, 115–116, 122, 199, 223
Mucklebauer, John, 36, 38–39, 218
multiculturalism, 112, 117, 130

neoliberalism, 26, 29, 59–59, 63, 90, 144, 147, 156, 160, 165–171, 203, 224–226
networks, 6, 9, 11, 15, 19, 30, 175–176, 182–183, 194, 204

object-orientated ontology, 12, 37, 182
Organization of the NorthEast (ONE), 56–58, 74, 86, 90, 102, 199, 206, 220

Paley, Julia, 75
persuasion, 5, 7–8, 10, 14–17, 19–21, 25, 27–30, 33–38, 40–41, 78–79, 106, 137, 144, 173, 175–176, 178, 188, 192, 195, 203–204, 208, 218
Pezzullo, Phaedra, 15, 174–175
place, 2, 6, 8, 16–21, 28–30, 31–65, 72, 82–83, 97, 107, 113–118, 124, 141–142, 146, 174, 202–205. *See also* places of invention
places of invention, 8, 19–21, 28, 31–65, 67, 82, 97, 113–118, 124, 139, 141–142, 198, 202–203, 205, 207, 218–219; definition of, 8, 16–17, 31–42; and democracy, 28, 30, 66–109, 113–118, 123, 141–142, 198, 202–203; and diversity, 113–118, 123, 136–140; and housing, 31–65; as visual topoi, 113–118. *See also* rhetorical invention
policing. *See* community policing; Chicago Alternative Policing Strategy
poor, 2, 22, 33, 42–44, 46, 49–52, 54, 56, 59–64, 71, 89, 91–96, 100, 123, 131, 145, 148, 186–188, 197, 199, 207, 209, 212–216, 219–220. *See also* poverty
Poor People's Coalition, 50
positive loitering, 30, 121, 143–171, 206, 224–225; definition of, 146, 152; history of, 151–152; and neoliberalism, 156, 165–171
poverty, 23, 42–43, 51–55, 58–64, 71, 74–80, 86, 93, 95–96, 110, 118, 131, 133, 142, 148, 170, 176, 214, 216, 219. *See also* poor
property, 31–33; rights, 167; owner, 22–23, 25, 97–105; tax, 21–23, 33, 97–105; value, 43–45, 80, 97–105, 148
public, 2–3, 5, 21–24, 35, 45, 50, 52, 64, 68, 108–109, 125–127, 136, 158, 167–168, 170, 173, 192–193, 196–198, 212; debate, 10, 12, 88, 201, 211; definition of, 10–12, 182; democratic, 9–15, 66–109, 115, 117, 123, 127, 133, 198–210; emotions, 30, 81, 144, 170, 172–177, 182, 186, 188–189, 192, 194–196; formation, 9–10, 23–24, 27, 30, 34, 136, 144, 174–197; good, 2, 9–10, 24, 31–32, 42, 66–67, 76, 82–83, 92–97, 105, 111, 146, 155, 171, 202–203, 216; modalities, 11, 78–79; online, 124–128; 175–197; subjectivities, 13, 15. *See also* democracy: and publics; public space; public sphere
public art, 8, 110–142; and democracy, 110–142; and invention, 113–118
public housing. *See* housing

public memories, 5–6, 114–115
public rhetoric, 2, 26, 33, 79, 163, 176–177, 196
public safety, 43, 71, 74, 82, 86, 93, 95, 97, 105, 148, 151, 153, 155–156, 166, 179, 183, 187, 193, 196–197, 212
public space, 3, 10, 26–30, 33, 64, 77, 110, 115–117, 122, 136–137, 141, 144–149, 161–164, 188, 196, 201, 213
public sphere, 66–67, 72–79, 87–89, 105–109, 115–118, 130, 136, 210, 217; critiques of, 11; definition of, 10, 76–77; as heuristic, 210, 221–222. See also democracy: and publics; public space; public welfare
public welfare, 6, 29, 31–32, 44, 50, 52, 64, 91, 100, 122, 126, 148, 153, 167–168, 220, 225

qualitative research. See ethnography; field methodologies; rhetorical fieldwork
Queer to the Left, 57, 60–61, 71, 74, 87, 90–92, 106, 166, 219
Quintilian, 16

racism, 11, 35, 52, 59, 61, 90–91, 100, 111, 113, 133–135, 169–170, 174, 181–182
Rancière, Jacques, 1, 201
Read, Sarah, 15
redistribution, 105, 133–134, 210
Reynolds, Nedra, 40, 164
rhetoric: and affect, 6–8, 10, 14–16, 28, 30, 34, 37, 65, 144, 154, 161, 170, 172–197, 203, 205; and circulation, 6–8, 11, 14–21, 25, 28–29, 32, 34, 37–43, 59, 79, 82, 114–118, 137, 139, 141, 144, 163, 173, 175–194, 203, 214; definition of, 5–7, 14–16, 39; and democracy, 2–3, 7–10, 14, 23, 29, 41, 63, 66–109, 134, 139, 158, 167–171, 203; and embodiment, 6–8, 14–15, 17–19, 27–28, 37–41, 65, 139, 144, 154, 163–164, 170–176, 192, 194–197; and emotion, 24, 30, 81, 144, 170, 172–177, 182, 185–186, 188–189, 192, 194–196; and empowerment, 60, 169–170; everyday, 2–3, 5–18, 24–30, 38–40, 64–65, 109, 117, 139, 141–144, 146, 161, 170–178, 182, 189–190, 196, 198, 202–203, 208, 210, 219; and materiality, 6–7, 10, 12–14, 17–18, 28, 30, 35, 39–42, 63, 118, 138–140, 154, 161–164, 217; spatial, 3, 17–18, 24, 30, 34, 37–43, 63, 65, 116–117, 160–164, 169, 182–183; and thing theory, 12, 161–162; vernacular, 11, 15; visual, 12, 110–142, 154, 162–164
rhetorical ecologies, 7, 11–13, 15, 19, 28, 78–79, 83, 114, 139, 176, 182–183, 189
rhetorical ethnography, 8, 15, 26, 33, 41–42, 203; definition of, 15; and embodiment, 17–19, 217–218; as heuristic, 20–21, 27; as method, 15–21, 26–28, 34, 41–42, 176
rhetorical fieldwork, 8, 15–21, 26–28, 176, 198, 218
rhetorical force, 5–7, 17, 20, 28, 38–39, 109, 139, 154, 163, 176, 183, 195–196, 202–203
rhetorical invention, 7–8, 16–18, 20–21, 27–31, 34–42, 57, 60, 63–65, 67, 71–72, 97, 106, 113–118, 123, 128–142, 176, 187, 198, 202–203, 205, 207–208, 218–219; definition of, 7–8, 34–42; and materiality, 35, 71–72, 82–83, 138–140. See also places of invention
rhetorical situation, 7–8, 16–21, 35–43, 67, 95, 114, 139, 161, 176, 182–183
Rice, Jeff, 15, 39, 175, 185
Rice, Jenny Edbauer, 7, 12–13, 15, 19, 21, 79, 82, 189, 194
Rickert, Thomas, 7, 139–140, 205
rights, 31–33, 42, 44, 63–65, 82, 88, 93–94, 105–106, 203
Roots of Argyle Mural, 110–113, 118, 127–140

segregation, 35, 47, 52, 133, 169
Selzer, Jack, 13–14
Senda-Cook, Samantha, 15, 17, 176
Shiller, Helen, 53–56, 67, 73, 84–86, 89–90, 100, 103, 105, 108–109, 121, 148, 179–180, 183–184, 187, 211–212, 219–220, 222–223
Siegal, Paul, 45–47, 219
slums, 35, 47, 49–50, 57, 73, 131–132, 219
Smith, Jane, 59
Smith, Neil, 132, 160, 219–220
social justice, 5–6, 13, 23–25, 29, 31–32, 42–44, 56, 64, 67, 71, 75, 78, 83, 87–92, 107,

109, 111–112, 117–120, 127, 130, 133–137, 140, 142, 158–159, 196, 202–206, 208, 214, 216, 221, 223
social space, 8, 10–11, 14, 16, 18, 24, 27–29, 34, 37–43, 64, 77–78, 105, 114, 116–117, 136–141, 146, 160–161, 163–164, 169–170, 182–183, 189–190, 204–205. *See also* built environment; rhetoric: spatial; spatial
space. *See* built environment; rhetoric, spatial; social space; spatial
spatial, 8, 10–11, 17–18, 24, 30, 34, 40, 59, 63, 65, 118, 133, 139, 160–161, 169. *See also* built environment; rhetoric: spatial; social space
Spinuzzi, Clay, 15
stakeholders, 42, 47, 59, 64, 67, 73, 75, 78, 127, 130, 134, 143, 171, 213, 220; definition of, 221
Stewart, Kathleen, 172, 194–195

Tax Increment Financing (TIF), 21–24, 58, 84, 95, 97–99, 107–108, 218, 222
taxpayer, 33, 42, 73, 76, 108, 223; as topos, 33, 83, 97–105
thing theory, 12, 161–162, 182
topoi, 8, 14, 16, 29, 34–41, 43–45, 83–109; 139–140; definition of, 16, 34, 36–41, 82–83, 139, 218–219; democratic, 8, 14, 23, 29, 32–35, 45, 53 58–65, 66–109, 113–122, 136–142, 156; diversity, 110–142; emotional, 173–177, 185, 189, 194, 196; housing, 32, 43–45, 53, 58–65, 216; property, 97–105; taxpayer, 33, 83, 97–105; visual, 113–142, 176–178, 180, 182. *See also* commonplace
Tracy, Karen, 1, 11–12, 15, 75, 201
Trainor, Jennifer, 15, 175

Uplift Mural, 110–113, 118–127, 130, 135, 138, 140, 223
Uptown Chicago Commission (UCC), 49–52, 56, 58, 220
Uptown neighborhood, 45–65; as class warfare, 51, 56; crimes rates, 149–151; and democracy, 25, 66–109; and diversity, 2–3, 5, 9, 29–30, 35, 47–49, 52–53, 56, 62, 80–81, 105, 110–142, 184, 188, 211, 218; history, 29, 31–65, 130–133; and housing, 31–35, 41–65, 79–109, 141–142; and immigration, 42–50; and political strife, 2–3, 9, 23, 34, 45–109; and public art, 110–142; and public formation, 9, 23–24, 172–197
Uptown Neighborhood Council (UNC), 58, 73–74, 86, 88–92, 94–95, 107–108, 199
Uptown Update, 108, 123, 175–197, 209, 212, 223, 225
urban development, 3, 5, 21, 26, 29, 42–43, 45, 49–52, 54, 56–57, 64, 68, 71, 83–88, 92–98, 100–101, 121, 130, 132, 137, 141–142, 146–148, 159, 179, 197, 199, 201, 211–213, 216, 220
urban renewal, 22, 27, 42, 47–53, 56–57, 92, 96, 115, 131, 148, 219

vernacular, 117; publics, 12, 77, 157–158; rhetoric, 11–12, 15, 18
violence, 10, 13, 23, 67, 76–77, 88, 112, 119–121, 128–140, 149–151, 175–177, 183–188, 201, 222, 224–226

Wacquant, Loïc, 24
welfare. *See* public welfare
Wilson Yard, 2–5, 23, 27, 29, 57–62, 67–109, 174, 186, 193, 199, 205, 209, 211, 219, 221–223